28.50

The Staging of Religious Drama in Europe in the Later Middle Ages: Texts and Documents in English Translation

*Translated by Raffaella Ferrari, Peter Meredith,
Lynette R. Muir, Margaret Sleeman, and John E. Tailby*

Edited by Peter Meredith and John E. Tailby

Early Drama, Art, and Music
Monograph Series, 4

MEDIEVAL INSTITUTE PUBLICATIONS
Western Michigan University
Kalamazoo, Michigan
1983

Printed in the United States of America

Introductions and Translations

Raffaella Ferrari   Italian
Peter Meredith   English and Latin
Lynette R. Muir   French
Margaret Sleeman   Spanish
John E. Tailby   German

CONTENTS

Illustrations

INTRODUCTION

This book has one very modest aim: to make available descriptions, stage directions, and records of religious plays of the Middle Ages from all over Europe in modern English translations. It is not intended to give a comprehensive coverage but rather by drawing attention to the more interesting references that we have come across to give an idea of the range and type of information that exists. The book arose from our own joint work in medieval drama at the Centre for Medieval Studies in the University of Leeds and from the feeling that much staging information, though published, was not widely known, often because of the original language in which it was written.

The term "Middle Ages" needs some comment. Anything relating to a play before 1500 we have accepted without further question as evidence for medieval staging, anything after that we have used if it seemed to us to throw light upon a tradition of staging current in the Middle Ages. The obvious example of the latter is Lucerne where the vast bulk of the material, texts and records, comes from the late sixteenth century, but it is also true of locations such as Chester where despite a very early tradition of performance the main sources of information date from after 1550, the earliest manuscript of the complete text indeed dating from 1591. While it is easy to show that both of these plays stem from a tradition already flourishing in the Middle Ages, there remains the possibility that any particular piece of information may be a late addition. All we can do is give readers that warning and leave them either to rely on our judgment or, more importantly, to begin to search out the truth for themselves.

Predominantly the extracts that have been chosen are drawn from records and descriptions rather than stage directions. This is because we have attempted to choose references that are not only significant but also explain themselves, and too often stage directions indicate the doing of something but fail to say how it is to be done. They refer to Calvary or Jerusalem or *domus* or *tentum* without explaining how such a structure (if indeed it is a structure at all) was constructed, or call a character "bishop" or "thief" but give no idea, apart from the words of the text, how the audience knew. We have also included material such as the Toledo accounts, in which the very accumulation of a large number of detailed entries gives an idea of how something was done. We have sometimes omitted an apparently promising reference because its significance cannot be understood without a lengthy context.

We have chosen extracts because of what seems to us their intrinsic value in suggesting a tradition or a way of managing some piece of stagecraft. We have not limited ourselves to what might strictly be defined as "plays" because often the tech-

1

niques of processions and "shows" throw light on the staging of
true plays. In almost every case the extracts we have chosen
are not readily available in a modern English translation. Occasionally, however, we have included items already translated,
either because a translation has seemed to us inadequate or
because of the importance of the reference. Since our intention
is that the book should introduce the evidence for medieval
staging to the interested reader unfamiliar with the whole range
of scholarship on the subject, it has seemed wrong to exclude
material which might suggest an important tradition of staging
or method of organizing a performance simply because a translation existed. We have, however, kept these to a minimum.

We have deliberately avoided specific interpretation of the
material while accepting that any translation is inevitably an
interpretation, and, in order to give emphasis to the material
itself, we have made the linking passages as brief as possible.
The aim in translating has been to keep close to the original.
We have attempted to be clear in our own minds what a passage
meant before deciding how to translate it, but have used this as
a way of selecting the appropriate word rather than as a means
of slanting a whole translation in a particular direction. One of
the dangers of this approach is that awkwardnesses in the original remain in the translation, but this has seemed preferable to
the inevitable interpretation involved in ironing out problems or
in making a translation stylish. If ambiguities still exist, they
are the ambiguities of the original. Occasionally a word is
glossed but in the main we have left technical terms in a modern
English form rather than take interpretation further. In the
case of English texts, the same general principle has been ap-
plied, though in many cases the sentence structure remains the
same with only a single word or two translated. In all language
areas there have been some extracts in which either an uncommon word or phrase has proved impossible to translate, or a
colloquial mode of expression has created an ambiguity impossible of solution.

The introductions have been divided up according to language. Though it is of importance to know what is happening in
places close to each other, there is no way in a book of this
kind that it is possible to accommodate such a geographical division. It is equally impossible to use national boundaries when
dealing with so long a period of time, though we realize that a
certain awkwardness arises from our division according to
language, which joins Lucerne with Admont or Paris with
Rouergue. What the introductions attempt to do is to give some
idea of the range of staging information in a particular
language-speaking area so that the references that appear in
the main body of the text will not be totally without a context.
In the case of Cornish there is some inconsistency as well as
some unfairness in placing it under English; however, as the
only important example of Celtic drama from the period and,

despite its distinctiveness, one which is closely related to English, it has seemed most appropriate to place it there. In view of the small number of translations from Dutch and Greek plays, we have not provided introductions to these two traditions. The introductions are not intended to be potted histories of drama in an area or a language.

ENGLISH AND CORNISH

In the Latin *Visitatio Sepulchri* of the tenth century *Regularis Concordia* (not included here), England has one of the earliest descriptions of a play in medieval Europe, but apart from the Latin liturgical drama (and excepting the Anglo-Norman *Adam*) there is little information about the staging of plays in England until the very end of the fourteenth century. From that time the growth of the vernacular civic plays and the survival of both civic and guild records provide a scattered mass of material from the cities. Chester, Coventry, and York in particular demonstrate in considerable detail the workings of an annual processional staging of biblical plays. Each is similar in dividing up the play into a series of pageants, in using a number of separate wagons for the performance, in relying for the financing of the play on the craft guilds, and in performing at a number of stations in the city (a tradition rightly unshaken despite the recent attacks on it). The number of separate pageants varies: at York from 48 to 52, at Chester 24, at Coventry an unknown but possibly even smaller number. The performance date also varies: at York and Coventry on Corpus Christi day itself, at Chester (at least as far as surviving records are concerned) on the three days of Whitsun. The overall nature of the plays also differs from place to place: at York very much a civic-controlled exercise in public display, at Chester much more of a combined product of City and Church.

They vary most, however, in the nature of the surviving evidence. Most of the evidence from Chester, for example, is of the second half of the sixteenth century and stems primarily from three guilds--the Painters, Glaziers, Embroiderers, and Stationers'; the Smiths, Cutlers, and Plumbers'; and the Coopers' (with some information from the Cordwainers and Shoemakers')--and comes mainly from their financial accounts. On the other hand, York is rich in City material from the end of the fourteenth century and in the records of a single guild, the Mercers', from early in the fifteenth century. To these can be added the Bakers' records from the middle of the sixteenth century.

As a result of this varied evidence we have from Chester detailed information for the later sixteenth century about costumes and properties, payments to actors, methods of setting up and taking down "carriages" (the Chester name for the wagons), and also about food consumed during the various activities. There is, however, very little certainty about the pageant route and the relations of guilds and City. From York, on the other hand, there is little information about costumes and properties (except for the lucky chance of the survival of the Mercers' indenture), no detailed information about payment to individual actors, information over a long period about the development and repair of a single "pageant" (as the wagons were called in York) and of a single "pageant-house" (the store for the wagon), very detailed information on the pageant route for very nearly two centuries, and a considerable knowledge of the relationship between City and guilds. Coventry is to some extent a combination of York and Chester with detailed guild information about actors, properties, and costumes but also with considerable information about the part played by the City.

Information coming from the texts of the plays themselves is mainly in the form of stage directions, and there are again marked differences. The full Chester texts are all antiquarian copies dating from after the last performance of the play, but they possess a full and extremely interesting series of stage directions; York, on the other hand, possesses a complete text dating from the late fifteenth century but containing almost no stage directions at all. Only two pageants survive from the Coventry play, one in an early nineteenth-century edition, but they contain a number of interesting (and in one case well-known) stage directions. The importance of stage directions comes most to the fore, however, in the case of the N. Town plays (otherwise known as *Ludus Coventriae* and sometimes Lincoln plays). The manuscript is a composite one containing a number of different types of plays from different sources--a pageant series like York, a linked stationary group, and a two-part Passion Play. The most important of these for its information about staging is the Passion Play. This is intended for a place and scaffold set (fixed location staging) and contains not only detailed evidence for the use of scaffolds, but also information about costume, properties, and sets. Unfortunately its information is of value mostly through the accumulation of detail, in many cases needing considerable interpretation, and therefore little of it has been included here.

The records of other cities, towns, and villages suggest that the processional and the place and scaffold methods of staging were the two major traditions in English plays, but there was also considerable variation and interplay between them. In East Anglia, place and scaffold performance either through combinations of villages or in the smaller towns, and often in aid of church funds, seems to have been common. Something similar also appears in Kent (e.g., New Romney). On the other hand, Norwich certainly had a pageant series, while Canterbury seems to have had a single pageant play, though as with Lincoln it is difficult to be sure whether the play had spoken lines or was merely a tableau or mime. Information at present accumulating through the work of the Malone Society and Records of Early English Drama seems to suggest that fixed location staging was far more widespread than processional.

The greatest of the English place and scaffold plays is not a biblical or saint's play but a morality, the *Castle of Perseverance*, with its frequently reproduced stage plan. Like the *Castle*, the Cornish plays also make use of a circular acting area with possibly a series of scaffolds around the perimeter. Plans exist in the manuscript for each of the three parts of the Cornish *Ordinalia*--the *Origo Mundi*, *Passio Domini*, and *Resurrexio Domini*--and the plays contain an interesting series of stage directions, though these are not as full as those from the other major Cornish biblical play, the *Creation of the World*. The play of *St. Meriasek*, like the *Ordinalia*, contains a diagram indicating a circular playing area with apparent scaffolds around the edge.

No clear evidence has survived in English medieval theatrical sources for the large-scale fixed location type play in a civic setting such as appeared at Mons or Romans, or at Lucerne. Nor is the evidence for the staging of English plays anywhere as detailed as from those places. It is becoming clear, however, that almost everywhere in England (and this appears to be true of English-speaking Scotland as well) drama of some kind was being performed during the later Middle Ages and through into the sixteenth century. As ecclesiastical pressure grew, however, in the latter part of that century not only the great civic cycles but also the Summer-games and King-plays were squeezed out of existence, so that the final references to staging, and they are often very revealing ones, are to such things as selling off costumes or to wagons in decay. One such was the pathetic Norwich Grocers' wagon which, having been pushed out into the street for non-payment of rent, became "so weather-beaten that most of it was rotten . . . and now one piece was torn off it and now another" until it was finally handed over in part payment of the outstanding rent, and taken to pieces.

FRENCH

There is little information available about the staging of French vernacular drama before 1400 apart from the directions in the twelfth-century Anglo-Norman *Adam* and *Seinte Resurrecion* plays. As the former is available in many English translations, only brief quotations are used in this book; the Resurrection play has also been previously translated but there is no extant English version of the complete texts of the two staging prologues so they have been quoted in full.

From about 1400 through to the end of the sixteenth century, there is an enormous wealth of material including the texts, council minutes, and full accounts of the productions at Mons (1501) and Romans (1509). Especially valuable is the Mons text since it is a producer's copy with very full stage directions for the actual per-

formance. Many other play texts contain useful directions for staging, and there are also town records which provide details about
finance and organization while contracts with carpenters and painters
give precise descriptions of the size and construction of stages,
audience stands, scenery, and special effects. Eye-witness descriptions and personal comments in chronicles and epistles add another
dimension to this great bulk of material, of which necessarily only a
small fraction can be included here.

In the majority of cases, the information relates to big
civic productions of the Old or New Testament plays, but there
are also references to saints' plays and episodes from the Bible
on a smaller scale. Despite a steady flow of editions and studies in the last few years, there are still a number of plays that
have never been edited, and many references in city records
are only available in the century-old *Les Mysterès* by Petit de
Julleville. The work of G. Runnalls on the Auvergne/Mont-
ferrand tradition and the staging studies by Rey-Flaud and
Konigson have added a considerable new body of material to
that previously available and also suggest the probability that
much yet remains to be discovered in city archives and libraries
all over France.

An outstanding feature of the French civic productions was
the use of special effects or *feintes:* their preparation and execution was entrusted to a specially skilled man who was well paid for
his work. The large, solid timber stages made it comparatively easy
to construct elaborate machinery and trap-doors (*secrets*) even for
outdoor performances, and productions were sometimes so spectacular, especially in the presentation of Heaven and Hell, that they
were talked of for years afterwards.

A short time before the performance a parade or *monstre*
might be held to advertise the play. After it was over, the stage
would be dismantled and the timber and properties sold to help de-
fray the costs. Though there were exceptions, in most cases actors
seem to have provided their own costumes. The actors were drawn
from all walks of life from artisans and guild members to clergy and
aristocracy; there are even a number of references to women acting
in civic plays though this was by no means a universal practice.

It is noteworthy how much variety of actual staging is recorded. Plays on carts drawn by oxen or horses are recorded from
northern France, but the more usual practice was to use a large
multiple set, which might consist of one great stage with a series of
mansions on it as at Mons or Valenciennes, a series of platforms and
mansions as in the play of St. Crispin or the Montferrand Passion, a
combination of mansions and a *platea* or playing area as at Rouen,
the use of an amphitheater as at Bourges, or a theater in the round
as in the fifteenth-century Fouquet miniature of the martyrdom of
St. Apollonia. In many cases the descriptions are susceptible of
various interpretations.

Medieval town councils, like their modern counterparts,
were particularly concerned with finance, and a great many of

the records concern payments of some kind. France is the only
country in Europe where it was the normal practice to charge
for admission to the plays, and a semi-professional attitude to
the financing of even religious drama is already evident in the
Royal Charter granted to the Brotherhood of the Passion in
Paris in 1402. In translating the financial references, the original French money of account--the *livre, sou,* and *denier*--has
been rendered in £ s d, with an occasional T added as in the
French to indicate that it is the *livre tournois* that is meant.
The *livre parisis* is only mentioned rarely. The other common
unit of currency used in the records is the *florin*, which
equalled twelve *sous* or *grossi*.

The money was provided from a variety of sources, including local churches and church dignitaries, the city councils,
admission charges, contributions by the actors (which gave them
also a right to a share of any profits), or individual patrons.
The play was generally produced by a *régisseur* or *conduc-
teur*, sometimes a specially imported and paid professional,
sometimes a local man. In a civic production there was often a
group of councillors or *echevins* appointed to supervise the
play. The performance might last from one to forty days,
though the length of each session seems to have varied considerably: from as little as 1200 lines to over 5,000. Sometimes
the "days" were consecutive as at Mons, an eight-day play, and
sometimes a series of consecutive Sundays or feast days as in
the five-Sunday Montferrand Passion or the forty-day Acts of
the Apostles at Bourges in 1536.

Although most performances were in the summer months and
on Sundays or feast days, there is little evidence of a special association with any one feast comparable to the Corpus Christi plays
of England or Spain. Nor do we find many examples of regular
annual or even decennial large-scale civic performances such as the
English guild cycles or the Lucerne Passion play. In almost every
case, the great plays seem to have been one-time occasions, inspired
by gratitude to God for deliverance from the plague, by a desire to
celebrate the prosperity of the town or to honor the local saint, or
by a mixture of similar and other reasons. Even after the ban on
religious plays by the Brotherhood of the Passion in Paris in 1548,
they continued to be performed in the provinces through the sixteenth century and even later in France itself, though in French-
speaking Flanders--in Lille, for example--religious plays were banned
by Philip of Spain in 1563 because of their subversive tendencies.

GERMAN

The preponderance of material from Lucerne over that from
the rest of the German-speaking area in this book reflects the
volume of extant material from this city regarding the staging of
the Passion play there compared with the relative paucity of

information about details of performances elsewhere. The recent important book by Bernd Neumann (*Zeugnisse Mittelalterlicher Aufführungen im deutschen Sprachraum,* 1979) increases greatly our knowledge of the range of locations at which plays were performed in the German-speaking area between the twelfth century and the early seventeenth century. Municipal accounts from various locations in the German-speaking area seem to reveal a fairly consistent pattern: in the week following Easter a group of local citizens performed a Passion play on a wooden stage erected for this purpose on the market place and taken down again after the performance. Both the erection of the stage and the provision of major props attracted municipal subsidy. This is precisely the situation in Lucerne, about which much more detailed information is extant.

It also seems that plays' texts and props were lent and borrowed commonly over relatively short distances. In this way there developed in many areas groups of plays with regional similarities. Such has long been recognized to be the case in Hessen, where definite links exist between several extant manuscripts (e.g., those associated with Frankfurt am Main and Friedberg) even though the precise details of the relationships are less easily discerned. The same is true of the Passion plays from South Tyrol, where only now are reliable editions of the texts being published in accessible editions which will make possible examination of the relationships. Consideration of this group of texts and associated material was deliberately omitted from this book.

The extant evidence reveals that the Lucerne Passion Play was performed at regular intervals from about 1450 until the late sixteenth century and then finally in 1616. Locally the play has always been referred to as the "Easter Play" since it was performed in Easter week. From about 1530 these performances lasted two days, and the version which can be reconstructed from the surviving partial texts requires two days of twelve hours each for performance. Texts, overlapping but each individually incomplete, survive from the performances in 1545, 1571, 1583, 1597, and 1616. The Zentralbibliothek Luzern also contains volumes of material relating to the performances from 1538 onwards. These together with the stage directions and other details in the manuscripts are the sources of the detailed information presented here.

Within the corpus of material from Lucerne that relating to the 1583 performance is especially significant since it includes the director's copy of the first quarter of the text (i.e., the first half of the first day including several elaborately staged scenes from the Old Testament) as well as the plans for the stage on both days drawn up by the director and Town Clerk Renward Cysat and also the list of measurements of the structures on the *Weinmarkt* square made by Uolrich Hardmeyer on Cysat's instructions on the day following the performance. Most of the material translated relates to this 1583 performance, but details concerning the 1571, 1597, and 1616 performances are included where they provide additional information.

Names for several parts of the staging area on the *Wein-markt* square recur frequently in the material from Lucerne. Translations for these have been chosen which avoid words such as "station," "booth," and "mansion" which have other connotations for English speakers: *hoff*, the wooden pens in which most of the actors remained seated throughout the day's twelve-hour performance when not involved in the current scene, has been translated as "stall"; *brugi* (pl. *bruginen*) is translated "stand" not only when it refers to structures occupied by spectators but also to others such as the Temple; *gerust* has been translated "scaffold" or "scaffolding"; *ort*, denoting the place where people stood when not involved in the action who had no "stall" of their own, is translated "position"; *stand* is translated "role" or "part"; and *platz* is translated "square" although the connotation "acting area" is also present.   The originals for these translations are not repeated each time they recur.   The building across the upper, eastern end of the square has been referred to throughout as the *Haus zur Sonne*, modernizing without translating Cysat's usage; by 1583 it had already ceased to be "The Sun Inn." While Lucerne is referred to as a "city" and its council as the "City Council" etc., the English term "Town Clerk" has been used for the office held by Cysat.   A separate note on the translation of the plans is contained in Appendix II.

Among the most familiar documents relating to medieval German theater is the *Frankfurt Director's Roll*, now known to date from the period 1315-45 and not to be an autograph of Baldemar von Peterweil.   This text, unusually but not uniquely in the form of a scroll 436 cms. long on two wooden rolls, shows signs of repeated use including erasures and alterations.   It consists of approximately four hundred incipits for song and speech in German and in Latin, constituting in all almost five hundred lines of text besides the stage directions.   The latter--somewhat disappointingly for our present purpose--record most frequently what happened when instead of the manner in which effects were achieved.   The same is true to an even greater extent of several other important medieval German play texts such as the *Alsfeld Passion Play* and the *Künzelsau Corpus Christi Play*, which therefore are not quoted at all.   By contrast, stage directions from the relatively unknown *Admont Passion Play*, which survives in a late sixteenth-century manuscript probably from Admont in Styria, South Austria, are particularly enlightening for our purpose of discovering how effects were achieved.

ITALIAN

The extant vernacular religious drama from Italy in the thirteenth through fifteenth centuries is mainly of two kinds. The *laude* or short liturgical plays associated with the church festivals were organized and performed by the *disciplinati*, re-

ligious confraternities based on a particular town such as
Perugia. The presentation was very simple as we can tell from
the costume and properties lists which have survived. The
sacre rappresentazione, on the other hand, were longer, with
more elaborate character and incident development; they were
often written by well-known authors and might be performed by
civic or religious groups in any town. In Florence the actors
were often young boys. We have very little information on their
staging apart from a few stage directions. Two plays stand
apart from this tradition. One is the Passion play performed in
the Coliseum in Rome on Good Friday annually from 1460 to 1540
of which the text and some records have survived. The second
is the *Revello Passion play* containing a number of very interesting directions, which was performed in 1489 and which
shows strong French influence on both the text and the staging.

In addition to the play texts, however, there are a number of
descriptions of plays being staged with very elaborate machinery as
in the Ascension and Annunciation plays in Florence (Section D). In
his life of Brunelleschi, Vasari describes machinery which the great
architect designed for such productions; his account has not been
included here as it is widely available in English.

A popular form of outdoor staging in Italy was the processional such as that described for the feast of St. John the Baptist in
Florence. These spectacles made use of a combination of horse-
drawn wagons and groups of people on foot or on horseback, as can
be seen in the Modena Nebuchadnezzar or the Florentine plays (Section D). Everywhere, the hallmark of the Italian productions of the
fifteenth century was magnificence and spectacular effects, especially the use of lights in the Church plays.

LATIN

Latin, which transcends limitations of area, is the original
language of a number of the extracts translated in this book, but
only three extended pieces can truly be said to be within the Latin
tradition.

The Latin religious drama of the later Middle Ages, as of
the earlier, was mainly the drama of the Church. We have included here some of the developments of liturgical traditions in
Latin for comparison, but our main concern has been with the
vernacular drama. The *Cividale Planctus* is mainly of interest
because of its detailed concern with the use of gesture in sung
drama; the Easter ceremonies from Barking in Essex are essentially extensions of one of the earliest of the tropes, the *Quem
queritis;* while the elaborate and stately Presentation play of
Philippe de Mézières represents the composing within a liturgical framework of a new drama.

SPANISH

In broad outline, the main types of theater found in medieval Spain were (a) drama more or less closely associated with the liturgy, hagiographic plays, etc., performed in church, and (b), the processions, tableaux, and later plays, what one might loosely call "street-theater," associated with Corpus Christi.

The eastern Catalan-speaking part of the Peninsula fostered a particularly rich tradition of liturgical and Church drama, and we include examples which throw light on different methods of staging. From Majorca, we include the translation from Catalan of a ceremony or play contained in a sacristan's book of ceremonial (*consueta*), and performed as part of the liturgy on Easter Tuesday in Palma Cathedral. Although a late version (early sixteenth-century), it is a full one, describing the movements of the participants and giving information about such matters as payment and costume (it includes an unusual and dangerous use of candles as part of an angel's costume).

Elaborate sung vernacular plays associated with the feast of the Assumption of the Virgin were a feature of the east of the Peninsula. We include in translation the text (probably early fifteenth-century) of the Valencia play, performed over two days. Although basically Mary's part only with cues, it gives information about the melodies to be used, movements, gestures, etc. A stage (*cadafal*) was set up, and raising and lowering machines are mentioned but not described. Some idea of these machines can be gained from Valencia Cathedral accounts concerning their construction and from a description from city records of a machine used at a royal entry in Barcelona in 1519. The survival to our own time of the two-day sung *Elche Assumption play* allows us to form an impression of the Valencia play. At Elche, both the singing of the dialogue and the use of elaborate machines contribute to slow down the action and produce a rather slow, stately style of performance, thus providing satisfying sessions on two consecutive days.

The stage-directions of a group of forty-nine plays from Majorca on a variety of religious subjects contain important information about the use and arrangement of multiple stages in churches (see the *Majorca Esther play, Majorca Last Judgment play*, etc.). The directions reveal too that at least some were sung to liturgical melodies. The manuscript, discovered by Gabriel Llabrés in 1887, is a copy made at the very end of the sixteenth century, but some of the plays are believed to be much older. A similar method of staging was known in mainland Catalonia judging by the opening rubrics of the *St. Eudalt play*. *The Prades Assumption play*, dating probably from the early fifteenth century and also from the mainland, may be yet another example of the same method of staging. In the case of these last two plays, however, the place of performance is not specified.

The other examples of church drama included here give an idea of staging to the west of Catalonia. Church records from Saragossa give glimpses of a Christmas play performed before Ferdinand and Isabella in 1487. From these we learn that the Holy Family was played by a family in real life. The text of the sixteenth-century *Robles Nativity* gives the "choreography" for what amounts to a danced play. The Burgos Passion sequence, again sixteenth-century in date, shows unusual treatment of familiar material.

An interesting example of theater in a domestic context is the simple Magi ceremony acted by members of the household of Miguel Lucas de Iranzo, Constable of Castile, in 1462 and again in 1463. The description, an eyewitness account, of this and other ceremonies is contained in a chronicle of the family's activities which is replete with descriptions of such private entertainments.

Civic drama to celebrate a particular event was rare in the Peninsula. There is, however, one very interesting example in a play organized for open-air performance at Alcalá de Henares near Madrid in 1568 to mark the return of saints' relics. Two eyewitness accounts give a clear picture of the construction of a large wheeled wagon stage (*carro*) with railings and also a less clear but interesting description of a Heaven. The efforts of Spanish towns were more usually directed towards the traditional processions, tableaux, and later plays, put on at Corpus Christi. Often the plays were performed in church before being taken into the streets. A bird's-eye view of the order of the enormous Barcelona procession and biblical pageant of 1424 can be gained by reading the account contained in the city's *Llibre de les solemnitats*. The same source additionally tells us which floats or groups were supervised by which church, and there is a group of floats attributed to no authority, which may be city or guild floats. A closer view of the Barcelona spectacle is obtained from a contract for the renovation of three floats (*entramesos*) some thirty years later. At Valencia the spectacle was, to begin with, a biblical pageant, but plays were performed from the sixteenth century. Another contract, between a guild and a group of dancers, gives a glimpse of the celebration in Seville.

The most important breakthrough of recent years has been the discovery in Toledo of the Cathedral's records of expenditure on plays for Corpus Christi. The texts of the plays have not survived, but the accounts for 1493 (included here) give detail quite literally on the nuts and bolts of putting on the performance. The Toledo floats (*carros*) had railings and were carried, as are those at Seville in Holy Week today. The organization of the play was in the hands of Alonso del Campo, a member of the Cathedral clergy, until his death in 1499, when outsiders were brought in.

Although the ecclesiastical authorities increased their control over the plays during the second half of the sixteenth century, many traditions survived. In Valencia, for example, plays were performed at Corpus Christi until the end of the nineteenth century. Some traditions have survived to the present day, providing an opportunity unique in Europe to experience the atmosphere and excitement of the older forms of theater.

EDITORIAL PRACTICE

Editorial material is printed in italic, and translations in roman. Where editorial material appears within a translation, it is enclosed within square brackets and printed in italic. Where a "technical" word is used in the original text, it is underlined and included in parentheses (round brackets) immediately after the word or phrase in translation. Where there is uncertainty about the meaning of a word or phrase we have either given the original in parentheses (round brackets) preceded by a question mark (?) or a further explanation in parentheses (square brackets) also preceded by a question mark (?). If it has been impossible to give a translation or if the word only exists in its original form (e.g., *maravedis*), the word is given in the original language and underlined.

Where equivalents exist for measurements they have been used, but we have left all currencies in their original form. Occasionally the text will use, for example, pound Tournais besides pounds not so designated. In this case we have followed the original usage.

All personal names (except first names in the English texts) have been left in the form in which they appear in the original text. Place-names have been modernized, and where a modern English form exists it has been used.

Quotations of dialogue from medieval plays are placed within single quotation marks, while all other quotations appear within the usual double quotation marks.

We have normalized "u" and "v" according to modern usage.

REFERENCE TITLES AND DETAILED BIBLIOGRAPHY

Each place, play, or record has been given a reference title. These are printed in capitals in the linking passages and are listed, with notes and full bibliographical references, in the *Reference Titles and Detailed Bibliography*.

We have attempted to make the reference titles brief and the elements consecutive, in the order: place or personal name followed by ceremony. Occasionally this pattern has not been retained because of the natural word order of the linking passage. In two cases the order of the elements is reversed: CHRISTMAS PLAY . . . SANCHEZ DE BADAJOZ; EASTER CEREMONY . . . GRANADA (p. 157). These will be found in the list under: SANCHEZ DE BADAJOZ CHRISTMAS PLAY and

GRANADA EASTER CEREMONY.
   The reference titles are also used in the list of contents.
   The short titles and the abbreviations for names of series used in this section are given in full in the Select General Bibliography.
   When dates are given by century, the standard EDAM abbreviation is used. Hence, sixteenth century is abbreviated as 16c.

SELECT GENERAL BIBLIOGRAPHY

Included in the Select General Bibliography are abbreviations and short titles used in the Reference Titles and Detailed Bibliography.

Bergmann, Rolf. "Spiele, Mittelalterliche geistliche," in *Reallexikon der deutschen Literaturgeschichte*, 2nd ed. Berlin, 1958- . IV, 64-100.

Brett-Evans, David. *Von Hrotsvit bis Folz und Gengenbach: Eine Geschichte des mittelalterlichen deutschen Dramas*. Grundlagen der Germanistik, 15 & 18. Berlin, 1975. 2 vols.

Chambers, E. K. *The Mediaeval Stage*. London, 1903. 2 vols.

Cohen, Gustave. *Histoire de la mise en scène dans le théâtre religieux français du moyen age*, 2nd ed. Paris, 1925.

Corbató, see: H. Corbató. *Los misterios del Corpus de Valencia*. University of California Publications in Modern Philology, 16, no.1. Berkeley, 1932.

D'Ancona, see: Alessandro D'Ancona. *Origini del teatro italiano*. 1891; rpt. Rome, 1966. 2 vols.

De Bartholomaeis, V. *Origini della poesia drammatica italiana*, 2nd ed. Turin, 1952.

Donovan, see: R. B. Donovan. *The Liturgical Drama in Medieval Spain*. Toronto, 1958.

EETS: Early English Text Society.

Froning, see: R. Froning. *Das Drama des Mittelalters*, Kürschners Deutsche National Litteratur, 14. Stuttgart, 1892. 3 vols.

Konigson, Elie. *L'Espace théâtrale médiéval*, CNRS. Paris, 1975.

Linke, Hansjürgen. "Das volkssprachige Drama und Theater im deutschen und niederländischen Sprachbereich," in *Europäisches Spätmittelalter, Neues Handbuch der Litera-*

turwissenschaft, 8. Wiesbaden, 1977. Pp. 733-63.

Llibre de les solemnitats, see: *Llibre de les solemnitats de Barcelona*, ed. A. Duràn i Sanpere and J. Sanabre. Barcelona, 1930-47. 2 vols.

LTM Facsimiles: Leeds Texts and Monographs, Medieval Drama Facsimiles.

Mélanges Cohen, see: *Mélanges d'histoire du théâtre du moyen âge et de la Renaissance, offerts à Gustave Cohen.* . . . Paris, 1950.

Michael, Wolfgang F. *Das deutsche Drama des Mittelalters.* Grundriss der germanischen Philologie, 20. Berlin and New York, 1971.

Neumann, Bernd. *Zeugnisse mittelalterlicher Aufführungen im deutschen Sprachraum.* I. Die Erforschung der Spielbelege (diss. Cologne, 1979); II. Dokumente (not yet published).

Newton, Stella Mary. *Renaissance Theatre Costume and the Sense of the Historical Past.* London, 1975.

"Orígenes del teatro catalán," see: M. Milá y Fontanals. "Orígenes del teatro catalán," in *Obras Completas.* Madrid, 1888-96. Vol. VI.

Petit de Julleville, see: L. Petit de Julleville. *Histoire du théâtre en France. Les Mystères.* 1880; rpt. Geneva, 1969. 2 vols.

PMLA: Publications of the Modern Language Association of America.

REED: Records of Early English Drama.

Rey-Flaud, Henri. *Le cercle magique.* Paris, 1973.

Shergold, see: N. D. Shergold. *A History of the Spanish Stage.* Oxford, 1967.

Southern, Richard. *The Staging of Plays before Shakespeare.* London, 1973.

Teatre hagiogràfic, see: *Teatre hagiogràfic*, ed. Josep Romeu. Barcelona, 1957. 3 vols.

TLF: Textes littéraires français.

Tydeman, William. *The Theatre in the Middle Ages*. Cambridge, 1978.

Wickham, Glynne. *Early English Stages 1300-1660*. London, 1959. Vol. I.

Young, see: Karl Young. *The Drama of the Medieval Church*. Oxford, 1933. 2 vols.

REFERENCE TITLES AND DETAILED BIBLIOGRAPHY

For abbreviations and short titles, see Select General Bibliography.

ABBEVILLE   1466; record of performance for the entry of Charles the Bold; town accounts.
In: Petit de Julleville, II, 196.

ADMONT   Passion play with elaborate music and stage directions; MS. found at Admont, Styria, S. Austria, and probably originating from there. Late 16c.
Das Admonter Passionsspiel, ed. K. K. Polheim (Paderborn, 1972), with facsimile including music.

AIX-EN-PROVENCE   1444; contract for the stage and effects for a performance of play of SS. Peter and Paul.
M. Raimbault, "Une représentation théâtrale à Aix en 1444," *Revue des Langues Romanes*, 67 (1933-36), 263-74.

ALCALA MARTYRDOM OF SS. JUSTO AND PASTOR   Play commissioned by the Church authorities and intended for outdoor performance (for details of context see Section D).   1568; text accompanied by a detailed report of the proceedings, containing description of wagon and Heaven.   Stage directions proper give cues for music and indicate that some dialogue was sung.
J. P. Wickersham Crawford, "Representación de los mártires Justo y Pastor de Francisco de las Cuebas," *Revue Hispanique*, 19 (1908) 428-54.
Extract from eye-witness account of festivities to celebrate the return of the relics (see Section D). Morales was a historian and also Professor of Rhetoric at the University of Alcalá.
Ambrosio de Morales, *La vida, el martyrio . . . y las translaciones de los gloriosos niños Martyres san Iusto y Pastor . . .* (Alcalá, 1568), fol. 122^r and fols. 141^v-42^v.

ALENÇON   1520; carpenters' contract for building of stage.
G. Despierres, *Le théâtre et les comédiens à Alençon aux XVIe et XVIIe siècles* (Paris, 1892), 16 pp.

AMBOISE   1507; council records.
In: Petit de Julleville, II, 90.

AMIENS   1499; council records.   This production of the Passion used the text borrowed by Mons in 1501.
In: Petit de Julleville, II, 78.

18

ANGLO-NORMAN ADAM   Play text with extensive stage di-
rections; MS. of 13c, now in the library of the city of Tours.
Le Jeu d'Adam (Ordo representacionis Ade), ed. Willem Noomen,
Classiques français du moyen âge (Paris, 1971).

ANGLO-NORMAN RESURRECTION   Play text with verse pro-
logue describing the staging; 12-13c.
La Seinte Resurreccion, ed. T. A. Jenkins, J. M. Manly, *et al.*,
Anglo-Norman Text Society, 4 (Oxford, 1943).

ATHIS-SUR-ORGE   1542; contract with painter to provide the
properties for a triple bill: "Solomon," "Joseph," and a morality
play, at Athis, a small village near Paris.
S. W. Deierkauf-Holsboer, "Les représentations à Athis-sur-Orge
en 1542," in *Mélanges Cohen*, pp. 199-203.

AUNAY-LÈS-BORDY   see ROYAL EXONERATION

AUTUN   1516; description of a stage made for a play of St.
Lazarus, contained in the *Catalogus Gloriae Mundi* of Bartolo-
meus Cassanaeus (Frankfurt, 1579).
French translation in Petit de Julleville, I, 405.
(The Latin text is printed in the Appendix.)

BARCELONA 1394   Extract from municipal archives referring
to Corpus Christi procession; obstruction of streets.
In: "Orígenes del teatro catalán," p. 366.

BARCELONA 1424   Extract from entry in city's *Llibre de les
solemnitats* which gives ordering of procession and other details
for 1424.
In: *Llibre de les solemnitats*, I, 12-21.

BARCELONA 1443   Corpus Christi procession postponed because
of rain; extract from *Llibre de les solemnitats*, I, 138.

BARCELONA 1453   Agreement dated 20 April 1453 between
members of Barcelona City Council and a priest, Johan Çalom,
concerning the renovating of floats.
Ed. A. Balaguer, in "Orígenes del teatro catalán," pp. 368-70.

BARCELONA 1519   Description of royal entry of Charles I in
1519.
In: "Orígenes del teatro catalán," p. 251.

BARKING ABBEY   Directions for liturgical plays at Barking
Abbey; contained in the 15c Ordinal but probably dating from the
late 14c.
In: Young, I, 164-66 and 381-84.

BAUTZEN   St. Dorothy play; town records show a performance
associated with the saint's day as an established tradition by
1413.
[H.] Schachner, "Das Dorotheaspiel," in *Zeitschrift für deutsche
Philologie*, 35 (1903), 158 (quoting K. v. Weber, *Archiv für die
sächsische Geschichte*, 4, pp. 115ff).

BODLEY RESURRECTION   Early 16c text of two-part verna-
cular play of "Christ's Burial" and "Resurrection." Stage direc-
tions mainly in Latin.
*The Late Medieval Religious Plays of Bodleian MSS. Digby 133
and e Museo 160*, ed. Donald C. Baker, John L. Murphy, and
Louis B. Hall, Jr., EETS, 283 (London, 1982).
Also a facsimile of the MS.: *The Digby Plays*, ed. Donald C.
Baker and J. L. Murphy, LTM Facsimiles, 3 (Leeds, 1976).

BORDEAUX   Contract for building the stage for a performance
of the Passion play in 1525. Transcribed from the unpublished
text in the Archives of Bordeaux by Charles Mazouer.
(The French text is printed in the Appendix.)

BOURGES   see also ISSOUDUN AND BOURGES

BOURGES EFFECTS   1536; list of all the properties, scenery
and effects required for the performance of the "Acts of the
Apostles."
*Mystère des Actes des Apôtres: Extraict des fainctes qu'il
conviendra faire pour le mistère des Actes des Apostres*, ed.
Auguste-Theodore de Girardot, Annales Archéologiques (Paris,
1854), pp. 8-24.

BOURGES PARADE   1536; eye-witness description of the parade
(*monstre*) that preceded the performance of the "Acts of the
Apostles."
Jacques Thiboust, *L'ordre de la triomphante et magnifique monstre du mystère des Saints Actes des Apostres faite à Bourges
1536* (Bourges, 1838).

BROTHERHOOD OF THE PASSION   Records of royal charter
and parliamentary decrees relating to the *Confrérie de la Passion*, Paris.
In: Petit de Julleville, I, 417-18, 425.

BURGOS PASSION   Play divided into three short scenes (*pasos*).
Directions describe the action of the play and give detail of
gestures.
Joseph E. Gillet, "Tres pasos de la Pasión y una égloga de la
Resurrección (Burgos, 1520)," *PMLA*, 47 (1932), 949-80.

CANTERBURY   Early 16c records in English of the civic show

of St. Thomas performed on a pageant wagon.
Records of Plays and Players in Kent, 1450-1642, ed. Giles
Dawson, Malone Society, Collections VII (Oxford, 1965), pp.
188-98.

CASTILIAN TRIAL IN HEAVEN AND NATIVITY   Play with
brief stage directions. Texts of songs. Authorship and
date of composition not indicated in MS. On basis of language, probably written in second half of 16c.
J. P. Wickersham Crawford, "Comedia á lo pastoril para la
noche de Navidad," *Revue Hispanique*, 24 (1911), 497-541.

CATALAN SAINTS' PLAYS   see CATALAN ST. EUDALT,
MAJORCA ST. CHRISTOPHER (Conversion of), and MAJORCA
SS. CRISPIN AND CRISPINIAN

CATALAN ST. EUDALT   Play with extensive stage directions
and list of parts with names of actors. MS. notes melodies to
which dialogue is to be sung. According to text, play "written"
in April 1549 at San Juan de las Abadesas, but play itself
probably earlier than this (see Romeu, I, 56).
Consueta de Sent Eudalt, in: *Teatre hagiogràfic*, II, 67-120.

CHALONS-SUR-MARNE   1507; town records.
In: Petit de Julleville, II, 9.

CHALON-SUR-SAONE   Council records for the performance of
a play of St. Sebastian in 1497.
In: Petit de Julleville, II, 73.

CHELMSFORD   15c-16c churchwardens' accounts in English,
containing payments for plays performed in the town, costume
lists, etc. Cox dates the inventory 1562; Coldewey, 1563.
J. Charles Cox, *Churchwardens Accounts* (London, 1913), p. 277;
John C. Coldewey, "The Digby Plays and the Chelmsford Records," *Research Opportunities in Renaissance Drama*, 18 (1975),
107.

CHESTER   Mid-16c records in French, Latin, and English of
civic cycle play performed from early 15c to late 16c. Text of
play from late 16c and early 17c; stage directions in Latin and
English.
Chester, ed. Lawrence M. Clopper, REED (Toronto, 1979).
The Chester Mystery Cycle, ed. R. M. Lumiansky and David
Mills, EETS, s.s. 3 (London, 1974).
Facsimiles of two MSS., ed. Lumiansky and Mills, in LTM Fac-
similes, 1 (1973) and 6 (1980).

CIVIDALE   *Planctus* text for five singers with music and extensive directions for gesture written within the stave, above and

below the notes, and indicating the precise relationship between
words and actions. The MS., of the 14c, was formerly in the
Chapter library of Cividale Cathedral, and is now in the town
museum. It is incomplete and the end of the *planctus* is miss-
ing.
In: Young, I, 506-12.

CLERMONT   1492; archives of the Puy-de-Dome.
André Bossuat, "Représentations théâtrales en Basse-Au-
vergne," in *Mélanges Cohen*, pp. 177-83.

CORNISH CREATION   *The Creation of the World with Noah's
Flood* (*Gwreans an Bys*), MS. dated 1611. Play text in Cornish
with English stage directions.
Gwreans an Bys. The Creation of the World, ed. Whitley Stokes
(London, 1864).

CORNISH ORDINALIA   *Origo Mundi, Passio Domini, Resurrexio
Domini*; a 15c Cornish play text with Latin stage directions.
The Ancient Cornish Drama, ed. and trans. Edwin Norris (Oxford,
1859), 2 vols.

CORONATION OF FERDINAND OF ARAGON   1414; eye-witness account by Alvar García de Santa María, contained in a
MS. in Bibliothèque Nationale, Paris, and quoted in Shergold,
pp. 119 (Death's costume) and 121 (Death on a cloud).

COVENTRY   15c and 16c records in Latin and English of civic
cycle play performed from the late 14c to the late 16c. Text
of part of play only, from 16c. Stage directions in English.
Coventry, ed. R. W. Ingram, REED (Toronto, 1981).
Two Coventry Corpus Christi Plays, ed. Hardin Craig, 2nd ed.,
EETS, e.s. 87 (London, 1957).

DIEPPE   1443; account of the celebration of the English defeat
in *Histoire des Marionnettes* by Ch. Magnin.
In: Petit de Julleville, II, 193.

DUTCH WISE AND FOOLISH VIRGINS   Play text with stage
directions.
Het Spel van de V vroede ende van de V dwaeze Maegden, ed.
M. Hoebeke (The Hague, 1979).

ERLAU   Magdalene play, one of five plays and a *planctus* in a
MS. dating from the first half of 15c, found at Erlau in Hun-
gary; now cod. B.V.6 of the Archiepiscopal library at Cheb,
Czechoslovakia.
Erlauer Spiele, ed. K. F. Kummer (Vienna, 1882). Magdalene
play is Play IV, fols. 116^r-21^r in MS.

FLORENCE 1304   Town records of bridge disaster during play.
In: D'Ancona, I, 94-95.

FLORENCE 1439   Greek description of the festival of St. John
the Baptist. The MS. that contained the description is no longer
in the library at Turin.
In: D'Ancona, I, 230-31 (in Italian translation).

FLORENCE 1454   Town records of St. John the Baptist processional plays.
In: D'Ancona, I, 228-29.

FLORENCE ANNUNCIATION AND ASCENSION   From the Russian MS. of the diary of Archbishop Abramo of Souzdal which we
have been unable to trace. The present translation is made from
the German of Wesselovsky and compared with the Italian of
D'Ancona (I, 246-53).
A. Wesselovsky, "Italienische Mysterien in einem russischen
Reisebericht des XV. Jahrhunderts," *Russische Revue*, 10 (1877),
425-41.

FRANKFURT   A director's roll (*Frankfurter Dirigierrolle*), a
series of *incipits* and stage directions for a Passion play. Used
for several performances in earlier half of 14c in Frankfurt.
Formerly ascribed to Baldemar von Peterweil.
In: Froning, II, 340-74.

FRENCH SS. CRISPIN AND CRISPINIAN   Verse prologue to the
play text of 1443.
(The French text is printed in the Appendix from the edition of
the Chantilly MS. by O. Ostrowski, Greifswald Dissertation,
1909.)

FRENCH ST. LAWRENCE   Play text of the 16c with stage
directions.
Le Mystère de saint Laurent, ed. W. Söderhjelm and A. Wallen-
sköld (Helsinki, 1891).

FRENCH ST. LOUIS   Play text with stage directions.
Le mystère de Saint Louis, ed. F. Michel, Roxburghe Club (London, 1871).

FRENCH SS. PETER AND PAUL   15c play text with stage
directions.
*Le cycle de Mystères des Premiers Martyrs du MS 1131 de la
Bibliothèque Sainte-Geneviève*, ed. G. Runnalls, TLF (Geneva,
1976).

GRANADA EASTER CEREMONY   (Bird-song in Section B.10).
From a MS. in the archives of Granada Cathedral, a late copy

of a document which describes a ceremony established in the
first half of 16c.
In: Donovan, pp. 61-62.

GREEK PASSION   Part of possibly 12c text with stage directions of a Passion play probably performed in Cyprus.
The Cyprus Passion cycle, ed. A. C. Mahr (Notre Dame, Indiana,
1947).

HESSE NATIVITY   MS. of play text probably written in Friedberg in Hesse around 1460; other such plays are known in the
area at that time.
In: Froning, III, 904-39.

IRANZO   (Dragon in Section B.5, and Magi ceremony in Section
D). Extract from chronicle which describes life in the household
of Miguel Lucas de Iranzo, Constable of Castile, in the second
half 15c.
Anon., *Relacion de los fechos del mui magnifico é mas virtuoso
señor Don Miguel Lucas, mui digno Condestable de Castilla*,
Memorial Histórico Español, 8 (Madrid, 1855), pp. 54-55 (dragon), pp. 75-76, 108 (Magi ceremony).

ISSOUDUN   1535; verse epistle by Jean Boucher, making sug-
gestions about staging and production.
In: Petit de Julleville, II, 128-30.

ISSOUDUN AND BOURGES   16c chronicle of Swabian Counts of
Zimmern relates the episode as a digression from reporting the
travels of two young members of the family in the Low Countries.
Zimmersche Chronik, ed. Karl A. Barack, Bibliothek des Lit-
terarischen Vereins, 91-94 (Tübingen, 1869), III, 226-28.

LILLE   15c town records of organization and production of
plays.
Leon Lefebvre, *Les Origines du Théâtre à Lille aux XVe et
XVIe Siècles* (Lille, 1905).

LINCOLN   16c records in English of city dramatic activities:
St. Anne's Day show and, later, play of Tobias. City and guild
records.
Records of Plays and Players in Lincolnshire, 1300-1585, ed.
Stanley J. Kahrl, Malone Society, Collections VIII (Oxford, 1974).

LUCERNE   Passion play performed at regular intervals from
c.1450 until late 16c, then finally in 1616. Locally called "Easter Play" since performed in Easter week. Under auspices of
city; many details of the elaborate staging in late 16c survive as
a result of the work of Renward Cysat, the Town Clerk and

Director of the play. Two-day performances from about 1530.
MSS. in Zentralbibliothek Luzern: Texts (overlapping but each
individually incomplete) from performances of 1545, 1571, 1583,
1597, 1616; records from 1538 onwards in MS. 167, I (1538,
1545, 1560); MS. 170 (1560, 1571); MS. 172, I (1583); MS. 172, II
(1583, 1597); MS. 172, III, IV, V (1583); MS. 172, VI (1583, 1597);
MS. 172, VII (1597); MS. 174 (1571, 1583); MS. 177 (1571, 1583,
1597); MS. 178 (1545, 1571, 1583, 1597); MS. Zu 178 (1571, 1583,
1597, 1614-16); MS. 179, I, II, III (1597).
M. Blakemore Evans, *The Passion Play of Lucerne: An Historical and Critical Introduction* (New York & London, 1943); German translation (+ some different illustrations) *Das Osterspiel
von Luzern* (Berne, 1961). Section by Gustave O. Arlt on
Judengesänge (+ illustrations of "song-tablets") in Blakemore
Evans, pp. 68-76. *Das Luzerner Osterspiel*, ed. Heinz Wyss
(Berne, 1967), 3 vols.

MAJORCA ESTHER   Play with extensive stage directions which
indicate use of multiple stages in church, liturgical melodies to
which dialogue is sung, and cues for music. One of 49 plays in
the Majorca Codex (now MS. 1139 in Biblioteca Central, Barcelona) discovered towards the end of the 19c in Majorca by
Gabriel Llabrés. MS. is a late 16c copy, but many of the plays
are believed to be considerably earlier.
Consueta del Rey Asuero, in: *Teatre bíblic: Antic Testament*,
ed. Ferran Huerta Viñas (Barcelona, 1978), pp. 237-82.

MAJORCA JUDITH   One of the plays of the Majorca Codex
(see MAJORCA ESTHER). Sparse stage directions which suggest,
however, the use of multiple stages. Cues for music and some
use of liturgical melodies for dialogue.
Representatió de Judith, in: *Teatre bíblic: Antic Testament*,
pp. 201-35.

MAJORCA LAST JUDGMENT   Play from Majorca Codex (see
MAJORCA ESTHER). Exceptionally full stage directions indicate
use of two stages in church. Cues for music, and dialogue sung
to liturgical melodies.
Consueta del Juy, ed. Gabriel Llabrés in *Revista de Archivos,
Bibliotecas y Museos*, 3ª época, 6 (1902), 456-66.

MAJORCA ST. CHRISTOPHER   1. Conversion: one of the
plays of the Majorca Codex (see MAJORCA ESTHER). In the
MS. followed by Martyrdom and they may have formed a single
unit. Stage directions do not give a clear idea of how play was
staged, but do indicate that some of the dialogue was sung to
liturgical melodies. Texts of songs.
Consueta del gloriós Sant Christòfol, in: *Teatre hagiogràfic*,
III, 65-82.
2. Martyrdom: very similar to above in music and stage

directions.
Consueta del martiri de Sant Cristòfol, in: *Teatre hagiogràfic*,
III, 83-115.

MAJORCA SS. CRISPIN AND CRISPINIAN   Play from Majorca
Codex (see MAJORCA ESTHER).   Unusually full stage directions
which show use of three stages, and gestures for actors.   Cues
for music, *incipits* for pieces sung; some dialogue sung to liturgical melodies.
Consueta de Sant Crespí y Sant Crespinià, in: *Teatre hagiogràfic*, III, 153-209.

MAJORCA ST. FRANCIS   Play from Majorca Codex (see
MAJORCA ESTHER).   Prologue and seven short scenes (*pasos*).
Later in date than many in MS., and ll. 43-44 of prologue show
that play was written for performance in a Franciscan convent.
Directions indicate use of stage and of smaller platform on a
higher level.   *Incipits* of psalms.
Consueta de Sant Francesc, in: *Teatre hagiogràfic*, II, 121-58.

MERCADE VENGEANCE   Unedited play text with stage direc-
tions.
(The French text is printed in the Appendix from the Chatsworth
MS.)

METZ   Chronicles of the city record various performances:
1437, Passion; 1468, St. Catherine; 1485, St. Barbe.   Memoirs of
supervisor give details of 1513 play of the Sacrament.
In: Petit de Julleville, II, 12, 32, 48, 103.

MICHEL'S PASSION   Play text with stage directions; first per-
formed at Angers in 1486.
Jean Michel, *Le Mystère de la Passion (Angers 1486)*, ed. O.
Jodogne (Gembloux, 1962).

MODANE   Partial text and records, including contracts for two
performances, of the Antichrist play in 1580 and 1606.
Louis Gros, *Etude sur le mystère de l'antéchrist et du juge-
ment de Dieu* (Chambéry, 1962).

MODENA   1556; city records of Corpus Christi wagon play.
In: D'Ancona, I, 358-60.

MONS   Producer's copy of text, with full accounts and extracts
from the council minutes for performance of Passion play in
1501.
*Le Livre de Conduite du Régisseur et Le Compte des Dépenses
pour le Mystère de la Passion joué à Mons en 1501*, ed.
Gustave Cohen (Paris, 1925).

MONTFERRAND   Records of performances of Passion plays in
the 15c, especially in 1477.
A. Bossuat, "Une représentation du Mystère de la Passion à
Montferrand en 1477," *Bibliothèque d'Humanisme et Renaissance*,
5 (1945), 327-46.
G. Runnalls, "Le théâtre à Montferrand au Moyen Age," *Le
Moyen Age*, 3-4 (1979), 465-94.
La Passion d'Auvergne, ed. G. Runnalls (Geneva, 1982), pp. 29-42.

NEWCASTLE UPON TYNE   15c to 16c city and guild records
of dramatic activities in the city.
Newcastle upon Tyne, ed. J. J. Anderson, REED (Toronto, 1982).
John Anderson, "The Newcastle Dragon," *Medieval English Theatre*, 3 (1981), 67-68.

NEW ROMNEY   Records in English of town play of the later
16c.
Records of Plays and Players in Kent, 1450-1642, ed. Giles
Dawson, Malone Society, Collections VII (Oxford, 1965), pp.
202-06.

NORWICH   Later 16c records in English of civic cycle play,
performed 15c to 16c. One pageant text only survives, from
16c.
Non-Cycle Plays and Fragments, ed. Norman Davis, EETS, s.s. 1
(London, 1970), pp. xxii-xxxvi, 8-18.

N. TOWN PASSION   Late 15c play text in English contained in
composite MS. Not attached to any particular town or city.
Stage directions in Latin and English.
Ludus Coventriae, ed. K. S. Block, EETS, e.s. 120 (London,
1922).
Also a facsimile of the MS.: *The N-Town Plays*, ed. Peter
Meredith and Stanley J. Kahrl, LTM Facsimiles, 4 (Leeds, 1977).

PALERMO   Description of performance and costumes in 1581.
E. Di Marco, *Drammatiche rappresentazioni in Sicilia* (Palermo,
1876), pp. 17-37.

PALMA EASTER CEREMONY   Description of ceremony performed in Palma Cathedral on Easter Tuesday as part of liturgy.
Contained in sacristan's book of ceremonial (*consueta*), dated
1511.
In: Donovan, pp. 133-34.

PARIS ENTRY   1502-15; records of performances given as part
of celebrations.
In: Petit de Julleville, II, 201-02, 205.

PARIS RESURRECTION   15c unpublished play text in Biblio-

thèque Nationale, Paris, MS. fonds français 972, of unique Resurrection play with detailed stage directions for effects. Sometimes called "Michel Resurrection."
(The French text is printed in the Appendix.)

PERUGIA   1339; inventory of costumes and properties owned by the guild of St. Dominic.
E. Monaci, "Uffici drammatici dei Disciplinati dell'Umbria," *Rivista di filologia romanza*, I, No. 4 (1872), 257-60.
Ciro Trabalza, "Una lauda umbra e un libro di prestanze," in *Scritti vari di filologia dedicati a Ernesto Monaci* (Rome, 1901), pp. 188-89.

PERUGIA SERMON   1448; chronicles of the city.
In: D'Ancona, I, 280.

PHILIPPE DE MÉZIÈRES   Elaborate description of his Presentation of the Virgin play; contained with other liturgical material relating to the feast in a MS. belonging to de Mézières himself.
William E. Coleman, *Philippe de Mézières' Campaign for the Feast of Mary's Presentation* (Toronto, 1981), pp. 84-107 (1385 description, pp. 110-11).

PLAY OF ST. JOHN AND ST. PAUL   1485; play by Lorenzo de Medici with staging prologue.
Alessandro D'Ancona, *Sacre Rappresentazioni dei Secoli XIV, XV e XVI* (Florence, 1872), II, 237.

PRADES ASSUMPTION   Play with extensive stage directions which indicate the use of several structures (a Hell, a curtained Paradise, etc.). Cues for music, note of melodies to which dialogue to be sung. Play contained in MS. written at Prades, Province of Tarragona, and dated 1420. Editor believes it could be earlier.
Joan Pié, "Autos sagramentals del sigle XIV," *Revista de la Asociación Artístico-Arqueológica Barcelonesa*, 1 (1896-98), 673-86, 726-44.

REVELLO   15c play text with stage directions.
La Passione di Revello, ed. A. Cornagliotti (Turin, 1976).

ROMANS   Text and full accounts for the preparations (1508-09) and the performance of the play of the "Trois Doms" in 1509.
Le mystère de Trois Doms joué à Romans en 1509, avec des documents relatifs aux représentations en Dauphiné de 1400 à 1535, ed. U. Chevalier and A. Giraud (Romans, n.d.).
Le mystère des Trois Doms, composition, mise en scène et représentation etc., ed. U. Chevalier and A. Giraud (Lyons, 1887).

ROME   1498; records of costume, etc., for the Passion play
performed at the Coliseum; from the archives of the *Confrater-
nità del Gonfalone di S. Lucia.*
M. Vattasso, *Per la storia del dramma sacro in Italia* (Rome,
1903), pp. 93-101.

ROUEN   1474; stage directions at the beginning of the MS. of
a Nativity play performed at Rouen.
*Le Mystère de l'Incarnation et Nativité de Nostre Sauveur . . .
Jésus-Christ représenté à Rouen en 1474,* ed. P. Le Verdier
(Rouen, 1884-86), 3 vols.

ROUERGUE   15c play texts with stage directions, including a
play of the Last Judgment.
Mystères provencaux du 15e siècle, ed. A. Jeanroy and H.
Teulié, Bibliothèque Méridionale, III (Toulouse, 1893).

ROYAL EXONERATION   Two letters of remission granted by
the king after fatal accidents caused by cannon during the preparations for plays at Paris (1380) and Aunay-lès-Bordy, near
Paris (1384). Two of the earliest texts relating to performances
in Paris.
A. Thomas, "Le Théâtre à Paris à la fin du XIVe siècle,"
Romania, 21 (1892), 606-11.

ST. GENEVIEVE   Paris; early 15c MS. including biblical and
saints' plays. May have been repertory of the Brotherhood of the
Passion. 1. Nativity: stage directions in texts.
La Nativité et les Trois Rois, ed. R. Whittredge (Bryn Mawr
diss., 1944).
2. Passion: stage directions in text.
*Le mystère de la Passion Nostre Seigneur du MS 1131 de la
bibliothèque Sainte-Geneviève,* ed. G. Runnalls, TLF (Geneva,
1974).
*A Critical Edition of La Passion Nostre Seigneur from MS 1131
from the Bibliothèque Sainte-Geneviève,* ed. E. J. Gallagher
(Chapel Hill, 1976).

ST. OMER   1456-83; references in town accounts to perfor-
mances on carts and at drama festivals.
Justin de Pas, *Mystères & Jeux Scéniques à Saint-Omer aux
XVe et XVIe Siècles* (Lille, 1913).

SANCHEZ DE BADAJOZ CHRISTMAS PLAY   Mid-16c alle-
gorical play by Diego Sánchez de Badajoz which combines shepherds' announcement of Christ's birth, the *Ordo Prophetarum,* and
a sibyl's announcement of a tournament between Virtues and
Vices. Full stage directions which indicate performance in
church. Cues for music, texts of songs. Much of action takes
place off-stage.

Farsa del juego de cañas, in *Recopilacion en metro del Bachiller Diego Sanchez de Badajoz, reimpresa del ejemplar único por . . . D. V. Barrantes* (Madrid, 1882-86), II, 267-90.

SARAGOSSA   Accounts, authorized by the Archbishop and Chapter, which refer to a Nativity play performed before Ferdinand and Isabella and their children.   Schack writes that these accounts are "from the archive of the parish church of San Salvador."   The involvement of the Chapter suggests the Cathedral or a collegiate church.   The old Cathedral of Saragossa (*La Seo*) is dedicated to San Salvador.
Adolf Friedrich von Schack, *Historia de la literatura y del arte dramático en España . . . traducida . . . por Eduardo de Mier* (Madrid, 1885-87) I, 266-68.

SEMUR   1488; play-text with stage directions.
La Passion de Semur, text by P. T. Durbin, edited with an introduction and notes by L. R. Muir, Leeds Medieval Studies, 3 (Leeds, 1981).

SEURRE   Text and author's account of the production of the play of St. Martin in 1496.
Andrieu de la Vigne, *Le mystère de Saint Martin 1496*, ed. A. Duplat, TLF (Geneva, 1979).

SEVILLE   Contract of 1540 between the guild of tanners and the leader of a group of dancers for a danced representation of the coming of the Magi as part of the Corpus Christi procession.
C. López Martínez, *Teatros y comediantes sevillanos del siglo XVI* (Seville, 1940), p. 99 (quoted in Shergold, pp. 99-100).

SIENA NATIVITY   Scenario for a lauda, a liturgical play in the vernacular.
De Bartholomaeis, *Laude drammatiche e rappresentazioni sacre* (Florence, 1943), II, 208-09.

SUAREZ DE ROBLES   Danced Nativity play with very full stage directions.   Texts of songs.   According to stage directions, performed in church.
Joseph E. Gillet, "*Danza del santissimo nacimiento*, a sixteenth-century play by Pedro Suárez de Robles," *PMLA*, 43 (1928), 614-34.

TOLEDO   1. Corpus Christi procession and plays: very detailed accounts noting expenditure by Toledo Cathedral in 1493.
2. Extract from inventory of the possessions of Alonzo del Campo (member of the clergy of Toledo Cathedral and director of the Corpus Christi plays), drawn up in 1500, after his death.
Carmen Torroja Menéndez and María Rivas Palá, *Teatro en Toledo en el siglo XV*, Anejos del Boletín de la Real Academia

Española, 35 (Madrid, 1977), pp. 185-92 (accounts) and pp. 193-97
(inventory).

TURIN   1429; play of St. George. List of properties with cost.
From the royal accounts at Chambery, capital of Savoy.
Giuseppe Boffito, "Antica drammatica piemontese," *Giornale
storico della letteratura italiana*, 30 (1897). 344-46.

VALENCIA ASSUMPTION   Text (probably early 15c) contains
Mary's part and cues as well as detailed information on movements, processions, gestures, music to which dialogue is to be
sung. Play performed over two days, in church. Stage machinery used.
E. Juliá Martínez, "La Asunción de la Virgen y el teatro
primitivo español," *Boletín de la Real Academia Española*, 41
(1961), 179-334. Pp. 313-20 are a photographic reproduction of
Baron Alcahalí's edition of the text, based on the MS., now
lost. We have translated from the Alcahalí edition rather than
from the more recent one by M. Sanchis Guarner (see VALENCIA
CATHEDRAL) based on Alcahalí only.

VALENCIA CATHEDRAL   Extract from Valencia Cathedral
records (mid-15c) which refer to expenditure on machines for
raising and lowering (the *araceli* and angel's *peanya*, 'pedestal').
Published by J. Sanchis Sivera, "La dramática en nuestra catedral," *Almanaque de las Provincias* (Valencia, 1908), and quoted
in M. Sanchis Guarner, "El misteri assumpcionista de la catedral
de Valencia," *Boletín de la Real Academia de Buenas Letras de
Barcelona*, 32 (1967-68), 97-112.

VALENCIA CORPUS CHRISTI   Valencia City Council's agreement to a request from the King of Aragon that properties be
lent for the Coronation.
Corbató, p. 147.

VALENCIA CORPUS CHRISTI PROCESSION   Extract from the
accounts for Corpus Christi procession in early 15c (animal
suits).
M. Carboneres, *Relación y explicación histórica de la solemne
procesión del Corpus, que anualmente celebra la ciudad de Valencia* (Valencia, 1873), pp. 23-26.

VALENCIA DEPOSITION   Extract from records of 1517 for a
lost Deposition play performed at Corpus Christi, which refer to
payments to stage hands.
Corbató, p. 152.

VALENCIA ST. CHRISTOPHER   Extract from note on costumes
and properties in a late 17c copy of an older (lost) play performed at Corpus Christi (St. Christopher's costume).

Corbató, pp. 91-92.

VALENCIENNES   Contract agreed with the actors for the performance of the Passion play in 1547.   Written at the end of the
unpublished MS. of the play, Paris Bibliothèque Nationale fonds
français 12536.
In: Petit de Julleville, II, 144-56.

VIEL TESTAMENT   Compilation of plays on Old Testament
subjects. The Creation play has important stage directions.
Le Mistère du Viel Testament, ed. Baron James de Rothschild,
Société des Anciens Textes Français, (Paris, 1878), 6 vols.
*La Creacion, La Transgression and L'Expulsion of the Mistère
Du Viel Testament*, ed. Barbara M. Craig, University of Kansas
Publications, Humanistic Studies, 37 (Kansas, 1968).

VIENNA EASTER PLAY   Name taken from location of MS.;
language suggests that this play, dating from 1472, was written
down in southern Silesia.
Das Drama des Mittelalters, ed. Eduard Hartl, Deutsche Literatur
in Entwicklungsreihen (Stuttgart, 1937), pp. 74-119.

VIENNA PASSION   Incomplete MS. dating from about 1330;
apparently the work of a Bavarian scribe using a source from the
central Rhineland.
In: Froning, I, 305-24.

WYMONDHAM   16c guild records in English for dramatic activities of a small town.
Records of Plays and Players in Norfolk and Suffolk, 1330-1642,
ed. David Galloway and John Wasson, Malone Society, Collections
XI (Oxford, 1980/1), pp. 119-32.

YORK   14c to 16c records in French, Latin, and English of
civic cycle play performed from late 14c to late 16c.
Text survives from 15c, but few stage directions, all in Latin.
York, ed. Alexandra F. Johnston and Margaret Rogerson, REED
(Toronto, 1979), 2 vols.
The York Plays, ed. Richard Beadle (London, 1982).
Also a facsimile of the MS.: *The York Plays*, ed. Richard
Beadle and Peter Meredith, with a note on the music by Richard
Rastall, LTM Facsimiles, 7 (Leeds, 1983).

A. THE PRELIMINARIES

1. ARRANGING THE PLAY

The initial impetus for a performance might come from any one of a variety of sources. At MONS *in 1501, the idea came from an* ad hoc *group of townspeople:*
There was a discussion of the request made by some of the townspeople to be granted permission to perform the Passion, also to be able to enclose the area (place) of the said stage (hourt), and that the town should grant them help with the expenses, including the stage being built at the expense of the town. Agreed that they should be given reason to hope (leur bailler espoir), and that information should be sought on how things had been done in similar cases.

At MODANE *a group of individuals paid to acquire a text before asking the community to put on the play:*
May it be to the honored praise of God. Amen. Since it is so that certain individuals from Modane, moved by a sense of devotion, have paid out a certain sum of money to have and acquire (havoir et retirer) the books (les livres) of the mystery of the Judgment, intending this mystery to be played in the said place and seeing this mystery not being set forward (ne soy mettre en avant), have called on worthy Claude Torne and Jean Albert currently officers of Modane (modernes sindics d'Amodane) to inform them whether the community of the said Modane intend to play it or not, with the intention and purpose that if they are informed that the said community wants to play the said mystery, they will offer the said text to this community on their guaranteeing them (en les guarantissant) the money employed to acquire the said text without asking for expenses or remissions (vacations). Otherwise they have been asked to hand over the said books elsewhere, which they will do.
To which the said officers did not wish to give any reply without having first heard the will of the people of the said Modane, as the said officers have truly affirmed above.

For this reason, today, the 21st of the month of April 1577, in front of me, the ducal notary here undersigned, and in the presence of the witnesses named below at the request of the said officers, the said dwellers and inhabitants of Modane named below being assembled by the ringing of the bell in the usual manner, in the square in front of the church of the said place, having first of all invoked the name of God, on coming out of the church, being asked by the said officers whether they intend to perform the said mystery of the Judgment with the help of God, replied individually as is set down hereafter, in the

35

presence moreover of Maître Jean-Michel Chinal, ducal notary of
the said Modane, lieutenant of the Lord Castellan (seigneur
chastellain) and of Catherin Clerc, ducal officer (sergent ducal)
present in the interests of his Highness [the Duke of Savoy],
as follows:
[140 people are listed as being present]. All the above-named
agree and are of the opinion that, with divine help and all being
done devoutly and for the instruction of the people (l'instruction
du public), the community of Modane should perform this mystery and to this end retain the said texts, have them corrected,
and generally carry on as the matter requires until any other
decision be taken by the community.

And the said Benedict Nuer and Jean Jordain, butchers, have
protested that they understood the costumes of the actors (accoutrements des ystoriens) were to be provided at the expense
of the community.

Mathe Valloyre agreed to the above except that he does not
consent to the costumes being provided by the community at the
expense of the said community. François Lanfrey, Mathe Pinet,
and Claude Torne said that if they were thought fit to have
parts (capables faire personnages) they would not be able to
undertake (emprompter) them.

Claude Villet du Mollar and Jean, son of the late Jean Bernard,
said they were prepared to accept all the expenses but did not
want to act (faire personnages).

Master Michel Replat, ducal notary, agrees to act but does not
want the community to provide the costumes.

Claude, son of the late Pierre Coct, says he has enough to pay
without that and does not agree to it.
   [Formulas of signing.]

   The preliminaries might involve obtaining permission from
appropriate authorities. This might be given directly by the
king, as with the BROTHERHOOD OF THE PASSION in Paris in
1402:
We, Charles etc., make it known to all present and to come,
that we have received the humble supplication of our well be-
loved brothers, the Masters and Governors of the Brotherhood
of the Passion and Resurrection of our Lord, based on the
Church of the Trinity in Paris, setting out that for the performing of various plays (misterres) of saints, both men and
women, and especially the play of the Passion which they have
recently begun and prepared to perform before us, as they
have done previously, which they have not been able properly

to continue because we were not then able to be present; for
which performance and play the said Brotherhood has laid out
and spent much of its goods as have also the Brothers each one
in proportion; saying further that if they played publicly to the
community (en commun) it would be to the profit of this Brotherhood, which they may not properly do without our leave and
permission, they request our gracious granting thereof. We
who will and desire the welfare, profit, and advantage of the
said Brotherhood and the rights and revenues thereof to be
increased and augmented with favors and privileges so that
everyone as an act of devotion may and should join them and be
of their company; to those Masters, Governors, and Brothers of
the said Brotherhood of the Passion of our said Lord, we have
given and authorized, give and authorize with special favor,
power, and royal authority, this time for all time and always in
perpetuity, by the tenor of the present letters, authority,
leave, and permission to perform and play any play at all, be it
the said Passion and Resurrection or any other of saints both
men and women, that they shall select and put on whenever and
as often as they please either before us, before our commons,
or elsewhere either in rehearsal (en recors) or otherwise and to
meet, unite, and assemble in whatever place or space lawful for
this purpose which they find either in our town of Paris or in
the surrounding districts (la Prévoste, Viconté ou Banlieue
d'icelle) in the presence of three, two, or one of our officials as
they select, without thereby committing any offence against us
or justice. And these Masters, Governors, and Brothers above-
mentioned and each one of them during the days on which is
performed the said play that they are playing, either before us
or elsewhere, either in rehearsal or otherwise, thus and in the
said manner may go, come, pass, and return peacefully,
dressed, garbed, and equipped (ordonnez) each one of them as
the case shall require and as is appropriate, according to the
ordering (ordenance) of the said play without let or hindrance;
and for the greater confirmation and surety of our most abun-
dant favor we have taken these Brothers, Governors, and Masters under our protection and safeguard during the course of
the said plays (jeulx) and while they are playing only, without
any harm to them nor to any one of them on this occasion or
otherwise however it may be to the contrary.

*Local secular and ecclesiastical authorities, separately or
together, were often approached.*
At AMIENS *the council* (eschevinage) *met on 3 February 1499,
when two members* reported on the interviews they had had with
the king's officers about the Mystery and the Passion of our
Lord Jesus Christ which it was planned to perform this year;
they [*the officers*] had responded favorably but as for the Lord
Bishop and the Chapter, it seemed from their excuses and criti-

cisms that they were not favorably disposed nor wished to contribute.
Having debated the matter, the councillors decided that if the
royal officials are in favor of the performance, without further
discussion with the aforesaid bishop and chapter they will have
the Passion of Our Lord Jesus Christ performed at the forth-
coming feast of Whitsuntide.

At CLERMONT *in 1492, the townspeople refused to join
the canons in organizing a performance of a morality play:*
Let them perform it at their own expense, for there is a threat
of pestilence and the town has many problems (de grans af-
feres).

*Permission might be obtained only very shortly before the
performance.* MONS *town council, June 1501. The performance
was in July:*
And it seemed also good to ask his grace of Cambrai [*bishop of
the diocese in which Mons lay*] for license to perform the said
play.

*Sometimes permission to perform might be given only on
certain conditions, as for the performance of the "Viel Testament" by the* BROTHERHOOD OF THE PASSION *in Paris in
1542:*
[*On the understanding that*] they shall charge each person only
2s admission to the theater (théâtre); only charge 30 escus
for the rent of each box for the duration of the said mystery;
there shall be performances only on feast days that are not
Solemn Feasts (non solennelles); they shall begin at one hour
after midday and finish at five; they shall ensure that there is
no scandal or riot; and since the people will be attracted away
from Divine Service and this will diminish the alms-giving, they
shall pay to the poor the sum of a thousand pounds, unless a
larger sum is ordered.

An application for permission to perform in LILLE *in 1590
indicates that similar restrictions were in force in the Spanish
Netherlands:*
We, Jaspar Flameng etc., all actors in plays and comedies (com-
édies) of this town of Lille, in order to attract the youth and
the people of this town away from the taverns and wineshops on
Sundays and holy days and to keep them in the town on these
days without their leaving it, and also to avoid the rows and
arguments (noise et questions) which often occur on these days
as a result of drinking, these petitioners have the intention,

with the help and assistance of their fellow actors and the
permission of the most honored lords, and indeed to provide an
edifying example for the salvation of the said community, to
present and perform at the next season of Easter in the town of
Lille on the said Sundays and holy days at the accustomed
hours, as has been done in times past, the Passion of Our Lord
and Savior Jesus Christ, as has been done in the past in the
Court of Our Lord and King [*the Palais du Rihours*] and in
other places; and the said petitioners promise to submit these
[*texts*] beforehand and have them inspected and approved by
the worthy Doctor Cupette and to submit them to you, my
lords, at a time and place agreeable to you and to the satisfac-
tion of your lordships. Having the intention also, in view of the
cost and expenses that will be involved in this task, to charge
6d T (tournais) for each person on the understanding that they
will pay to the poor of the town the sum of £4 P (parisis) for
each day that they perform, which the said petitioners would
neither wish nor dare to do without your lordships' permission,
which is the reason why these petitioners have addressed themselves to you, worthy and discreet gentlemen, beseeching you
most humbly that you should grant them permission for this
undertaking. And also they promise that in these plays they
will conduct and comport themselves as they have done in the
past in all honor and respectability without anything that can be
criticized. [*The permission was granted but the levy for the
poor was raised to £5 per playing day.*]

*Various reasons for organizing a performance, including
civic rivalry and the hope of financial gain, and also the getting
of permission from civic and religious authorities are recorded in
comments about the performance at* ISSOUDUN AND BOURGES.
Some rich citizens of a small town called Issoudun, ten French
miles from Bourges, decided to put on a Passion play (ein passion). For this purpose they built a proper theater (thatrum),
just as we read that the Romans did down to the days of Pom-
pey the Great. The costumes were also made expensively from
all kinds of silks. The nobility with their womenfolk rode from
great distances to see it. The organizers (spilhern) profited
greatly as did the citizens of Issoudun in general, for the play
attracted enormous crowds and everyone wanted to see it, for
nothing like it had been seen in France in many years and it
was therefore valued for its rarity.
. . .
The Passion play at Issoudun could scarcely have been finished
before it was known that the citizens there had done such good
business that several thousand francs were left, over and above
all expenses, besides the praise which had also accrued to
them. Thereupon the leading citizens of Bourges held a meeting
and decided that, since everything had gone off so well and so

profitably at such a small place as Issoudun, all that could well
be put on with great honor and magnificence at Bourges, and
that besides they had space for a theater (theatro) and other
possibilities (gelegenhait) in every way better than those at
Issoudun. The French court had indeed been accommodated
here several times. They conferred together on all these matters and decided that not only they who were meeting the costs
would benefit from it greatly, but that all the citizenry would
derive great profit from it. And when they had requested and
obtained from the court permission and privilege they began
serious preparations with the intention of putting on (spilen)
the Acts of the Apostles.

Now at Bourges there was on one side an astonishingly large
ditch at a place in the town which was somewhat on an elevation; the old people said that once many years ago a tower stood
there. . . . This ditch or the open space (platz), which as I
have already mentioned was said to have been the base of a
tower, the citizens obtained from King Francis as a theater
(theatro) and since it had a large ward (?bezirk) and also plenty of space around it, the citizens began to fit it out as an
amphitheater (amphitheatro) of a pretty good size, in any es-
timation almost as large as the capacity of the Colisseum at Rome.
Also on the ground they had their channels through which they
could secretly direct the water into the acting area (caveam)
and out again. The extent of their expenditure on the costumes
and other items can well be judged from the fact that several of
them were almost ruined by the expense, for the simple reason
that immediately after Easter in that same year 1535 [final 5 is
editorial addition] war broke out between the Emperor Charles
and the King of France, so that the greater part of the nobility
was called on to perform feudal service, and in addition there
were all kinds of trouble in France. This proved a great hindrance to this play, so that they could not make so much money
from it as would have been the case otherwise.

      In LUCERNE, the performance planned originally for 1592
took place only in 1597; the official response to the formal request for this performance is contained in the minutes of the
City Council for 9 August 1596, and as elsewhere is coupled
with arrangements regarding the sharing of costs:
Today the City Council at the instigation and request of our
local parish priest (H. Lüttpriesters) on behalf of the brethren
of the Brotherhood of the Coronation agreed to the playing and
performance next Easter of the story of the Passion, which is
called the Easter Play. But in order that not all expense, particularly such great expense as occurred previously, shall fall
on the Councillors and their City, the Council will nominate
certain of their own members to join those gentlemen nominated

by the Brotherhood, who will be in charge and will keep the
expenditure under review as to how much can be saved (wie vil
darüber gan möge) and how much the Council will be required
to contribute beyond the fees paid by the participants; and
since war or pestilence might occur, it shall remain within the
competence of the Council until after Christmas to cancel this
performance.

*Even in a city where performance was fairly regular, the
decision had still to be taken and those taking part notified.
The notification of the craft guilds by the mayor at YORK was
very formal:*
The schedules of the pageants (sedule paginarum) [*the brief
descriptions of each short play*], written out by the Common
Clerk, are to be delivered annually to the crafts by six ser-
geants-at-mace of the mayor in the first or second week in
Lent, in the form subsequently below-written [*the descriptions
follow this note*].

Occasionally the schedules (usually called "billets") were recalled:
And in consideration of the said plague, it is agreed that the common officers of this city shall immediately take into their hands the
billets that were sent out for the Corpus Christi play; and the said
play for the said consideration to be given up and not to be played
this year [*18 May 1550*].

*The arrangements made at ROMANS in July 1508 for the
performance of the "Play of the Three Martyrs" included a specific agreement on the sharing of costs:*
And firstly it was said that the gentlemen of the Chapter and
those of St. Maurice will pay half of all the cost and expense
which will be made, both for making the book and for the production (pour fere joyer) of the said play. That is to say that
the gentlemen of the Chapter will pay two thirds of the half and
the gentlemen of the Chapel of St. Maurice will pay one third of
the half; thus the town will pay the other half of the said expenses.

*Major construction work was sometimes treated separately.
At MONS in April 1501:*
There was a discussion on the Mystery of the Passion to determine whether the town would have the stage (hourt) built at
the town's expense. Agreed to assemble those who are taking
part (qui ont parchon) next Sunday to learn if all will be ready
for Whitsun and then ask the carpenters if they could complete
the stage within the said time.

Later in the month it was agreed in the matter of the Mystery
of the Passion that they should send for Master Collart Ghossuin
together with some of those who are organizing (s'entremetent)
the said Mystery to learn the cost of the stage (hourt), the es-
timate and the way of doing it (quelle conduite il y auera) in
order to report to the next council, *at which there was* further
discussion of the Mystery of the Passion: whether it will be
done and at whose expense. Agreed to perform the Mystery as
soon as possible (à toute diligence) and the town to construct
the stage (hourt) and to ask permission from the Central Authority (de la main); appointed commissioners: De le Val and
Engherant, with the town clerks of works (maistres des ouv-
rages).

         *At NEW ROMNEY, Kent, in 1560 all the inhabitants were
expected to share in the labor and costs of setting up the
stages, and their individual responsibilities were listed, for
example:*
In primis--Mr. Simon Padyham, Bailiff: his own stage;
Item--Mr. Cheseman; 20s, provided that he is not charged with
anything or any office relating to the play;
Mr. Holton: builds Heaven;
. . .
Thomas Ederycke: four loads with his wagon and four days
work;
. . .
Richard Godfrey: his part of the stage;
. . .
[*Most of the inhabitants offered a number of days' work.*]

         *At LUCERNE in 1583 as usual the City Council paid for the
construction of the stage and other woodwork: [See also the
lists of expenditures below, Section C.]*
This is what the City Fathers (Mgh) are having prepared for
the Easter Play in 1583:
         Heaven, the woodwork
         Item: the general stands (brüginen)
         Item: the Mount of Olives and Thunder
         Item: everything required for the Manna
         Item: the Rock from which water flows
         Item: the bier, and another one for John the Baptist
         Item: the altars and tables
         The stand (brügi) for the Temple
         The River Jordan
         The pit for the sick (Siechengruob)
         The grave of Lazarus
         The general burial place on the mountain
         The Crosses, of which there are four

Financial contracts were sometimes made between players and organizers, as at VALENCIENNES *in 1547:*
It is to be noted that to provide for the expenses and organization of the said Passion, the said companions elected in Valenciennes twelve [*later the MS. says* thirteen] supervisors both to be their masters and leaders and to ensure peace and unity if there should be any division or argument among them, and the said supervisors could punish and fine the said actor-companions (compagnons jueurs) for any misdemeanor without recourse to the magistrates.

Item: it is also to be noted that the said thirteen undertook the business, all agreed to pay any expenses incurred, if by chance there should be some disaster (mortalité) or war so that they could not act or carry out the said enterprise; in addition, if anyone undertook to perform a role and then did not want to fulfil his undertaking, they could distrain on his person and his goods. And the said contract (obligation) was made and signed on Thursday (le jeudy absolut) and they began the performance the following Whitsuntide.
[*Here follow the names, particulars, and chosen roles of the thirteen supervisors, the three authors and revisers of the text* (originateurs) *and the thirty-three actors who signed the contract; followed by the names of all the other actors involved including five girls, one of whom played the Virgin Mary. Then the contract itself is given, as follows*]:

1. Order for the play and mystery of the Passion and Resurrection of our blessed Savior and Redeemer Jesus Christ to be played, God willing, in this city of Valenciennes, beginning on the Monday of Whitsuntide, in the year 1547.

2. Item. All the actors (jueurs) will be obliged to swear an oath and make a contract before a representative of the overlord (homme de fief jurez de Catel) and a notary to act on the days decreed by the supervisors unless they are excused by illness.

3.   Item. The actors will be required to accept the roles offered to them by the supervisors and authors.

4. Item. The actors will be required to attend rehearsals (records) on the days and times appointed; if there is no reasonable excuse, each time they fail to appear they will be fined three farthings (patarts).

5. Item. Each actor will be required on playing days to attend and appear on the stage (hourdement) to rehearse, on pain of six farthings.

6. Item. Each actor will be required on playing days to be on the stage at 12 noon and ready in place to begin, on pain of 10 farthings.

7. Item. All actors are forbidden to meddle with or be so bold as to murmur against the supervisors ordained and deputed to manage matters so that everything may be achieved by fair agreement and unity to the honor of God and the town, on pain of such fine as the said supervisors shall exact.

8. Item. No actor shall leave the acting area until after the second session (cambre) without leave of the supervisors or reasonable excuse, on pain of ten farthings.

9. Item. No actor shall stand at the gate or meddle with taking the money but leave this to those deputed to do so by the said supervisors, on pain of 6 farthings.

10. Item. All the actor-companions given a role by the said supervisors shall be required to hand over each of them one gold écu [= £6] or equivalent when they accept the first role as contribution to the expenses if they wish to participate in the profits or losses (au bon et au maulvais), and also to pay any fines they may incur, and at the end each one will get back what he contributed unless there is a loss.

11. Item. That no actor-companions shall make up groups or drinking parties on playing days either before, during, or after, but shall be satisfied with the refreshment (rechinet) provided by the said supervisors on the spot (la place).

12. Item. That if any dispute or argument should arise between actor-companions they shall be required to wait until the matter is settled and arranged by the said supervisors without going to law, on pain of ten farthings.

13. Item. That the actors who do not wish to contribute the aforementioned gold écu shall agree to await whatever the supervisors shall give them for each day at the end of the performances.

14. Item. As for the gain and profit, if there is any, it shall be divided in two parts--i.e., one half fairly and equally between all those who have contributed money: supervisors, actors, or administrators, and if one has paid out more than another he shall not therefore receive any larger amount; and the other half shall be divided among the actors and administrators only by shares as ordained, according to their merits, by the said supervisors, and no actors or administrators shall [re-

ceive a share] without the agreement of at least seven of the said supervisors.

15. Item. That no man or woman should be admitted to the play without paying except the supervisors, actors, and administrators only, not including their wives, children, or family.

16. And as for the construction and cost of the works (ouvriages) both inside and outside, they shall be exclusively at the order of the said supervisors.

17. Item. That the said supervisors shall assemble as summoned to the number of at least seven to give order for anything needful and proper.
[*The legal details of the signing are given here.*]
Given on 8 April 1546 before Easter [*1547*].

18. Item. To provide for what is laid down in the eleventh article of the above agreement (ordonnance), was distributed to each person, supervisor, actor, administrator, old and young, girls as well as men, the sum of eighteen pence for refreshment and food between the two sessions, together or separately and at the said place both audience and actors could purchase wine, strong ale, and small beer (cervoise forte et petite) and everything necessary for refreshment.

19. Item. That the little children who were angels but had no other role received for their refreshment 6 pence.

At LUCERNE *the increase in costs in the later sixteenth century provoked the innovation for the 1597 performance, first mooted in the Deliberations* (Beratschlagungen) *of 1592, that the actors should contribute towards the costs on a sliding scale:*
Since in such an excellent and splendid performance (Actu) or play (Spil) many and diverse things are necessary as regards costume, equipment, and other things, some of which concern a whole group [*i.e., those together in a scene*], some only individuals, which individuals or persons do not have the necessary wealth (vermögens) or whatever is necessary and useful for taking such a role, and also in order that moderation prevails and also that the City Council is not overburdened and is kept willing to do the best with the major costs, therefore at the first general meeting, before the texts of the parts are handed out, a collection shall be made towards these general costs and each person shall be charged as follows:

From each of the principal parts	40s
From each of the important but not principal parts	30s
From a moderately important part	20s

From a minor part   12s
From one of the very minor parts or from each of
      the pupils in the schola judeorum   8s

Each shall hand over this money before he receives his text
(Spruch). For this purpose a treasurer shall be nominated by
the Committee who, as regards such receipts and all expenditure
which occurs on the orders of the Director or of the Committee,
shall keep good record. But in this matter consideration and
pity as regards the poor shall also be exercised.

    For smaller-scale regular performances, a fixed contribu-
tion might be made by a secular or religious authority. In
ROME the Brotherhood of the Banner-Bearers of St. Lucy:
deliberated and agreed that the producers [*of the play*] be allowed to spend every year twenty ducats or more for the said
passion, not including the meals [*for the musicians*], . . . and
to have it performed on our site (luogo) at the Coliseum or on
any other site the company may decide upon.

    In England, the civic cycle plays, though organized by
the city, were usually financed by the individual craft guilds
through a fixed charge levied on their members. Because of
this financial responsibility, the crafts made every effort to
ensure that the city did not allow non-guild members in related
occupations to escape payment. At YORK exceptionally the
Innholders' pageant was partly financed by the City. In 1484
three citizens took over the "bringing forth" of the pageant for
eight years:
provided that those who keep inns but have no signs pay as
well and as much yearly to the repairing of the said pageant
and bringing forth of the same as the said innholders that have
signs do, that is to say every one of them annually, 4d; and
also that every person that provides fodder for the horses of
visitors who come to this City pay in like manner every year 4d
for bringing forth of the said pageant; and that also the said
William Robynson, Robert Shyrley, and Andrew Blyth have
yearly from the Chamber of the City during the said eight years
for bringing forth of the said pageant what the ordinance about
it states, that is to say 2s.

    Whole crafts that were not responsible for a pageant were
also normally made to contribute to a craft that was, even
though the occupation might be totally unrelated; as at CO-
VENTRY in 1507:
Memorandum that it is ordained at this council meeting (Lete)
that the craft and fellowship of Bakers shall be contributory and

charged henceforth with the craft and fellowship of Smiths, and
to pay yearly to them towards their pageant at the time of
Corpus Christi 13s 4d, and so to continue from henceforth yearly.

*Separate arrangements were sometimes made for the prepa-
ration of the text of a play. In MONS, the text was borrowed
from Amiens and copied:*
There was a discussion of the request made by those who want
to perform the Passion who are asking for 30 florins [*£18*] to
have three copies (en trois parties) of the Mystery of the Passion made and that they should also be given 10s towards meeting their expenses. Agreed to have them recopied and to give
them for their salary (sallaire) from the town £60 [*error for
£6?*] and the rest to be discussed at the next council.

At this meeting was read a note of the expenses sustained by
Anthoine Vinchant in going to Amiens in the matter of the Mystery of the Passion, amounting to £15 7s. No agreement was
reached because he would not leave the council while the matter
was discussed.

Discussion of the texts of the Passion (livres de la Passion) and
returning them [*to Amiens*] by the promised date. Agreed to
collate the manuscript copies (kayers) and return them.

*The commissioning of the text and the subsequent pay-
ments at ROMANS in 1508 were recorded in a series of entries in
the Town Council's accounts:*
Primo. Paid for a collation enjoyed in the Town Hall (meyson de
la ville) on 15 August 1508 when the officials (commys) inspected (visitaient) what Canon Pra the author had done with
the book of the first day, amounting to 4s.

Paid to Jehan Moliera because on the above-mentioned day it was
agreed by the officials to go to Vienne to fetch Master Chivallet
to be co-worker with the said Canon Pra to prepare the book of
the Three Martyrs, which amounts to 33s 9d.

Paid the 25th August to Master Chivallet, poet (fatiste), of
Vienne, for his coming and for his return journey, because he
did not want to work with the said Canon Pra, amounting to 10
florins 8s.

Paid the last day of August to the said Canon Pra as part of
what can be owed to him because of the said book, the sum of
30 florins.

Paid the said day [*4 November 1508*] to Jehan Milliart for three quires of good paper (fin papier) for the said book, amounting to 2s 3d T.

Paid the 13th day of November to Ponson Rollan for copying out (en deduciun) the roles of the said book, amounting to 2 florins for the town's share [*2 florins more on 23 December. Many expenses references for Canon Pra. He was paid 12 florins a month*].

9th day of December. Paid to Master Jehan Astier for a skin of parchment to cover the books of the Three Martyrs, 6 liars [= 1½ *sous*].

From TOLEDO *in 1493 the accounts include an entry for paper:*
five quires (manos) of fine paper for the giants' collars and for four caps which were made, also for writing out parts (para coplas) and for other necessary items. at twelve maravedis the quire, makes sixty.

At CHESTER *in 1561 the Smiths paid:*
for paper to copy out the individual parts (parcels) from the book, 5d;
. . .
spent at delivering the parcels and getting players, 4½d.

From MONS *the minutes of the Town Council and the accounts together give information regarding publicity and additional entertainments under various dates in 1501:*
1 June. Notice was given at the said meeting that Hughes [*lawyer at the High Court of Hainault*] had been to see the organizers (eschevins) and told them that the Lord Bailiff [*regent of Hainault under the Duke of Burgundy*] had advised that authorization should be obtained to notify the good towns that whoever wanted should come and perform plays and entertainments (jeux et esbatement) in the evenings during the period of performance of the Passion and there should be some prizes and trophies appropriate to this (aucuns pris et juweaux à ce servans).
Item: it seemed good to the said Lord Bailiff that safe conduct be given to the inhabitants of the good towns of this region who come to see the Passion against any debts that these said towns might have, and although the Lord Bailiff has indeed the power to grant such safe conduct, yet it seemed to him to be a good idea to obtain this authorization from the Prince who in this way would be informed of the performance of the said Passion.

16 June. Also write again to the Lord Bailiff that there should
be watchmen (guet) at the town gates and at the Town Hall;
that the iron chains should be hung around the market place
(du Marchiet) during the performance; that everyone should
keep his dogs in the house; and that inn-keepers should report
the names of their guests each night.

19 June. There was talk of having a prize for each day, in the
evening after the end of the said Mystery, to be played for;
the first of three ounces of silver, the second of two ounces of
silver, and the third of one ounce. Agreed to award the said
trophies and to have the performances near the fountain without
touching the stage (hourt) of the said Mystery.

26 June. Discussion of the watchmen during the Mystery of the
Passion, that there should be two men on guard at the wicket
(resteau) and there should be a guard on the gates at night.
Agreed to have a guard of eight men at the gate and that the
gatekeepers (portiers) and the men on guard should be on the
right of their barriers (au destre de leurs barieres) and to
know what people entered the town. Also that guard should be
kept at the Town Hall (Maison de la Ville), and the innkeepers
should report each night the names of their guests to the guard
at the Town Hall, and that the chains should be set up at the
entrances to the market place so that no one could bring carts
(ne puist cariet) onto the market place.

17 July. To Gerosme Fosset, for the fee for his journey to the
towns of Valenciennes, Douai, Arras, Amiens, and Cambrai to
carry letters from the honorable eschevins in connection with
the said mystery and poetry festival (Jeu de Rhetorique) which
took five days on horseback at 25s per day, entered here, in
addition to the £4 T already given him for the said journey,
45s. [*Three other similar entries for 3 July list a total of
eleven other towns to whom letters were sent.*]

3 July. To Hanin le Joly, clerk to Wibert Descolieres, for his
fee for having prepared 16 letters (lettres missives) sent to
various good towns to inform them of the date fixed for the said
Mystery and of the prizes for the poetry festival, 44s.

26 June. To Sire Jehan Bouchart, priest, for having made six
notices to attach to the six gates of the town to advertise the
date fixed for the performance of the said mystery play, 12s.

28 August. Item: the request of Colin Rifflart who is asking
for payment for having made and copied twenty-two letters sent
to various towns in this region in connection with the Mystery
of the Passion.

In ROME *the Brotherhood of the Banner-Bearers of St.
Lucy made use of sermons to publicize their Passion Play:*
Item: the said Lord Guardians (Sigg. Guardiani) shall be obliged to proclaim [*the play*] in the customary places (loci) and
above all through the preachers: the latter must be urged to
expedite their sermons in such a way as not to impede the said
Passion.

In LUCERNE *the invitation to participate was issued by
the preachers:*
To be announced from the pulpit that the play is to be performed so that those who are desirous of taking part can make
themselves known to the appointed Clerk [*i.e., Cysat himself or
one of his assistants*] and have their names noted.

*Inevitably, bad weather conditions sometimes caused post-
ponement, as at* BARCELONA *in 1443:*
on the day of the feast of the Sacred Body of Jesus Christ,
after the honored Governor of Catalonia, Councillors, and leading citizens had heard Mass in the Church of St. James according to custom and had had breakfast in the City Hall, they were
attending Mass in the Cathedral when there was such a down-
pour that the procession had to be postponed until the following
Sunday; and the floats (entramesos) which had already been
brought to the cathedral cemetery had to be taken back to the
store (casa) where they are kept.   And on the Saturday after
the said Thursday, those mentioned above walked to the Cathedral with the accustomed ceremony to hear vespers, and the
clergy celebrated matins in the evening, as is the custom on the
Wednesday.   And after vespers, the horse was ridden past the
stopping places (lochs) of the procession, with the trumpeters;
and on the Sunday morning, the said honored Governor, Councillors, and leading citizens heard Mass in the said Church of
St. James and afterwards went to the City Hall for breakfast as
was the custom, proceeding afterwards to the Cathedral, and
then the procession took place in the normal way.

Similarly at METZ *in 1485:*
Then on the said 24 July the aforesaid play was performed in
the [*Place*] en Chambre.   And the people went to take their
places at 4:00 in the morning.   And they were supposed to be
playing three consecutive days, i.e., the Sunday, Monday, and
Tuesday.   But on Tuesday about 2:00 in the afternoon the
weather was so appalling that it was almost dark and they had
to stop the performance, and could not complete it till the following Sunday because of the rains.

[*The leading role was taken by a young apprentice barber, who did so well that he was adopted and educated by a local canon.*]

The performance of the St. Martin Play at SEURRE *in 1496 had to be postponed several times for various reasons, including plague, war, harvest, weather. See Section D below.*

2. ORGANIZING THE PERFORMANCE

The difficulties inherent in the task of casting a play are evident from the notes made by the LUCERNE *director, Cysat:*
When the permission for the performance has been made known, nobody is to give assurances or make promises regarding the roles, but above all everyone is to be referred to the Director, who is to have no other authority than to record each person's name and request and to refer these matters to discussion and decision of the Brotherhood and of the religious and secular members of the Committee (verordneten) appointed by the City Fathers and by the Brotherhood, and this for the sake of the best and of the avoidance of unfriendliness, disorder, and antagonism, and also to avoid the burden falling on one individual.

In large scale plays the casting was often the responsibility of a committee, as in CHALON-SUR-SAÔNE *in 1497:*
Also it has been agreed that they shall attend all the rehearsals that are held and that if they decide any actors are not competent to play the roles allotted to them, they can make changes and give other roles to those whom they consider appropriate or do all that they consider proper within reason.

After 1476 in YORK *the decision whether to accept or reject a performer was put into the hands of the four most experienced actors in the City:*
Ordinance regarding the Corpus Christi Play.
Also it is ordained and established by the full consent and authority of the Council aforesaid, the day and year within written [3 April 1476], from this day forward perpetually to be observed and kept; that is to say that yearly in the time of Lent there shall be called before the Mayor at that time four of the most skillful (connyng), prudent (discrete), and able players within this City to test, hear, and examine all the players and pageants of the play throughout all the craftsmen connected with the Corpus Christi Play. And all those that they shall find adequate in appearance and skill, to the honor of the City and credit of the said crafts, to accept and authorize, and all the others, inadequate in skill, voice, or appearance, to discharge, remove, and dismiss.

In LUCERNE *the Committee took note of previous good performance or even of a hereditary claim on the role. The following paragraph follows immediately after the one already*

quoted regarding the proclamation of the play from the pulpit:
Then when the Director thinks there are enough names on the
list, as many as are needed, he is to arrange as speedily as
possible for a meeting of all members of the Committee, secular
and religious, to be held. At the meeting the list of names is
to be examined and compared with the index (Register) of names
and parts in the previous Passion Play, gone through, and then
there is to be considered what is to be allocated or what response is to be given to each individual.

If anyone who had a certain part in the previous one or more
Passion Plays and played it well and unobjectionably and who
asks for the part again, he is not to be refused it in so far
as appearance (gstalltsame) and the nature of his position and
age and also of the role which he is to play make it appropriate
and acceptable.

Also in cases where such persons are no longer fit for the same
roles, or have died but have left legitimate sons or brothers
who would be fit, these may be allowed to take advantage of
this and have the same parts. However, this is not therefore
to be a rule, but to be left to the free choice and decision of
the Committee, according to the way in which they think they
can best make provision; and whatever they decide in such a
case, that is how things are to be left, with no further tussle
(zühen), by virtue of the freedom and authority invested in
them by the City Fathers.

*Nevertheless, the physical appearance of the actors was taken
into consideration:*

pro futuro. That parts are to be according to the persons with
the right stature (statur) and appearance (gestalltsame), particularly those who have to walk and perform beside one another.

On voices: those who have much to say but do not have good
comprehensible voices are to be changed or exchanged.

*The large number of roles involved sometimes made doubling
necessary:* People should not be misled when on occasion two
or even three parts have been given to one person; this has
happened for the sole purpose of reducing the number of actors, for otherwise the whole square (platz) would be full just
with actors, being as it is far too restricted, and such a play
would otherwise require over four hundred people.

The ensuing problems only became evident during rehearsals:
Ozias cannot speak in the leading-out scene as he is Centurio.
Longinus cannot speak in the scene with John the Baptist as he

is Lucifer.

*Even in a small-scale play, roles might be shared as is
seen from the cast list in the* CASTILIAN TRIAL IN HEAVEN
AND NATIVITY:
The names of the shepherds are Cremente, Pascual, and Hu-
mano.
He who plays the part of Man can also be Joseph.
He who takes the part of Desire can be a shepherd.
He who takes the part of the Godhead can be Our Lady.
He who takes the part of Justice can be a shepherd.
He who takes the part of Mercy can be another shepherd.
He who takes the part of Peace can be an angel.
He who takes the part of Truth can be another angel.
Love.
The Eternal Word.

At METZ *in 1513, three short plays were performed on
consecutive days in Whitweek, during which Philippe de Vig-
neulles' son played five parts:*
. . . I, Philippe, was one of the organizers (gouverneurs) and
collected the money which was levied on the stages and scaffolds
(hours et eschaffaulx) and the total amounted to 23 francs, and
my son Andrieu played five parts in the three days.

*In Florence the actors were sometimes young boys. Aware-
ness of their inadequacies is seen in the prologue to the* PLAY
OF ST. JOHN AND ST. PAUL (1485):
The Company of our St. John
celebrates this festivity;
and we are but young:
therefore forgive our tender age
if these verses are not good or well recited,
for we know not how to wear the clothes of lords,
nor can young boys represent old men, or women;
and yet we shall do our best, with zeal;
forgive a few mistakes due to youth.

*The allocation of roles did not always pass unquestioned.
In* LUCERNE *this dissatisfaction provoked a rebuke from the
City Council:*
The City Fathers also require once and for all (endtlich) that
each individual is satisfied with the parts allocated to him and
that he refrain both privately and publicly from criticizing,
blaming, maligning, accursing, being hostile to, or hating the
members of the Committee or those concerned with the matter,

either collectively or individually, whoever they may be. Since in these matters they are doing merely what the City Fathers and Council (Hundert) have commanded and sanctioned, whose sole aim is that everything be done to the glory of God, the edification of the common people, and the praise, honor, and renown of the City of Lucerne, for so many good Christians both outsiders and those from the City, for their consolation and the good of their souls.

Attitudes to women on stage varied enormously. In LU-CERNE, *efforts were made to prevent their entry into the acting area totally:*
And any participants in the play who at any time need anything getting or fetching are to plan and give instructions that it is done by a male person to avoid inappropriate doings with the to-ing and fro-ing of women and serving maids across the square from one stall to another throughout the play, as has happened in the past.

What evidence there is from England (and there is very little) suggests that women's parts were played by men, at least in the civic plays. COVENTRY, *Smiths', 1499:*
Item: paid to Dame Percula [*Pilate's wife*] for his wages, 2s 8d; *and later elsewhere in the same year:*
Item: paid to Pilate's wife for his wages, 2s.
1495: Ryngold's man, Thomas, that played Pilate's wife.

In France, however, there are a number of instances of women taking important roles, as in METZ *in 1468:*
The play was performed in the courtyard of the Dominicans (grans Prescheurs) during the three feast days of Whitsun [*probably Sunday, Monday, and Tuesday*]. And it was put on and performed at the expense and charge of Lady Catherine Baudoiche. And the role of St. Catherine was taken by a young girl aged about eighteen, the daughter of Dediet the furrier, and she performed her task marvelously well to the pleasure and delight of everyone. Yet this said girl had twenty-three hundred lines in her part, nevertheless she knew them all perfectly (sur le doigt), and this girl spoke so clearly and movingly that she made several people weep and pleased everybody. And as a result of this, the girl made a rich marriage with a noble soldier of Metz, called Henry de Latour, who fell in love with her because of the great delight he took in this.

In SARAGOSSA *in 1487 the Holy Family was played by a* husband, wife, and son so that the play (el misterio y repre-

sentacion) should be acted with greater devotion. *For this they*
were paid: To the woman who took the part of Mary, to Jesus
and Joseph . . . the Chapter ordered payment of two gold
florins, or 32s.

The payment of actors was not uncommon in Spain, as can
be seen from the TOLEDO *records from 1493 where the cast of*
each play is listed with the payment made; see Section D.

In England too there are numerous records of payments to
actors. CHESTER, *Smiths' etc., 1546 [or, according to Clopper,*
1553–54]:
We gave to the Doctors, 3s 4d; we gave to Joseph, 8d; we gave
to the little God, 12d; we gave to Mary, 10d; to Dame Anna,
10d; we gave to the angels, 6d; to old Simeon, 3s 4d; we gave
to Barnes and the singers, 3s 4d.

COVENTRY, *Smiths' 1478:*
Corpus Christi
Paid to Jesus, 20d; paid to Herod, 4s; item, paid to Pilate, 4s;
paid to Caiaphas, 2s 7d; paid to Annas, 2s 2d; paid to the
beadle, 3s; paid to Percula, 2s; paid to two knights, 4s; paid
to Peter, 4d; paid to Pilate's son 4d; paid to Malchus, 4d; paid
to Demon, 16d.

CHESTER, *Painters' etc., 1568:*
Item, paid to Joseph, 10d; . . . Item, for Our Lady's wages,
8d; item, to four shepherds' boys, 2s 8d; . . . Item, to the
eldest shepherd, 2s; item, to the second shepherd, 20d; to the
third shepherd, 20d; item, to Troll [*the shepherds' servant*] 2s;
item, to Troll's boy, 6d.

Actors were occasionally paid in France, as in AMBOISE *in*
1507:
To Messire Jehan Bardeau, priest, who had the role of Our Lord
to play in the Passion, has been allotted and paid the sum of £8
T for his efforts and recompense in having rehearsed the said
role for four months ending on 15 March 1506 [*1507*] which is a
rate of 10s T per week.

In France actors normally provided their own costumes.
At CHALON-SUR-SAÔNE:
[*Thirty inhabitants*] swore on the Gospels . . . to accept will-
ingly the roles offered them in the Play and Mystery of St.
Sebastian and to perform them and costume themselves at their
own expense and cost (frais missions et deppens); each as is

appropriate and necessary to the character portrayed. [*Failure to do so incurred a fine of 10* escuds tournois.]

They might receive assistance from the organizers. MONT-FERRAND *1477:*
I, Sir Guillaume de Keboul, priest, canon of the Church of Our Lady of Montferrand, admit that I have had and received from the noble consuls (messeigneurs les consulz) of Montferrand and from the hands of Jehan Perchero, one of the said consuls, the sum of 15s which was to help me pay for my costume as Death to play on the day of the Resurrection . . . given on the day of St. Peter in August [*1 August*] 1477.

Alternatively, wealthy patrons were approached, as at CHALONS-SUR-MARNE *in 1507:*
Item: a request has been made by the man who is playing the role of Lucifer and who is poor, that some of the gentlemen who are not taking part should help him to costume himself (acoustrer). The clerics (les abbez), the bailiff of Chalons, and several wealthy men from the said Chalons who are not taking part have offered and promised to costume at their expense the man who is playing the role of Lucifer because he is poor and a good player.

At LINCOLN *in 1515 and again in 1521 fear of the plague prevented the City from borrowing costumes from the surrounding countryside as they had been accustomed to do for the St. Anne's day show.*
1515: Also in this presence it is agreed that whereas various garments and other adornments are yearly borrowed in the country for the setting forth of the pageants of St. Anne's Guild, now the knights and gentlemen are afraid because of the plague so that the Graceman [*of the St. Anne's Guild*] cannot borrow any such clothing. For which reason every alderman shall prepare and provide in the said show two good gowns; and every sheriff-peer, one gown; and every chamberlain-peer, one gown; and the people with them are to wear the same.

1521: Also in this said presence George Browne, one of the aldermen of this City who has been elected in the place of the Graceman of St. Anne's Guild, complains that because the plague is reigning in this City he cannot get such garments and other adornments as should be in the pageants of the procession of St. Anne's Day. Wherefore it is agreed that Mr. Alanson shall immediately be asked to borrow a gown from my Lady Powes for one of the Marys, and the other Mary to be dressed in the crimson gown of velvet that belongs to the same guild.

In England, there is occasional evidence that the craft guilds who financed them provided costumes for actors, either hired or specially made. COVENTRY, *Smiths' etc.,* 1489:
Item, paid for a gown for Herod, 7s 4d; item, paid for painting and coloring it, 6s 4d; item, paid for painting Herod's garment that he walked in the procession in, 20d; item, paid to a tailor for mending Herod's gown, 8d; item, paid for mending hats, caps, and Herod's headgear (?crest) with other associated odds and ends (smale geyr belongyng), 3s.

1488: Item, paid for hiring a scarlet hood and a rochet for one of the bishops, 5d.

The use of clerical actors necessitated a dispensaton for them to allow their beards to grow, as at AMBOISE *in* 1507:
To obtain from my lord of Tours [*the Bishop*] or his representatives (ses vicaires) dispensaton for the clerics (gens d'église) who have parts to play in the said Mystery of the Passion to allow their beards to grow, has been paid, 12s 6d. . . .

Information on rehearsals is relatively scanty. There is evidence of expenditure involved in regular rehearsal at ROMANS:
Paid on 23rd December for coal to burn (pouter) at the Cordeliers to hold the rehearsals, 9 liars.
[*Similar entries, for coal or wood, for rehearsals occur on 5 and 11 January, 11 February.*]
Paid on 18th March for a meal provided at the Oficiala [*archbishop's courthouse*] during the rehearsal, 7s 9d.
[*Similarly 9, 14, 15, 21, 22, 29 April; 6 and 7 May. The performance was at Whitsun.*]

There is evidence from COVENTRY *that actors were sometimes paid for rehearsal. Cappers',* 1555:
Paid to the players at the first rehearsal, 18d; spent at the said rehearsal, 3s 2d.

At MONS *regular rehearsals were held in the Town Hall. On at least one occasion dinner was provided:*
To Jehan Billet, for 48 days when he summoned the players to assemble for all the meetings for rehearsals made from the beginning of the said Mystery in the Town Hall entered here by agreement with him £6. To Jehan Barbet . . . who was re-

imbursed for what he had paid for a dinner (desjeuner) at the
Stag, the day that they tried out God and the two thieves on
the Cross, 19s.

There are frequent references to rehearsals in the guild
accounts from England, but almost the only activities specifically
mentioned in relation to them are eating and drinking.
CHESTER, *Smiths' etc., 1561:*
Paid to John Byrth for beef for the general rehearsal, 6s 8d.
. . .
for six crocks for ale at general rehearsal, 10s; a crock of
small ale and two gallons, 20d; a measure (hoppe) of wheat for
the general rehearsal, 2s 3d; to James Tayler for bread and
cakes for general rehearsal, 2s 7d; for wine for the said rehearsal, 2s 7d.

COVENTRY, *Smiths' 1490:*
This is the expense of the first rehearsal of our players in
Easter week: in primis in bread, 4d; item, in ale, 8d; item, in
kitchen [*meat, fish, etc. to eat with the bread*], 13d; item, in
vinegar, 1d; summa, 2s 2d. Item, paid at the second rehearsal
in Whitsun week, in bread, ale, and kitchen, 2s 4d.

The difficulties involved in organizing rehearsals are evi-
dent from various entries in the LUCERNE *records:*
These can rehearse separately: Moses with his group, Ozias
with his group. . . .
The torturers with the Crucifixion.
The beheading of John [*the Baptist*]; item, the hangings of
Haman and of Judas are to be tried out in good time. Likewise
David with Goliath.

The following are to be assembled on a separate occasion: all
women's and girls' parts except: Judith, Veronica, Esther,
Herodias, Bala, Virgin Mary, Magdalene, Martha, Elizabeth.
Likewise: all the angels, all the boys' parts, all the maids, the
four page boys (Cämmerling), to look them over and to examine
and instruct them separately, and to dismiss any who are un-
cooperative.

People are to learn their parts better and not leave everything
to the Director, also to come more conscientiously than hitherto
to rehearsals.

For the 1597 performance a system of fines for specific offenses
was introduced:
Nobody is to contradict the Director, but in what the rehearsal
entails and reveals to him everyone is to obey him, with the

possibility of correction by the Committee; on pain of the aforesaid fine [10s]. From now onwards anyone who fails to appear
at rehearsal without good cause when he has been notified, he
is to be fined, the first time 6s, the second time 10s. The
third time the Committee is to be notified. Anyone who gives his
role to someone else or exchanges it without the knowledge and
approval of the Committee, or who loses the text of his role
through carelessness, is to pay 10s fine.

Nobody is to change the text of his role, either add to it or
subtract from it, without express instruction from the Committee, but is to speak it as is written in the rehearsal text (dem
probier Rodel glych), on pain of 10s fine.
On the days when the play is being rehearsed, nobody who is a
participant in the play is to go drinking, on pain of a fine of
10s to the general funds of the Brotherhood.

Similar restrictions on the actors are included in the
VALENCIENNES *contract already quoted.*

At NEW ROMNEY *in 1555 the actors were legally bound by
a recognizance to pay £5 each if they failed to fulfill certain
conditions set out in English, thus:*
The condition of this recognizance is such that where the
above-bound parties have taken upon themselves to be players
in the stage play at New Romney aforesaid, to be played by the
grace of God at the feast of Whitsun next coming, and have
received players' speeches or parts in the said play, that is to
say: John Tyre, the part of Herod; George Gerrard and William
Brouker, Herod's knights; [blank], Herod's messenger; Robert
Edolf, Clement Stuppeny, Lawrence Stuppeny, Simon Padyam,
James Grenewaye, and John Hollocke, tormenters; Edward
Honey, Pilate; John Fyndall, Pilate's messenger and Caiaphas'
messenger; Robert Davye, Caiaphas; John Plomer, Annas and
the second devil; and John Crockey, Annas' handmaid, if they
and every one of them do learn before the said feast of Whitsun
their parts before appointed and be ready to play the same, and
further do at every time of the rehearsal of the said play come
to Romney aforesaid and rehearse their said parts without any
deceit--God, the king and queen's majesties, and no reasonable
cause preventing them--that then this present recognizance
shall be void, but otherwise shall remain in all its full strength
and power.

At METZ *in 1485 they seem to have had a walk-through on
the stage:*
And the scaffolds (eschaffauts) were erected a week before in

the Place de Vezegneuf on which they acted and did the whole
play without speaking.

      The director's task was never easy. The thirteenth-cen-
tury GREEK PASSION *begins with a charge to the director in-*
dicating his duties:
You, who are master of the present production (diataxis) and
are going to direct the others, must before the beginning of the
action organize in proper order the things such an enterprise
requires and have them all ready, so that when it is needed
each thing is at once ready and prepared. Furthermore you
must make individual contact with each actor and costume each
according to the character he is to represent, from Christ and
the Apostles to the other men and women. And similarly for the
Jews and everyone else. The performers must be selected,
choosing those who are suitable to perform and present the
types of characters. In addition they must be able to ask and
answer in writing. And instruct them to play their part in such
a way as not to excite laughter and mockery, but with piety and
great attention in the fear of God. Let them take heed not to
interrupt each other or cut in so that confusion follows, but let
each one, as you wish it, ask or reply in proper form. Further
let them not make any alteration nor say anything which might
make the spectators laugh. But let all things be done to
arouse awe or fear.

      There is little clear evidence from England for directors,
but occasionally individual citizens would take over the control
of a particular pageant by agreement with the masters of the
guild. COVENTRY, *Smiths', 1453:*
. . . accorded and agreed on Monday immediately before Palm
Sunday, in the thirty-first year of the reign of Henry VI, that
Thomas Colclow, skinner, from this day forth shall have the
control of the pageant until the end of twelve years next following, he to provide the players and all that is associated with
them for the whole of the said term; except that the Keeper of
the Craft shall have the pageant brought out and shall provide
the cloths that go around the pageant, and provide rushes for
it. And every Whitsun week those who are Keepers of the
Craft shall dine with Colclow and every master shall lay down
4d, and Colclow shall have for his labor yearly 46s 8d. And he
to bring in to the Master on Sunday immediately after Corpus
Christi day the original [*text of the pageant*] and fetch his
seven nobles. And Colclow must bring in towards the end of
the term all the garments that belong to the pageant in as good
a state as when they were delivered to him.

3. AUDIENCE

Wooden stands were sometimes constructed specifically for the spectators; at METZ in 1437 there were simple tiers of seats:
In the said year [1437] in the month of July the play of the Passion of our Lord Jesus Christ was played in Metz in the Place des Changeurs [*now the Place Saint Louis; plays were normally performed in this square*]. The theater (le paircque) was constructed in a very noble manner, for there were nine tiers of seats like steps all around, and behind were large and long seats (grands sièges et longs) for the lords and ladies.

At ROMANS in 1509, the audience accommodation was extremely complex and even included privies, as is shown in the carpenter's contract:
Item: the above-named carpenters shall undertake to construct all round (tout a lentour) the said platform sloping tiers (pantes couches en deppendent) six fathoms (toises) in width approximately (de langeur ou environ), which shall be made of large pieces of wood, good and strong, set closely side by side (pres l'un de l'autre) each four pieces being held by a beam (postz), furnishing the four angles (quatre quarrés) of the said slopes with wood and beams in the form of right-angled brackets (en maniere d'arpie); and between each beam (post) shall be provided pieces [*of wood*] called planks (doblis) good and proper for the work and for seats appropriate to it (a cella duysantes) as the commissioners require, and they shall make two gates (portes) to the said slopes for going in and out and shall make a privy (ungz retraitz) in the said platform if it is needed.
Item: the said carpenters shall undertake to make above the said slopes (au dessus des ditz pantes) eighty rooms (chambres) or more if possible as the said commissioners require, and the rooms shall be supported on rooms (chambres sur chambres appilles) with good large pieces [*of wood*]; and the said rooms shall be floored with planks (planchees) so that one cannot see between the beams; and between each two of these rooms shall be wattle walls (y aye listellement closes), and on the side of the entrance to the said rooms shall be solid timbers (soit tout poste) in order to put a lock (un sarralhe) on the door of each room. And on the viewing side (sur le regard du jeu) they shall undertake to put a barrier to prevent falling and a beam across on account of the small children.
Item: in addition the said carpenters shall undertake to make on the entrance side of the said rooms a gallery with wooden railings (gardes de boys) and at each end of the said galleries they shall make a privy where the said commissioners shall ad-

vise, and similarly they shall make ladders to ascend to the said
galleries of the said rooms as the commissioners shall advise
them to do.

*At AUTUN in 1516 a specially constructed auditorium held
what is probably the largest audience recorded. They were also
particularly well-behaved:*
We, the people of Autun in the year of the Lord 1516, constructed an excellent and magnificent amphitheater in the
field of St. Lazarus, which is in the middle of our city. It was
made of squared timbers (ligno quadrato) constructed with ex-
traordinary skill at the expense of the church and the citizens.
There was nothing comparable in France. It had two hundred
and forty boxes in the upper parts, all divided by wooden partitions covered in paneling. There the churchmen, nobles,
senators, knights, gentlemen, and dignitaries of the city had
their places. In the acting area (cavea) or lower part, the
tiers (gradus) and seats were so arranged that the circuit increased in size as it rose up where the people were sitting
together under linen awnings (velaria lintea) which protected
the spectators, both sitting and standing, from the rain. The
actors were also covered by these in the middle of the acting
area (in medio cavee seu Theatralis scenae) and were separated
from the people by a ditch full of water and other barriers. In
this amphitheater eighty thousand people could be easily accommodated, and as the performance (spectacula) had been
publicized in the neighboring districts the spectators poured in
in almost endless numbers. The performance was perfect; given
in the honor of St. Lazarus, patron of Autun, whose life written
in excellent verse, not for vainglory but in honor of the Divine
Majesty and St. Lazarus, was performed (recitata) over four
days enthusiastically and free (vehementissime et gratis). And
God therefore granted that it was performed with no whistling
or uproar among the people or any mockery; also that it rained
overnight but all day no finer weather for those days had been
seen.

*It was customary in France to charge for admission to the
big civic plays with varying prices for the different stands, as
at MONS in 1501:*
There was a discussion of the auditorium (parcq) which seemed
too small and whether there should be stands (hours) from the
end of the auditorium going as far as the houses. Agreed to
make a stand from the end of the auditorium as far as the
houses but safeguarding the entrances of the houses; and to
keep the entrance to the Town Hall well cleared (ample) without
including it in the enclosure of the auditorium.

There was a discussion about the commissioners [who were] to
receive those who entered the stage enclosure (le cloture du
hourt): [four names] who for entry into the auditorium (parcq)
shall collect 12d from each person and as for those who are on
the stands (les hours) near the houses (marchissant as
maisons), they shall pay three sous each. And it was agreed
that no one should enter the auditorium (parcq) before nine
o'clock in the morning and that no admittance would be allowed
for children under ten, the old and infirm, and pregnant women.

At YORK *in 1417 the making of money out of scaffolds e-
rected for spectators at the stopping-places of the play (or "stations") caused the City Council to re-think the whole question of
the siting of the stopping-places and led to the system of free
bartering for stations which held good until the demise of the
play in the late sixteenth century.*
June 7, the Monday before Corpus Christi day:
. . . the Mayor, honorable men and all the said community, by
their unanimous consent and assent, ordained that all those,
who because of scaffolds (pro skafaldis) which they erect in
front of their doors on public ground at the aforesaid places
[the stations] receive money from people sitting on them (super-
sedentibus), shall pay every third penny of the money thus
received to the Chamberlains of the City to put to the use of
the community; and if they shall refuse to agree honestly with
the Chamber to pay such a third penny or other things, that
then the play (ludus) shall be transferred to other places at the
disposition and will of the then Mayor and Council of the Chamber of the City, without the contradiction of any to an ordinance of such a kind (nemine ordinacioni huiusmodi contra-
dicente); only a few owners of scaffolds (skaffaldorum) in
Micklegate being excepted.

June 12, the Saturday after Corpus Christi day:
And because the said matter was not able to be given full consideration because of the nearness of the said feast of Corpus
Christi and the shortness of the time, the aforesaid therefore
gathered in the Chamber of the Council . . . considering that
it was improper and contrary to the good of the community that
the aforesaid play should be played annually in those fixed
places and in no other when each person according to his means
carries the burden of sustaining that same play; therefore they
unanimously ordain for the advantage of the community that the
places for playing the aforesaid play be changed, unless those
before whose places it was formerly played pay a certain fixed
sum to the community, each individually for having this same
privilege thus annually; and that in all the following years,
while that play of plays (ludus ille ludi) shall be performed, it

shall be played in front of the doors and properties of those
who wish to pay more generously and profitably to the Chamber
and do more for the advantage of the whole commmunity for
having this same play there; not giving favor to any person for
some individual profit, but only what is considered the public
good of the whole community of York.   And the abovesaid reverend man, John Moreton, submitted himself for his properties
totally to the disposition and guidance of the Mayor and Council
of the Chamber, as to how much [*he should pay*] at the abovesaid play for [*having*] the play in front of the door of his
dwelling-house in the street of Micklegate and of his other
properties in the City.

In LUCERNE *the Director proposed an increase in the
audience accommodation for the 1583 performance:*
The large main stand behind the fountain might well be improved
in future, or else another be added behind it, so that it can
hold and bear more of the populace (<u>volcks</u>).   For the future
the City Fathers are to be requested that the stands for the
populace be somewhat improved, but particularly the main stand
behind the Fishmarket fountain be extended to the greater com-
fort of the populace.

Other details are mentioned in various documents:
Item.   The stands to be made all round the square (<u>allenthalben
ze machen umb den platz herumb</u>), and the three entrances with
closed trellises.   The stand in front of the old Courthouse is
not to be broader than 9½ feet. The scaffolds for the populace
and spectators are to be 8½ feet up from the alleyway (<u>gassen</u>)
and then above and to the back well-raised upwards throughout
(?<u>wol verhöcht durch uffhin</u>).

This stand above the stalls on the <u>Haus zur Sonne</u> is to be 6½
feet wide throughout.

The projecting roofs (<u>vortächlin</u>) on the <u>Haus zur Sonne</u> are to
have platforms fixed beneath them (<u>untersetzen</u>) in such a way
that the populace can sit.   The general stands in front of the
houses and also the palings (<u>schranken</u>) [*i.e., the rear walls of
the stalls*] are to be 8 feet away from the houses consistently.

From the Butchers' Hall upwards to the end double stands are
to be made, which the windows and roofs can accommodate, and
raised; for as far backwards as the entrances go, everything is
to be covered in stands (<u>verbrügenet</u>) over and over.

*Further enlargements proposed for 1597 seem to have been
vetoed by the City Fathers. They include a suggestion for a
"double-decker" stand:*

It can also be made double on top (Man kan sy ouch oben uff doplet machen).

Further information can be gleaned from the references to the treatment of distinguished guests:
Considered by the Council on Wednesday before Palm Sunday 1583:
. . . That visitors and particularly important people from other places in the [*Swiss*] Confederation and elsewhere, but pre-eminently the clergy, are to be given good accommodation, so that they can see comfortably and well. That is to be taken care of by the Committee members appointed by the Council.

. . . For visitors of repute who do not have their own reserved windows, a place and space (ort und platz) to be kept for them in the Butchers' Hall and the Old Courthouse. Namely, for the most important, rooms [*presumably those just mentioned*] or other comfortable windows, for the rest however the stands erected in front of the said windows.

. . . Two members of the Council are to be specifically nominated, with the instruction to see to the accommodation of the visitors in this way.

1597: Prepare a special place from where our clergy as well as visiting clergy can watch. By command and permission of the City Fathers it is ordered that this is to be towards the foot of the square (unden) behind the stalls, beneath the roof in front of Town Clerk Cysat's and the New Apothecary's houses.

Similar treatment of distinguished guests is recorded at MONS *in 1501:*
To Philippe Dervillers, echevin, has been repaid what he spent on the instruction of the echevins for the banquets offered each day of the Mystery to Madame de Chiervé, wife of the Bailiff of Hainault, who was in the upper room of the Town Hall (Maison de la Ville) each day [*of the play. This room overlooked the stage*].

At ROMANS *in 1509 certain groups involved in the pre-paration of the performance were given a free box; the cost of that given to the painter was deducted from his fee:*
For eighty-four boxes (chambres) rented at 3 florins each, total 252 fl. From which boxes must be deducted the following which were given [*free*]. To the Cordeliers: one box [*the performance was in their courtyard*]; then to the carpenters who made the scaffolds, one box; . . . then to Master François, the painter, one box, which was deducted previously from the 100 florins which he was paid. [*François designed and made as*

well as painted most of the decors and the special effects.]

The need to keep clear the route of a procession is evident from BARCELONA *in 1394, where people were forbidden to:* make or have made any structure or scaffold (<u>bastiment ó cadafal</u>) on the streets through which the procession is to pass. This is so that the streets may not be obstructed; neither are fireworks, including exploding fireworks (<u>foch gresch ne sclaffidors de foch gresch</u>) to be set off, on pain of a fine of 20 <u>sous</u> for each offense.

The danger in a lack of control over crowds gathered to watch performances is revealed in the following report of the collapse of a bridge in FLORENCE *in 1304:*
the inhabitants of Borgo San Friano [*?San Frediano*], accustomed since the old days to produce the most original and varied spectacles (<u>giuochi</u>), published a proclamation that whoever wanted to get news of the other world should make sure of being on the Carraia bridge and along the banks of the Arno on the first day of May; and they constructed stages (<u>palchi</u>) on barges and boats on the Arno, on which they built a representation and likeness of Hell, with fires and other punishments and torments, with men disguised as demons of most horrible appearance and others who appeared like people in the form of naked souls, and they were put to various tortures with very great shouting and screaming and storming; and this appeared like a most terrible and frightening thing to hear and see. Many citizens went to see this new spectacle, and the Carraia bridge, which at that time was made of wood on piles, was so overburdened with people that it broke in several places and collapsed together with the people who were on it so that many people died and were drowned, and many were injured, so that the spectacle changed from jest to the truth, and, as the proclamation had said, through death many went to get news of the other world.

Such accidents could occur at any performance where uncontrolled spectators crowded together. We owe the earliest mention of a play about the martyrdom of St. Dorothy being performed in BAUTZEN *to a reference to such an accident:*
On 8 February 1413 the schoolmaster with the consent of the cathedral chapter and the town council put on (<u>gab</u>) in the middle of the market place as usual on the Sunday before the feast day of St. Dorothy the annual performance of a play (<u>Comoedie</u>) about the martyrdom of St. Dorothy. When the play (<u>spiel</u>) was almost half-way through and large numbers of the excited populace had climbed onto the roof of the cloth hall near the clock-tower on the market, the roof gave way beneath them,

bringing down with it a section of brick wall and killing thirty
people, who were buried the following day with great weeping
and lamentation. Many were badly injured, receiving permanent
injuries to hands and feet.

Part of the fifteenth-century proclamation of the play in
YORK *is concerned with avoiding serious brawling amongst the*
audience:
We command on behalf of the King and the Mayor and Sheriffs
of this City that no man go armed in this City with sword or
with Carlisle axes or any other weapons of defense in disturbance of the King's peace and the play or hindering of the
procession of Corpus Christi, and that they leave their armor in
their inns, except knights and squires of good standing who
ought to have swords carried after them, under penalty of for-
feiture of their weapons and imprisonment of their bodies.

In the early sixteenth-century copy of the proclamation
from CHESTER, *the authority of the Church is added to that of*
the Crown in keeping audiences under control:
[*Henry Fraunces, a monk of Chester monastery*] got from Clement, then bishop of Rome, a 1000 days of pardon and from the
bishop of Chester at that time 40 days of pardon granted
thenceforth to every person coming in a peaceable manner with
good devotion to hear and see the said plays, from time to time
as often as they shall be performed in this City. And every
person or persons disturbing the same plays in any way to be
cursed by the authority of the said Pope Clement's bulls, until
such time as he or they be absolved from it.
    . . .   Wherefore Master Mayor in the King's name strictly
orders and commands that every person and persons of whatsoever estate, rank, or position he or they be, coming to the
said plays, behave themselves peaceably without making any
assault, affray, or other disturbance by which the same plays
shall be disturbed, and that no person or persons, whosoever
he or they be, use or wear any unlawful weapons within the
precinct of the said City during the time of the said play, not
only under penalty of cursing by the authority of the said Pope
Clement's bulls but also under penalty of imprisonment of their
bodies and paying a fine to the King at Master Mayor's pleasure.

B. THE PERFORMANCE

1. THE PLAYING AREA

Where the performance was on wagons or floats, preparation of the playing area itself was mainly concerned with cleaning or repairs. TOLEDO, 1493:
Firstly, to a man who cleaned the floats (carros) and shook out all the other things, one rreal.
For brooms, four maravedis.
. . .

Three master carpenters came because there was much to be done, and six assistants to move the floats (carros) to the church and erect the railings (verjas); the wages of the master craftsmen were six rreales, those of the assistants, another six.

COVENTRY, Smiths' 1471:
Expenses for bringing up the pageant into Gosford street among the Company, 8d; expenses for burnishing and painting the vanes for the pageant, 20d; item, clout-nails and other nails and tallow for the pageant, and for washing the said pageant and rushes, 6½d; item, at bringing the pageant out of the [pageant] house, 2d; item, nails and other iron gear for the pageant, 8½d; expenses to a joiner for workmanship for the pageant, 7d.

An agreement was made on 20 April 1453 between members of the City Council of BARCELONA *and a priest concerning the renovation of two floats in the Corpus Christi series:*
Firstly, the said priest Johan Çalom shall construct the float (entramés) of the Creation of the World in the following manner: from the base (buch) there will rise four pillars which will support a Heaven of clouds (un cel de nuvols). On two of these pillars there shall be an angel, and in the center of the Heaven shall be God the Father holding an orb in his left hand, and with his right hand raised. He is to be seated on a finely carved throne which is to be either gilded or silvered. Between the base and the Heaven there is to be a large revolving globe (un gran mon rodó qui rodará), half of which is to have the appearance of being covered with water, and, above the water, the other half is to be divided between a starry sky and land with a city on it. And on the floor of the float there is to be a wheel [or circular platform (rollo)] on which four angels are to stand, and there are to be four more at the pillars-- that is, one at each pillar--and they shall all sing.

Item: another float called Bethlehem or the Nativity of Jesus Christ, on the base of which he shall remake two canopied structures (porxes) with a space between them, each of which shall have four pillars which will support its canopy. And above each of the said canopies--that is, on top of each of the said pillars--there shall

71

be an angel, and the four [*innermost*] shall support a vaulted Heaven
(un cel rodó) with stars and clouds, in the center of which God the
Father shall be visible at least from the waist up. From him shall
descend rays of light or fire (raigs de foch ó de lums) which shall
pass between the said structures and reach down to where the infant
Jesus is lying. And on the floor of the float, on the left hand side,
there shall be a Nativity group (presebra), and in it the ox and ass,
and Joseph, kneeling. And in the other canopied structure, on the
right hand side, Mary shall be kneeling. And in the middle, between
the two structures, the infant Jesus, quite naked, shall lie, glowing
with light (lensant raigs de si mateix). Mary and Joseph shall as has
been said be kneeling, turned towards the Child, contemplating him.
And the angels mentioned above shall sing Gloria in excelsis. And
then the three Kings are to come up through the door of the said
float, climb the steps which Çalom shall have made, and shall adore
the infant Jesus.

    In CHESTER *in 1572 the Coopers' "carriage" (the term usually
used for a wagon in Chester) had to be substantially rebuilt as well
as taken apart again for storing:*
Item, cost of taking the carriage apart and bringing it up to the
steward's door, 18d.
Item, two sills for the carriage, the price 2s 8d.
More paid to John Croulay for making the carriage, and nails, 4s.
Item, for carrying the wheels to the water and from, and the under-
carriage (berygh) of the carriage, 7d.
More spent when the painters came to decorate the under-carriage.
. . .
Item, for iron and binding a wheel, and one staple, one new wheel,
and repairing one old wheel, which comes to 5s 1d.
More spent in greasing the carriage wheels, and grease for it, the
ladder [?*the sub-frame of the carriage*] and setting it up on the
wheels, 14d.
More for frets and for axle-tree pins, 8d.
Item, spent at bringing it up to the Minster Gate, for cords and pins
to set up the housing [?*the superstructure*] of the carriage, 2s.
. . .
Item, paid to John Croulay for taking the carriage apart, 7d.

    *For fixed location staging, construction work was necessary. A
number of carpenters' contracts have survived, including* MONT-
FERRAND 1477:
16 March. [*agreed with*] Michiel Crestin, Jehan Giolet, Jehan
Coraill, and Pierre Bicameys, carpenters, for making the scaffolds
(eshaffaulx) for the mystery of the Passion . . . for the price or sum
of £15 and in return for this sum the said carpenters undertake to
make the said scaffolds under the direction of Master Guillaume
Merichon, doctor, director (conduicteur) of the said mystery. [*The*

town was to furnish all wood and materials.]

1 April. Item: George Roullet . . . has received . . . the sum of
17s 6d as the price of two dozen poles (potz) which were used to
make the Limbo in Hell. [*Roullet's receipt is also extant in which
he admits having received the money: for two dozen poles used both
for Limbo and on the scaffolds as needed for the Passion.*]

23 May. Paid to Symon Daussot, woodman (fustier) . . . the sum of
27s 6d T for the sale of four dozen and 20 fir poles (potz) which
were bought from him to extend the scaffolds (eslargir les chaffaulz)
and do what was necessary for the mystery to play the Passion on
Whit Monday.
[*The Play was acted on six successive Sundays and holy days.*]

        The ROMANS *contract of 1509 contains the following stipu-
lations:*
30 December. Firstly, the afore-named carpenters shall be required
to make a platform 30 paces long and 15 paces wide, at two paces
to the fathom (toise), which platform shall be raised on pillars to
the height recommended by the commissioners (commis) for the said
play and mystery, secured (composta) by strong beams (postz) fixed
together and pegged (?clevellees).
Item. The said carpenters will undertake to enclose the said platform from the top downwards with planks well joined together so
that no one can see underneath the said platform; and from the
platform upwards to supply an enclosure of squared poles (bastons
quarres) in the manner of stakes (liteaux) with withies (?bignes) and
cross pieces (?doubles perses) to form a trelliswork (pour trellisser)
with the said poles inside (dedans) to the height of four feet or
thereabouts.

Item. The said carpenters shall undertake to make within (dedans)
the said platform: towers, turrets, castles, towns of wood, and
stakes and canopies (?chapiteaulx) as necessary with portals and
openings for the effects (ouvertures de feinte) and steps, and change
them from day to day according to the requirements of the mystery
(mistere); with the necessary seats (sieges); and to furnish the wood
and workmanship for the said effects (feintez) prepared according to
the instructions of the commissioners (commis).

Item. The said carpenters shall undertake to make Heaven and Hell
in wood with carpenters' work according to the instructions of the
commissioners as is suitable, with the entrances and exits and trapdoors (secretz) all of wood.

The whole playing area at ROMANS *was covered with awnings:*
Paid 27 April for eighteen pots (pos) of wine, total 6s, and for 3s
given for bread and meat (chert) to those who erected three wooden

poles (piesses de boes) at the Cordeliers to support the awnings
(tentes) and ropes. . . . Paid the same day for having several ropes
and mill-stones (?mofles) carried from Paradise as far as the Cordeliers to help erect the three wooden poles afore-mentioned, total
3d T.

18 May paid to the said Gregoire for a large square piece of iron
(gros fer carre) to set into the wall of the Church of St. Francis
[the church of the Cordeliers] to fix the awning (tentes) weighing $3\frac{1}{2}$
lbs., total 3s 6d.
More, I have paid to Guillaume Fores for the awnings for the play
(tentes du jeu) which he supplied . . . 61 florins 8s T.

ALENÇON 1520:
Contract for erection of a theater in Alençon, October 1520.
With Master Thomas Guitton, carpenter.
1. Complete a scaffold (chaffaulx) to serve as Paradise which will be
placed and set against the outer rampart (contre le boulevert) and
will be of three levels (estaiges) and as high as the rampart or more
if need be and the length and breadth will be such as the place
(place) will hold, the whole being closed in behind from the first
floor (plancher) to the last floor at the top. The said scaffolds
(chauffaulx) shall be rounded off (arondis) with curved canopies
(de pens tout ront) and there will be three floors (planchers).

2. Item. Another scaffold to serve for Hell, which will be at the
corner of the gate of the town wall and will be made and constructed of one level (estaige), the height and canopy of the said
scaffold being of the height of the rampart of the said gate and
made in the form of a lean-to (appentis). On the said lean-to shall
be made another small stage (estaige) to serve as Limbo.

3. Item. Between the said two scaffolds of Paradise and Hell shall
be made a scaffold level with the outer rampart (?comme est le
boulevert) and of three levels (estaiges) on top of each other as
much as there is empty space between the said scaffolds, and it
shall be six or seven feet broad.

4. Item. There shall be made scaffolds of one level (estaige) on the
wall of the street which is made to serve the said Mystery, which
level shall be the height of a man (a haulteur d'hommes) above the
said wall, and the said scaffolds will be borne on stages strengthened
by the said wall behind and in front by other timbers (postreaulx),
with canopies borne on the gates of fire (?portes du feu).

5. Item. There shall be made other scaffolds, one stage high, from
the corner of the wall (mur d'arrest) to go as far as the town wall
right across the ditches (fossés), which scaffolds shall be made
properly (convenablement); and the said scaffolds shall be made on
top (au dessus) of light squares of wood.

6. Item. There shall equally be made scaffolds behind from Paradise
as far as the wall of the town to give access (?pour entrer) and of
the same height as the whole structure.

7. On the side of the town walls shall be made other scaffolds similarly supported as above. For these there shall be equally a gallery
to give access to the scaffolds at the position of a tower which is
part of the said walls. There shall be only one gallery made to
serve the said scaffolds.

A further carpenter's contract comes from BORDEAUX, *1525:*
Today, 4 August 1525, being present and appearing in person Peyrotin
de Barety, broker (corratier) of the parish of St. Michael's, Bordeaux, and Guillem Bergeron, braid-maker (aguilletier), citizen of
Bordeaux, on the one part and Bernard Gasteau, master carpenter of
Saint-Project and Rousseau, carpenter (charpentier de gross fuste) of
the parish of Saint-Maxens of the said Bordeaux on the other part.
Between which parties has been made, passed, and agreed the following bargain, pact, and agreement. That is to say that the said
Gasteau and Rousseau have promised and will be obliged to construct
and set up on the ditch of St. Eligius (le foussé de Saint-Eliège),
in the place where the mystery of St. Eulalia was acted, the following scaffolds (les eschaffaulx) to act, with the aid of Our Lord,
the baptism and beheading of St. John the Baptist together with the
conversion of the Magdalene, death and raising of Lazarus, in the
following form and manner:

Firstly, to block off with boards (tables) the area and place where
the said mysteries shall be played from the walls of the community
house (maison commune) of St. Eligius towards the garden of Lestonar, to rise on the paving to a height of three paces in the said
paving (?monter sur le pavé de hault de troys pas dans ledit pavé)
and returning to the said wall at a water channel (?esguyer) which
emerges from the said community house of St. Eligius and this to a
height of ten feet (et ce de dix piedz de haulteur), which said
boards and scaffolding (chaffaudage) [*are to be*] at the same place
as the said scaffolds (eschaffaux) are customarily placed and set up.

Item. Further to cover with staging (chaffauder) all the area (place)
which is between the two towers of the said community house together with the areas which extend from the opposite side (depuis en
face) as far as the said wall of the town, and from the Paradise as
far as the wall of the Town Hall.

Item. Further to make a scaffold (eschaffault) for Paradise and
another for a Hell projecting eight feet and eleven feet in height
and those which are against the said wall projecting six feet (de six
piedz de saillie). Further, at the two corners of the paving
(pavé), at each corner a scaffold (eschaffault) twelve feet long

and of the appropriate height (<u>la hauteur que s'appartiendra</u>) and
four entrances (<u>portes</u>) where they shall think fit (<u>ou il leur
plaira ordonner</u>). And to level (<u>lisser</u>) the area (<u>place</u>) where
the said mystery shall be played wherever it needs it. Also to
make seats (<u>sièges</u>) high on the said paving (<u>hault sur le dit
pavé</u>) to seat the audience who come to the said play and
Mystery. All of which work the said Gasteau and Rousseau
have promised and promise, and will be obliged to supply
(<u>rendre</u>) all the scaffolding and set it up in the said place by
one week from tomorrow, and the said scaffolds thus made
shall be left set up (<u>en leur estat</u>) until the day of the feast of
the Decollation of St. John the Baptist [*29 August*] inclusive.
And this in return for the sum and payment of one hundred
Bordeaux francs (<u>francs bourdelois</u>) which sum of one hundred
Bordeaux francs the said de Barety and Bergeron and each of
them have promised, promise and will be obliged to supply,
give, pay, and deliver one for the other and each of them alone
and for the whole without benefit or division to the said Gasteau
and Rousseau on the said day and Feast of the Decollation of
St. John the Baptist next coming without any failure.

Item. Further it has been agreed between them that if there is a
great deal of rain on the feast days when the said mysteries are to
be played so that they cannot play at that time because of being
prevented by the rain, the said Gasteau and Rousseau shall be obliged to leave the said scaffolds (<u>eschaffaulx</u>) on the said place until
the completion of the five feast days next following during which
they determine to play the said mysteries.
Item. Further it has been said and agreed between the said parties
that if the said scaffolds (<u>exchaffaulx</u>) break through the fault and
blame of the said Gasteau and Rousseau, in that case they will be
held to belong to the said Barety and Bergeron; also if any boards,
sections (<u>membrures</u>) or other piece of wood were broken, spoiled,
damaged, or stolen after the said scaffolds (<u>eschaffaulx</u>) have been
made until the end of the said play, in that case the said de Barety
and Bergeron have undertaken and will be obliged to satisfy, make
good, and pay the said Gasteau and Rousseau for the said damage
and interest (<u>dommaige et interestz</u>).

*A number of different constructions and locations may be
erected in the playing areas. The verse Prologue to the twelfth-
century* ANGLO-NORMAN RESURRECTION *describes such a set; the
two manuscripts vary slightly, and both are given here:*
[MS. P]
In this manner, we recite the Holy Resurrection. First of all, we
make ready all the places (<u>lius</u>) and mansions (<u>mansions</u>), first of
all the cross (<u>crucifix</u>) and then the tomb (<u>monument</u>). There must
be a jail to imprison the prisoner. Let Hell be put on this side and
the mansions on the other side, and then Heaven. And on the plat-

forms (estals) first of all Pilate with his vassals (he will have six or
seven knights); Caiaphas will be on the next, and the Jews (la
Juerie) will be with him, then Joseph of Arimathea; in the fourth
place shall be Lord Nichodemus; each of them shall have his men
with him. In the fifth the disciples of Christ; the three Marys shall
have their place in the sixth. And let them arrange to make Galilee
in the middle of the playing area (place); let Emmaus also be made
there where Jesus had betaken himself to the lodging (hostal). And
when everyone is seated and there is quiet on every side, Sir Joseph, he of Arimathea, shall come to Pilate and say to him. . . .

[MS. C]
If you have the devout intention of presenting the Holy Resurrection
in honor of God and reciting it before the people, arrange that there
shall be room to make a very large acting area and also you must
make proper provision how you set out (aser) the places (lius), and
that the mansions (maisuns) which belong to it shall be properly
provided for. First of all the cross (crucifix) and after that the
tomb (monument), the men at arms who will keep watch there, and
the Marys who will come there. The disciples on their platform
(estage) should behave in a prudent way (cum sage), Nichodemus will
have his place there and Master Longinus, the blind beggar, and Sir
Joseph of Arimathea and Pilate with his knights, Caiaphas, Annas,
and the Jews (li Jeu). David's tower and Master Bartholomew and a
jail shall be put there to incarcerate the prisoners. Let Hell be put
on one side there, in which will be the devils together with the
patriarchs who shall be held there in bonds. You must not forget
Heaven where the angels must dwell. Let it be arranged that they
make Galilee in the middle of the playing area, and Emmaus, a little
castle, where the pilgrims will take their lodging. And when everyone is seated and there is quiet on every side, Joseph of Arimathea
shall come and say. . . .

        A *similar verse Prologue is found in the* FRENCH ST. LAW-
RENCE *play, 1499 (the dots and number show lines of text omitted):*
I want to show you the characters, the actors, and the stages too
(estages) so that you can understand what we want to make known
to you. This construction (habitacle) here shows Paradise and represents it. There is the one called God; it is right that the place
(lieu) should be beautiful. The angels are around him. Philippe the
Roman Emperor who holds all men under his rule is seated in his
high place. Beside him is his son Philippe and round them are their
knights . . . [11]. Lo, there is a great king of Gaul . . . [3] and
here is the defender of Rheims . . . [3]. Beyond you see the
domain of the great country of Spain . . . [8]. Decius is on this
side . . . [6] and in this place (lieu) are also seated four wicked
men, torturers . . . [5]. In this place lives and dwells the wise
provost Ypolite . . . [4]. You can see in this dwelling (repaire)

Sixtus, the holy father of Rome . . . [4]. The good widow in this
stand (estre) . . . [3]. See the goldsmith in this low place (bas
lieu) . . . [5]. On this side is Hell . . . [7]. My division is finished.
[A series of stage directions refer to individual scaffolds.]   Philippe,
the emperor, begins: first scaffold (eschauffault). . . . Servant,
knight, father of St. Laurens: the second scaffold. . . . Passevant
speaks before the stage (estage) of the king of Gaul, and Ancelot
[knight of Gaul] comes down and goes about the playing area (les
champs).

The FRENCH SS. CRISPIN AND CRISPINIAN play is introduced in a similar fashion:
Good people, so that you may be clear about what you are seeing
here, I will name each of the characters and also their condition
(estat).   Some of them are in this place down here (lieu bas cy) in
the open space (champ) which is both long and broad.   Several
others are also around here (cy entour) on these high stages (hauts
estages).   And to begin with a high place, first of all you see here
Paradise: God is here with his angels, Our Lady seated beside him
. . . [4]. The two good brothers who are called Crispin and Crispinian, behold them there in Rome . . . [5]. On this side here is
the town of Soissons where there are many Pagans and also more
than a thousand Saracens, both great and lesser . . . [4]. There you
see King Maximian and his councillors with him . . . [6]. The provost, whom I have mentioned already, you see there in great array
. . . [46]. Behold four of the torturers (tirans) I have mentioned
. . . [7]. In that place you see the jailer who keeps the prison
. . . [6]. In this place are two worthy people of good will and good
life . . . [16]. There you see the Pope in his house (manoir) . . .
[5]. There you see an archbishop also who serves God as a good
and worthy man . . . [11]. Sixtus whom it pleases me well to name.
Behold him there! I see him in his place . . . [19]. Then see there
stinking Hell! Inside are a swarm of devils.

The MAJORCA SS. CRISPIN AND CRISPINIAN play is described in similar terms:
Three scaffolds (cadefals) are to be made, and between them there
is to be much. . . . At one end of the scaffold there is to be the
palace (palau) of a Moorish king and, close to the palace, a chapel
(capella) in which there is an image of Christ crucified. At the
other end of the scaffold there is to be a church (sglésia) with a
belfry. On another scaffold there is to be the palace of the Emperor Maximian, and near his palace there is to be a governor,
called Kactioner. On another scaffold there are to be two shops
(botigas), one at each end. Also two hermit's houses (cases); in one
of them there is to be a very old hermit. On the same scaffold,
there is to be a little house (caseta) for two shoemakers, and a
table and two chairs.

The MAJORCA ESTHER *play has detailed stage directions at
the beginning which show how the scaffolds were arranged:*
To put on this play four scaffolds (cadefals) are necessary: that is,
two on each side of the church. The first is to be near the mayor's
bench and that is where King Ahasuerus shall stand, very richly
dressed, with a crown on his head and a scepter in his hand. In
addition, there shall be two doorkeepers, one on each side of the
scaffold. In addition there shall be seven eunuchs in the palace
(?presidēntia) with their hats in their hands. Further, there is to
be a table prepared so that they can eat when the time comes. The
total number of characters is ten: two doorkeepers, seven eunuchs,
the king.

The second scaffold shall be set up a little below the other and on
it shall stand Vashti the first wife of King Ahasuerus, richly dressed,
with her royal crown, and with two maids; in addition, two eunuchs,
and Hegai and Hatach, dressed in long robes. In addition, there
shall be Esther, after she has been made queen, with her two maids.
Before she becomes queen, however, she shall stand with Mordecai in
some other place (en algun loch apartat) in the church. The total
number of characters then is: Queen Vashti, two servants, two
eunuchs, Hegai, Hatach, Esther, Mordecai.
    On the other side of the church there shall be two further
scaffolds lined up facing the others. On the first, in front of King
Ahasuerus's scaffold, there shall be four sages with long robes and
white beards, and these are to be the King's councillors. Total: 4
sages.
    On the fourth scaffold Haman shall stand with two servants,
two messengers, an official, three soldiers, a trumpeter, an execu-
tioner. Finally, there shall be wood to make a gallows on that scaffold when the time comes. Total: Haman, two servants, one official, three soldiers, two messengers, one trumpeter, one execu-
tioner.

The PRADES ASSUMPTION, *written in Catalan before 1420,
begins with similarly descriptive directions:*
In the place (loch) where this play (representaciō) is to be presented, the organization is to be as follows:
Firstly, the Jews are to make a splendid house (una bella barracha)
for themselves. Similarly, Lucifer and the other devils are to make
a place which is to be a large Hell (un loch quey sīa infern gran).
And they are to take there an anvil (anclusa) and hammers (mayls)
to make a loud noise when the time comes. Also, Paradise (parays)
is to be fitted out with fine purple cloths, rich curtains, and ties
(?benes) where Christ is to be with angels and archangels. Also St.
John the Baptist, patriarchs, prophets, virgins, and other blessed
souls. Also, there is to be constructed a house (casa) for the Virgin

Mary in which there is to be a fine bed, furnished with good curtains, and in front of the house there is to be a fine oratory (un
bell horatori) where the Virgin may say her prayers. Also, there is to
be made in another place a fine tomb (un bell sepulcre) where the
Virgin Mary will be placed when she departs this life, and there are
to be some fine white garments which she will put on when Christ
raises her from the dead and leads her to Paradise. Also it is to be
arranged that when the angel who brings the palm returns to Paradise, there is to be a noise with explosions (esclafidos) and
cerredos.

*The relationship of the different structures to each other is in
some cases uncertain, as in* ROME, 1498:
The tribunal (tribunale) of Pilate with four round columns in front
and four square columns behind, with ceiling, frame (cornice), and
all its other fittings (fornimenti).
Item. Another small tribunal on four small, round columns for
Herod.

*Sometimes the structures are precisely positioned in relation
to the total playing area, as in* ROUEN, 1474:
[*Performed in the New Market Place* (neuf marchié]. And the
mansions (establies) were set in the northern part of the aforesaid,
from the house with the sign of the Crowned Axe as far as the
house with the sign of the Angel, according to the order given at
the end of this document (codicille). But the mansions of the six
prophets were away from the others in different places and parts of
the said New Market.

At MONS, *labels were used to identify structures on the
stage:*
To Jehan du Quesne for eighteen loads of turf (voyes de wazon) with
his horse and cart at 18d for each load: 27s. [*Another entry for 19
loads the following week--the week of the performance.*]
To Sir Jehan Portier, priest, for having made at the command of the
honorable organizers and commissioners (eschevins et commis) ninety-
eight notices (briefvés) in large letters (de grosse lettre) of the
places (lieux) on the stage (hourt): entered here by agreement, 48s.
For pins, this day, on the stage to attach a number of labels
(briefvets) 3s. [*15 July. First day of the play.*]

The ROUEN *locations were also apparently labeled:*
To avoid tedium we will not describe the locations (lieux); you can
recognize them by the notice (escritel) which you see above them.

In the course of the play a location that was no longer needed could be reallocated, as at MONS:
Henceforward, if desired, the house (logis) for Mary and the thirty-year old Jesus can be in Adam's house (logis).

Perhaps the most detailed description of a playing area is that from LUCERNE *in 1583, which should be read in conjunction with Cysat's plans of the stage for the two days of the performance* (Appendix II, pp. 283-85): Lay-out of the places of the Passion Play (Abtheilung . . . osterspils) held Anno 1583. Thus measured on the orders of Town Clerk Cysat by Master Uolrich Hardmeyer the carpenter, master of works (Werckmeister) in Lucerne, on the Friday after Easter Anno 1583, when the Passion Play had been performed on the preceding Wednesday and Thursday.

1. Hell at the bottom end of the square towards the Muligasse, between the fountain and the Cobblers' Hall, two feet away uphill from the door of the said Hall. In front two posts are to be dug in, on which the mouth is hung, drawn up, and lowered, 9½ feet wide. The first post is to be 3½ feet from the Hall. The mouth shall be level with the scaffold (dem gerüst eben) beside the fountain on the side facing the square. The length of Hell up to 6 feet away from the door of the Tanners' Hall, towards the fountain. Beside the door (darneben) it has a separate closed passageway out. Hell closed in, walled in, also covered over and raised at the rear. The space between Hell and the fountain is to be covered over and also have a stand over it (verbrügenet sin) as far as the post on which the mouth hangs--likewise also on the other side, what is free as far the post of the entrance--and forwards it tapers (werts verloren) as far as the pillar of the fountain.

2. King Saul's stall (hof) uphill beside it, near to Sebastian Knab's house, 11½ feet wide, and shall begin one foot away, beside and above the said doorway. Between Saul's stall and the corner of the stand (Brügi) which is erected on the fountain, the same passageway to Hell shall stretch (hallten) 9 feet. The stall shall stretch on the slant (schelbs) from the said doorway of the said house away towards the square as far as Judas' tree. The space from the scaffold (gerüst) forwards as far as this tree shall be 9½ feet. Between Sebastian Knab's house and this still shall be 6 feet.

3. Judas' tree shall be in front of the corner between Saul's and Herod's stalls, in front of the Apothecary's, 5 feet out from the stall.

4. Herod's stall uphill beside Saul's stall, 16 feet long upwards from Saul's stall and 9½ feet wide, and shall extend up to 5 feet from the doorway of the Apothecary's house.

5. Annas shall have his stall on the uphill side of Herod's, 11½ feet
long, reaching in front of Town Clerk Cysat's house, and 9½ feet
broad. 6 feet space behind the stall.

6. The apothecary's on the uphill side of the previous stall. It is
to have only one seat and a place where he can set up a small
scaffold or a frame (gerüstlin oder gstellin) for the apothecary and
his seat for his person only beside it. This place is to be 5 feet
broad and 9½ feet long. And behind it, 6 feet space, shall be precisely in front of Town Clerk Cysat's doorway.

7. The stall of the Virgin Mary shall be straight in front of Town
Clerk Cysat's house called the Haus zur Rose, uphill from the aforesaid apothecary's. Its length is to be 13 feet and its breadth 9½
feet, and behind 6 feet of space. Behind this stall there is to be a
comfortable (komlich) raised stand for the clergy: from the Parish
church (der stifft im Hof), Franciscans (Barfuosser), Capuchins, and
Jesuits, and if there is more room, visiting clergy, as many as there
is room for. This stand shall reach along the house almost as far as
the Brotschol.

8. Zacheus is to have his stall uphill from Mary's stall in front of
the old Courthouse. Its length is to stretch 14 feet according to the
suitable length of the table and both benches. And then in breadth 9
feet. Also to have boards (tili) on the floor so that the table and
the benches can conveniently stand.

9. Moses' stall also in the same place, as wide (wytt) as the arch of
the Brotschol reaches, namely to extend 14½ feet in width (wytte).
Is to taper (sich verlieren) at an angle from the corner and Mary's
stall, also Zacheus's stall, to the corner where John's prison stands.
Also from another page: The Brotschol is to be covered in or walled
in at the back.

10. John's prison, at the top, next to Moses' stall, 8 feet long, 7
feet broad, is to have the door at the front corner. *Also from
another page:* the door of John's prison is to be open at the top and
have wide gaps (wytte sprenzel) so that John is visible and can speak
outwards.

11. The stand (brüge) on the fountain shall cover the whole fountain in a rectangle. The height shall be as high as the fountain
is and one more piece of wood on top. In breadth 24½ feet. In length
backwards 32 feet. At the rear raised 3 feet as far as Barabbas'
prison (stoc). The pillar (sul) for the flagellation of Christ is
to stand 7½ feet away from this prison front. The lead cover (loden)
for the grave, 4 feet long, 2 feet broad, and is to be 7 feet from the
scaffold backwards towards the prison and 8 feet from the prison,
also 7½ feet towards Hell. And the steps (stäglin) to the grave
beneath the stand shall go straight by the stone pillar or corner

down towards Sebastian Knab's house. The small shed (schüwrlin) or Christmas Hut is to be at the bottom corner of this stand. It is to be 5½ feet broad and long and 7 feet high. And this small shed or Christmas Hut is not to have walls, but to be erected just with four posts and be open, have a simple roof of thatch (schoub) simply attached. The roof beam of the hut is to face towards the square, with a hole in it, at the back a small upright pole attached to it, 8 feet high, to which is attached the rope (schnuor) for the star. [To this should be added the note for 1597: curtains and the roof for the hut.] The desert of John the Baptist is also to be exactly on the same place. The stocks for the prisoners are to be at the front near the steps (stägen) where one goes onto the stand, 6½ feet long. For the crowning there is to be a small stool (gefiert stüelin), 1½ feet broad, 2½ feet long. This stand on the fountain is at the back to be boarded off (verwandet) from the high rear stand. Likewise also elsewhere on the other sides, downwards around the fountain.
The steps are to be from the corner of the alleyway (gesslin) towards the Fishermen's Quarter (gegen der fischer statt) 16 feet away, 5 feet broad, 15 feet long, at the bottom raised with a separate first step (unden erhöcht mit einem antritt): from the step to the end 7 feet on the other side.

12. The big main stand at the foot of the square behind the fountain begins next to the one on the fountain, is to reach to the corner of J. Hans Allmender's house reaching to the bottom of the lintel (gsims) of the window. At the front beside the fountain it is to be 12 feet high and reach to the Hall of the Tanners' guild (gsellschaft). And on the back of it, it is to have its good beams.

13. Heaven is to be high up, at the top of the square, raised between the two oriels of the Haus zur Sonne, in such a way that it reaches and includes the upper windows of the upper corridor above the first and lowest windows, and that people can go in and out through these said windows. It is equipped as usual and as is well known. The ladder for climbing up and down is to be leaned up on the outside and turned towards the Brotschol, with a hand-rail and a box (laden) underneath. Its bottom step (ansatz) shall reach just 6 feet away from the corner of the house which faces the Brotschol. Heaven is to reach outwards (usshin) 7½ feet; be 11 feet long along the front, and at that point 8 feet high; at the rear it is to reach as far as the window lintel. The floor is to begin at the lower lintel.
Other documents show that decorations for Heaven were provided from the store of the Parish Church, and, at least in 1597, that Heaven was furnished with curtains: Curtains for Heaven.

14. The Choir (Die Sengery) is to be just under Heaven. It is made in such a way that it just fits between the two oriels beneath Heaven and that what has to be beneath it also has sufficient space. It

encompasses all the same width and is to be 8 feet high.

15. The Doctors' (Leerer) stall is to be on the left-hand side of the Haus zur Sonne beneath the same projecting roof (vortächlin) towards the Cornmarket, and be 7 feet broad and 14 feet long. Note: in the future it is to be smaller, for there will be only four of them. But the horn blower (Harst Horn blaser) could be with them, and consequently the stable for the animals can be given more space.

16. The asses' stable is also to be there under the choir on the ground in front of the house doors, 4 feet broad, 7 feet long.

17. The Mount of Olives is also to have its position beneath Heaven and the Choir, just in front of that door of the Haus zur Sonne which looks out towards the Brotschol, next to the ladder leading up to Heaven, located 9 feet away from the house on the floor of the square. It is to be 11 feet high, one side 8 the other side 7 feet broad, on top 5 feet broad and 6 feet long.

18. The table or stall of our worships the Mayors (Unser Herren der Schulltheissen) and of the most eminent visitors is to be at the foot of the square at the corner beside the stand on the fountain, next to Hell. There, boards (Tili) are to be laid on the ground at an angle (schreg) towards Hell, so that they do not obstruct access to Hell. These are to be 16 feet long from that same corner of the stand as far as the steps which lead from the square up onto that same stand. At the other outer corner 9 feet are to be partitioned off for Isaac's stall.

19. The stall of Isaac as an old man is to be exactly in the middle, between the stall of the Mayors just mentioned and the steps onto the stand, taking up the remaining space. It is to have a made-up couch (?angemachte Gutschen) with a curtain round the back up against the front panel of the stand on the fountain, and this is to be 6½ feet long.

20. The Synagogue or Jews' School starts at the corner near the house of former Mayor (Herrn Allt Schulltheissen) Jost Pfyffer, uphill in the square. There, boards (Tili) are also to be laid on the ground, at the bottom 6 at the top 8 feet broad, 20 feet long. At the top end of the Synagogue there is to be a passageway (gang) between the Synagogue and the Temple, 3 feet wide.

21. The Temple is to be immediately up from the Synagogue, except that the passageway is between them, as just stated. The Temple shall be made open and the choir so that one can see into it, as is known, also have on the ground boards (Tili), 9 feet broad and 23 feet long to the Choir, which is to stand adjacent to the barrier (schrancken), be 5 feet long and rounded, divided into 6 cor-

ners.
Item. 2 pieces of wood (höltzer) on top of one another for the
seat on each side. The pillars on the choir are to be slender (?ring),
10½ feet high and with a six-cornered star on top of them. In the
middle a helmet-stand (helmstengli) 10 feet high. Then reduced in
size with hoops to form a circle (?Darnach mit Reiffstangen ver-
jüngt in die Künde) like the top or knob of a heathen or Old
Frankish tower. On the ground the Temple and the Choir are to
have barriers to a height of 4 feet up, hung round with carpets.
The door of the Temple at the bottom shall be made with two piles
from the river bank (schwirren) and arched.

*Additional information can be gained from other documents; for
1583:*
Item. The stand on which the Temple stands.
Item. That the Temple be properly arranged and decorated. Raabod,
Urias, Zacharias, and Josaphat are to arrange and decorate the
Temple. The Temple is to have a choir, but all so that one can see
into it, not closed in.
And for 1597 the following: Temple--all those in the Temple (Tem-
pel Herren) are to join together in decorating and preparing the
Temple except Raabod and Urias, who have other expenses. The
lower part is to be wooden palings 1½ ells high, with cloths laid
over it. The choir is to have its special arrangement as usual. In it
an altar, on which the tabernacle (sarch) is to stand and the circumcision is to take place. At the bottom on a small pole is to be
a little bell which is to be rung by the youngest of those in the
Temple for the council on the Second Day; also when the Savior
reaches the cross he is to draw up the curtain and draw it quickly
apart when he dies.

22. The Dammed (Schwemm) Pool of Siloam dug into the ground in
the square, low down towards the fountain, 11 feet away from
Judas' tree, all the steps from the Mayors' table (?alle gräde von
der Herren Schulltheissen Tisch dannen) up the square, 11 feet from
Herod's stall.
Additional information for 1597:
The Dammed Pool of Siloam is to be at the bottom of the square
enclosed within a wooden tub (büchi) made by a cooper to contain
the water, buried 1½ feet into the earth, level with the ground.

23. The seat and position of those in the Temple (Tempelherren) is
to be beside the top end of the Temple, 7 feet broad and 9 feet
towards the square.

24. Caiaphas' stall uphill from the seat of the people from the
Temple, 11½ feet long and 9 feet forwards towards the square, and
goes 1½ feet into the Butchers' Passage. There is also to be a
small stand (kleins brügelin) for the seat on which Caiaphas is to
sit, 3½ feet broad.

Additional information about this stand is given for 1597: The Butchers' Passage is to be walled (verwandet) so that the acting area is
more accessible for the stand (damit man mitt der brüge destbas
zplatz komen möge).

25. The Herald's (Proclamators) stall uphill from that of Caiaphas,
14½ feet long and 9 feet broad.

26. Place for the musicians (der Spillütten ort), they have the
remaining space which remains at the top of the square between the
Herald's stall and the door or trellis towards the Cornmarket, 19
feet long tapering in front and angled towards the passageway, and
the point of this place goes 4 feet beyond Heinrich Krämer's house
(bis 4 schuoch in Heinrich Krämers huss).

27. The Savior's cross is to stand exactly in the middle of the square
between the two oriels of the Haus zur Sonne, near the top end, 30
feet from that said house.

28. The two other crosses of the thieves shall each be 10 feet
away from the Savior's cross.
Additional information for 1597: Note of what the master carpenter
has to arrange. The actual cross on which the Savior is crucified.
Also the crosses of the two thieves. Item: ladders, forks (gabeln)
and all the equipment for the three crucifixions. He shall also have
the three crosses dug in, and particularly the base (stock) of the
Savior's cross.

29. Moses' Brazen Serpent and its cross shall have their place for
insertion 7 feet away from the Savior's cross. It comes almost in
the middle of the square. There a piece of pipe is put upright into
the ground, level with the surface.

30. The Annunciation and Magdalene's garden are in the same
place, namely uphill from the old courthouse, 8 feet away from the
aforementioned hole of the brazen serpent, and it is not walled in or
enclosed like a stand, but simply an enclosure with laths, and low;
also hung round with carpets, and at the back a lath nailed upright
to it where the Holy Spirit comes over Mary.
Additional information for 1597: Magdalene's garden is to be a
small enclosure, at the front, where Paradise stood [*on the first
day*], made with laths or enclosed.

31. The stall of the Savior and the Apostles at the top of the
square by the Haus zur Sonne, from that door of the said
house which looks out towards the Cornmarket, from thence forward
to the said corner, which gives the same length and then 7 feet
broad.

32. Paradise is at the top of the square in front of the Haus zur

Sonne on the side towards the Cornmarket, from the post of the
Apostles' stall outwards, 6½ feet wide and from the corner 10½
feet. Now it is to be across from the first post to the other 24
feet in length, on all sides (allenthalben) lengthened and enclosed
(?geschrenkt or = with crisscross timbers?). The pit in which Adam
and Eve lie hidden in Paradise is to be in the middle, from the Haus
zur Sonne to the middle of the square 25 feet, adjacent to the
Mount of Olives, in the middle of Paradise. The box tree is to
stand 2½ feet from the pit.
Additional information for 1597: The Garden of Eden is on the First
Day Paradise, on the Second Day the garden of the Mount of Olives,
where the Savior prays; is not to be high, nor woven (gflochten), for
the greater part with branches of greenery or small evergreen trees
stuck in all around it. The pit in Paradise in which Eve is hidden is
to be by the tree in Paradise.

*For some plays the layout of the playing area is linked in a
rubric or stage direction with other information such as costume and
grouping of the characters.*

The fifteenth-century Last Judgment play from ROUERQUE *has a
detailed opening rubric:*
And first our Lord should be seated on a throne (cadieyra) well-
adorned and shall display all his wounds in the presence of everyone,
all gilded (totas dauradas). Next there should be four angels, two on
each side, one carrying the cross, the next the column with the rope
fastened to the column, the next the nails and the scourge, and the
next the lance and sponge. And there shall be a well-adorned throne
for Our Lady to sit on at the appropriate time on her Son's right
hand. And there should be two angels, each with his trumpet, and
in Paradise should be St. Michael and a great number of angels with
him. And the saints should be on the other scaffold (escadafal) each
in his place, arranged on benches (ordenats an bancz). And St.
Peter should wear his tiara as pope and the emperors and kings as
becomes their condition, dressed according to their estate in garments of green and black and marten fur (mosa). And there shall be
emperors and kings and churchmen (glieza) and women dressed according to their estate; and Jews shall be together and the others
similarly and shall approach when summoned by the angels.

The devils shall be at the side (apart) when they have come from
Hell and been before Eternal God and heard their sentence. Our
Lady shall be all alone in her place (son loc), richly dressed, on the
large scaffold (escafadal gran) and shall be there until it is time to
approach. Justice and Mercy and Life shall be all together on the
large scaffold. Death shall be in its place on the scaffold. The
Jews shall be at the side of the large scaffold so [4 names]; the
idolaters shall be at the side of the scaffold, so [4 names] etc. the
bad Christians . . . the members of religious orders: Bernardines,

Carmelites, Augustinians, Dominicans, Cordeliers, Minorites. . . .
[*God summons angels who sound their trumpets and call on dead to
rise*] . . . and after when they have mounted to Paradise, the dead
shall rise, some from the tombs and the others from secret places
(de locs segretz), and shall all come before God and kneel in silence. After which, the saved shall mount a scaffold lower than
Paradise on the right-hand side, and the damned shall remain on the
large scaffold on the left-hand side. [*The angels are sent to sum-
mon Lucifer and the devils from Hell. Lucifer replies*] inside Hell,
without opening the door . . . [*dialogue of Lucifer and angels*], then
the angels go to Paradise and Lucifer speaks, lamenting, when he
has come outside and climbed onto the scaffold.

    There is a similarly detailed direction for the MAJORCA LAST
JUDGMENT *play:*
To perform this play there shall be constructed as large a scaffold
(cadefal) as possible in the chapel (capella) in the middle of the
church in such a way that it juts out a bit, and immediately behind
it there shall be set up another so that one can climb from one to
the other, and on it [*the higher*] shall be placed the following objects: firstly, a seat with a back, adorned with rich hangings (una
cadira de respalles molt ben empaliade), like a judge's chair, and, in
addition, three leather seats, two or so trumpets (trompetes) for
when they will be needed. In addition, there shall be placed there
a cross without a Christ crucified (una creu sens crusifici), two
banners with their poles (dos vexillas ab ses astes), placed on the
ground in readiness.

On the lower scaffold there will be nothing. Below this scaffold, if
possible, there is to be made a Hell-mouth (una boca de infern). If
this cannot be done, a curtain (una cortina) is to be hung there to
cover the lower part of the scaffold. That space will be Hell.

The characters will enter in the following manner: St. Michael is to
enter first, dressed in armor (vestit de arnes), with a drawn sword,
bareheaded, carrying a velvet cap, and wearing a gold chain round
his neck. Next, two guardian angels (custodis) shall enter side by
side, dressed in white albs and dalmatics with drawn swords in their
right hands and royal crowns in their left. Afterwards Christ and
Mary shall enter. Christ is to wear the following: a doublet (gipo)
of white satin, hose, and breeches (calses y calsons) of the same
stuff, and on this costume the wounds shall be shown by means of
something red (faran los [sic] plagues de alguna cosa veimella
[sic]). Over this costume he shall wear a white cape (cape blanca);
he shall wear a crown, as is the custom, and in his hand shall have
a drawn sword. Mary shall be richly dressed, like a queen. The
group of seven shall proceed to the higher scaffold in the following
manner: Christ shall sit in the canopied seat with Mary on his right.
Next, St. Peter, and behind him St. John, all on the same side. The

angels will remain standing, St. Michael in front of Christ looking at
his face. The guardian angels, one on each side, and nearer the
front of the stage, shall look towards Christ. Then three saved
shall enter in penitential garments carrying psalteries (saltiris). Then
Pride shall enter, dressed like a king with scepter and crown; after
him, Envy, well dressed, with spectacles (ulleres). Then, on the
right of Envy, Gluttony well dressed and carrying things to eat. On
the left, Anger, in armor (armada ab cuyrases) with a helmet (cer-
vellera) on his head. Then Lust, dressed as a woman, with a mirror,
and on her right shall walk Avarice in a long robe, an ink container
(tinter) at his waist, a purse (bossa) in his hand with objects inside
to make a sound like money jingling when he wishes, and a book
under his arm. On the other side of him shall walk Sloth in a short
jacket (giponet), in sagging breeches (en calsons de larch en larch),
with a pillow under his arm for having a rest when he feels like it.
And in this manner all ten will take their places on the lower scaffold: seven to the left of where Christ sits, and three to the right.

Then three devils shall enter in no particular order, helter skelter,
dressed in the usual manner except that Lucifer shall wear a crown
and carry a scepter. They shall carry manacles in their hands, and
in this way they shall enter from the Hell-mouth or from beneath
the curtain.
. . .
Now the saved and the damned shall fall down dead and enter behind
the scaffold, and shall change into the following costume: the saved
shall put on an alb (camis) and over it a light colored cape (capo-
tin), on their heads black wigs, bands on their foreheads, and on the
said bands a red cross. The damned are to wear black cassocks
(sotanes), and on their heads white, black, or reddish wigs. While
they are changing the angels are to blow their trumpets (trompetes),
and when they get word that the actors have finished changing, St.
Michael shall sing his words to the melody of Vexilla.

2. INDIVIDUAL LOCATIONS AND SETS

*Many locations and sets which contain machinery or special
effects appear below in sections 3 and 4. The most detailed descriptions of individual locations are those of Heaven and Hell. The
mouth of Hell is mentioned specifically several times:*
METZ in 1437: The gateway and mouth of Hell in this play was
very well made, for by a device (engin) it opened and closed of its
own accord when the devils wanted to go in or come out of it. And
this great head (hure) had two great steel eyes which glittered
wonderfully.

ROUEN in 1474: Hell made like a great mouth (guelle) opening and
closing as is needful. The Limbo of the Patriarchs made like a prison and they were only visible above the waist (du hault du corps).

MONTFERRAND in 1477: 20 March. Item: the said Percheron
[one of the town consuls] has given to the said Colas 15d for a
bundle of rings (faysse de cercles) to make the Hell's mouth.
Item: Pierre Noel acknowledges . . . having received . . . the sum
of 5s 3d T for the price of a cartload of thorn which was purchased
to put round the scaffold of Hell to play the play.

Hell's tower and Limbo are found in the PARIS RESURRECTON
(1419):
Here the Anima Christi should shove Satan from the top of the step
(marche) of the pit (puytz) inside, and Satan cries out horribly. This
pit should be made between the gate of hell and the tower of
Limbo on the side of the playing space (champ du jeu) so as to be
more visible, and the said pit must be made in such a way that it
seems from outside to be constructed of black dressed stone
(maconné de pierre de taille noire), and it should be made in such a
way that there are formed everywhere inside partitions of mortar
(bousilles) without them being visible. In one of the sections the
Anima Christi shall cast the devils, and from the other shall come
forth flaming sulphur, cannon-fire, thunder, and other fearful sounds
(tempestes) until Satan and the others shall all be cast in; after
which there will be silence, and then the Anima Christi will break
with his cross the door of the tower of Limbo, the fashion of which
tower is described hereafter, and as he does this the Anima Christi
shall speak the following:

> 'Up Adam and your companions,
> You shall come out of your prison,
> For we are the strongest ones inside here
> And you shall therefore come with me.'

Here the soul of Adam shall begin to sing this Responsory (respont)
Libera me . . . [several lines of Latin]. And the souls, singing
well, will help him to sing the responsory. And note that the Limbo
should be at the side of the platform (parlouer) of Hell which is
over the door in a dwelling (habitacion) which should be made like a
tall square tower surrounded by nets (rethz) so that through the said
nets one can see from the audience (parc) the souls who are inside
when the Anima Christi has forced his way inside there; but before
his coming the said tower shall be provided with black cloth curtains
all round which will cover the said nets and prevent them being seen
until the entrance of the Anima Christi, and then the said curtains
shall be cunningly pulled aside on small rings (annelez) so that the
people in the audience (parc) can see inside the said tower through
the said grills. And in addition at the coming of the Anima Christi
there shall be in the said tower several torches and lanterns or
great burning flambeaux. And behind the said tower there should be
people in some place crying out in a loud voice as lost souls
(desesperés) whom those in the audience cannot see, and this noise
should not last very long, and then the soul of the Bad Thief shall
say aloud, for himself and the other damned, what follows. . . .

The Hell at MONS was plastered with clay and decorated:
To Jehan Helle called Vacquenot, for three and a half days employed
in plastering Hell (placquier l'Enfer) at 12s per day, he and his assistant (varlet), 42s, and for the hair (poil) put into the plaster
(mortier) so that it can be painted on, 2s. Together 44s.
To Jaquemart du Bois, carter, for nine loads of clay brought by him
to the said stage (hourt). [Several more entries refer to this also.]
To Master Jehan Machon for a cartload of willow stumps (teste de
sauch) with his fee for having uprooted them, for two days, he and
his assistant (varlet), which [stumps] were used for the said Hell,
24s.

The BOURGES PARADE (monstre) had a float for Hell, preceded by
a group of devils:
After this infernal crew (diablerie) came a Hell, fourteen feet long
and eight wide, in the form of a rock on which was constructed a
tower, continually blazing and shooting out flames in which Lucifer
appeared, head and body only. He wore a bear skin with a sequin
hanging from each hair and a pelt with two [animal] masks (tymbre
à deux museaux) adorned with various colored materials; he ceaselessly vomited flames, held in his hands various serpents or vipers
which moved and spat fire. At the four corners of the rock were
four small towers inside which could be seen souls undergoing various
torments. And from the front of the rock there came a great serpent whistling and spitting fire from throat, nostrils, and eyes. And
on every part of the rock there clambered and climbed all kinds of
serpents and great toads. It was moved and guided by a certain
number of people inside it, who worked the torments in the [dif-
ferent] places as they had been instructed.

This was followed by a group of angels and a float for Heaven:
After them [angels and archangels] was brought a Paradise eight
feet wide and twelve long. All the way round it was a circle of
open thrones painted like passing clouds and within and without
small angels, such as cherubim, seraphim, powers, and dominions in
the round (éleves en bosse) with folded hands and moving continually. In the middle was a seat made like a rainbow on which sat
the Godhead (la Divinité), Father, Son, and Holy Spirit, and behind
two golden suns in the midst of a throne which turned ceaselessly in
opposite directions. At the four corners were the four Virtues--Jus-
tice, Peace, Truth, and Mercy--richly dressed, and at the sides of
the said Godhead were two other small angels singing hymns and
canticles to the accompaniment of the players on flutes, harps,
lutes, rebecs, and viols, who were walking along all round the Paradise.

Other references to the decor of Heaven include:
YORK 1433: A Heaven of iron . . . two pieces of red cloud and
stars of gold belonging to Heaven, two pieces of blue cloud painted
on both sides, three pieces of red cloud with sunbeams of gold and
stars for the highest of Heaven, with a long, narrow border of the
same work . . . nine smaller angels painted red to run about in
Heaven, a long thin cord to make the angels run about.

SARAGOSSA 1487: For half a pound of gold (oro de bacin) for the
heavens (cielos) and wheels (ruedas) of the angels, 6s.
For a sheet of tinsel for stars, 2s.
Three pounds of paste (aigua cuita) for sticking on the clouds and
stars, 1s 6d.

ROME 1498: Item, two breadths of cloth with clouds (anuvilate)
which were used for Heaven (paradiso).

ROUEN 1474: And Paradise is opened, made like a throne, with
gold rays all around. In the midst of which is God on an orna-
mented throne with on his right Peace, below her, Mercy. On his
left Justice, below her, Truth, and all around them nine orders of
angels one above the other.

Sometimes Earthly Paradise is described in detail as in the
PARIS RESURRECTION:
The outside of the walls of this Paradise should be white. And
within there should be trees, some in blossom, others laden with
fruit of different kinds such as cherries, plums, apples, pears, almonds, oranges, figs, pomegranates, and grapes. Other trees green,
such as rose trees, flowers, rosemary, and marjoram. And they
should be of such a height as to be visible above the wall all over

the playing area. And therein should be a fountain that will divide into four streams.

Paradise is also described in detail in the ANGLO-NORMAN ADAM:
Let Paradise be constructed in a high place. Let curtains and silk cloths be hung around it to such a height that the characters (per-sone) who will be in Paradise may be invisible up to the shoulders. Let sweet-smelling flowers and foliage be set (serantur) [*there*]. Let there be various trees in it and fruit hanging from them, so that it may seem a most pleasant place.

Fruit was also put on the trees in Paradise in MONS:
For withered and fresh (viezes et nouvelles) apples, also cherries, bought today for putting on the trees of Earthly Paradise: 5s.

See also below B.6, NORWICH Grocers' 1557.

3. MACHINERY

A very common use of machinery is for exits from and entrances into Heaven. The traditional Spanish araceli was an elaborate structure associated especially with the Virgin Mary. See Section D for the use of the araceli in the Valencia Assumption play. Mid-fifteenth-century records from VALENCIA CATHEDRAL refer to the construction of the araceli and to another machine used for transporting an angel.

I bought the following materials for the said play (representació): one thin sheet of wood used by sieve-makers to make the rays (raigs) of the Araceli . . . a dozen sheets of gold foil to cover the said rays; 14 quires of paper for the clouds (núvols) for the Araceli and for the pedestal (peanya) of the angel. . . .

. . .

Eight wax torches (antorches de cera) for the said play, so that it would be well lit . . . 24 smaller torches (antorchetes) to be held in the hand by the angels who were in the dome (cembori) with God the Father . . . and 28 thick candles (caneles grossetes) for the Araceli.

Similar machinery for Heaven is described in the records of various royal entries in Spain, e.g., the entry of Charles I into BARCELONA in 1519:

. . . the doors of the Heaven (cel) built over the Gate of St. Anthony opened, and the Heaven appeared as described below: there were three wheels (arcades) and in the middle of the upper one was God, to his right the Virgin Mary, to his left St. John, and then Elijah and Enoch to right and left respectively. On the second, middle one, there were six angels playing stringed instruments (instrumens de corda), three dressed in white albs, three with albs and red dalmatics belonging to the city, and all wearing angels' masks (cares) and wings. On the third, the lowest, were six angels dressed like the other six described above. And the doors and the back were painted with stars and cherubim, and the angels made sweet melody. When the King had almost reached the Cross by the Gate (?la creu del portal), the machine (caxa) attached to the beam (grua) began to descend with four singers in it dressed as angels without masks and wings, with wigs, and clasps and tunics of white cloth with gold adornment, and they began to sing as follows. . . .

From early in the fifteenth century is recorded a rather curious use of this machinery. At the banquet for the CORONATION OF FERDINAND OF ARAGON in Saragossa in 1414 there was a Heaven from which descended an angel in a "cloud," and then Death, also in a cloud. This appearance of Death must have been a success, for it was repeated after the Queen's coronation, and on this occasion a trick was played on a jester:

This jester was in the hall where the Queen was feasting, and when
Death appeared in the cloud (la nube) as he had done at the King's
coronation, as we have already described, the jester became agitated
at the sight of him and screamed at him not to come near him. The
Duke of Gandía sent word to the King, who was at the window
watching the Queen dine, that when Death came down and the jester
began to scream, he [the Duke] should lead him up and tell Death
to throw a rope down and pull the jester up to him. And this was
done. When Death came down in his cloud in front of the table,
Borra started to scream, and the Duke led him up; Death threw
down a rope, they tied it round Borra, and Death wound him up. You
wouldn't believe the racket Borra made, weeping, expressing his ter-
ror, and, as he was pulled up, he urinated into his underclothes, and
the urine fell on the heads of those below. He was quite convinced
he was being carried off to Hell. The King watched all this and
was greatly amused, as were all the others. And Borra the jester
went up to Heaven as Death's prisoner.

   The BOURGES EFFECTS (fainctes) list provides several examples of machinery for raising and lowering from Heaven:
There must be thunder in Paradise and a white cloud to come and
snatch up St. John preaching in Ephesus and transport him to outside
the door of the Virgin Mary's house. There must be another cloud
to snatch up the apostles in various countries and let them be
brought to the front of the said house.
. . .
A vessel (vaisseau) shall descend from Heaven full of all kinds of
creatures sent to St. Peter in prison; and God the Father and Son
shall speak, then the vessel shall return to Paradise.
There must be sent down from Paradise onto the said tomb a round
cloud in the form of a crown (couronne) in which are a number of
artificial angels holding naked swords and darts in their hands, and if
possible there should be living ones to sing.

   The only description of raising machinery for an English pageant wagon comes in the 1433 indenture of the Mercers at YORK
for their pageant of the Last Judgment:
Four irons to support Heaven; four pins for securing the ends (finale
coterrelles) and an iron bolt; a grid (brandreth) of iron that God
shall sit upon when he shall ascend to Heaven, with four ropes at
four corners; a Heaven of iron with a hub (naffe) of wood.
By 1526 this has become:
one iron seat with four ropes; one windlass with one rope.

   Christ's entry into Paradise after the Harrowing of Hell also
sometimes involves machinery, as in the PARIS RESURRECTION:
And he should be pulled gradually, and his legs should show below

the machine (engin), and above his head and joined hands, and over
the machine should be a cloth (toille) painted all over with the souls
of the holy patriarchs (who shall enter Paradise secretly by ladders
under Paradise). And the cords pulling the device (instrument) on
which is Jesus should be hidden by cloth looking like cloud (en
maniere de nue). And from the place where Jesus is there should
come forth above and below white and yellow manna (manne) like
large, white coins (blans) in the form of gold and silver. And the
Virgin Mary and her noble company, kneeling with joined hands,
should watch our Lord ascending thus until they have lost sight of
him.

   In ROME *in 1498 a variety of cloud-masked pulleys were
used, whose exact functioning the records do not make clear:*
An iron girdle with little hinges (a canchanetti) for Our Lady.
A pair of big iron bars (ferri) with two clouds reinforced with wood
(armati de legno) on which the angels come to the Cross, with its
beams.
Item: two iron strips to tie round the waist (da cegnere) with
pieces divided at the back (co li ferri dirietro spezzati), which are
hinged onto the aforesaid big iron bars for the angels.
Item: a construction of wood with nailed cross-members (de legno
carrato) with an iron bar (braccio) and a cloud.
Item: for the said angel, an iron to tie round the waist of the
angel, jointed, and to be hinged (snodato da impernare).
Item: a big iron rod with an iron cross-bar which ends in two hinges
(vanno in doi cancani) used on (in) a column in Santa Maria Maggiore
to make an angel appear.
Item: another, similar one, which was used for the appearance of
Our Lady of the Snows (a la Neve).
Item: four iron bars (ferri) for angels which were used in the cloud
or mandorla (amandola) when they play the Assumption of Our Lady,
with the cloud at her feet.
Two big iron bars for angels, joined together in a cross, which were
used (se operavano) at the feast of Santa Maria ad Martyres (?Santa
Maria Ritonna).
Item: a long iron bar with the girdle and a cloud at its foot for
Our Lady when she went up to Heaven (salliva a cielo).
Item: a hinged iron girdle (a canchani) for Our Lady inscribed twice
(scritta doi volte).
A construction of wood with nailed cross-members with which Christ
is taken to Heaven (paradiso) at the Resurrection.

   *The use of trapdoors in the stage was widespread in France
and, among other things, facilitated effective appearances and disappearances. At* MONS *several such "secrets" were used:*
Note that Cain must kill Abel directly over the hidden place (secret)
where the child representing the blood of Abel will be ready to cry

vengeance. . . . The child in the hidden place (<u>secret</u>) representing
the blood of Abel, lamenting.
Note for Jesus to disappear by the <u>secret</u> of St. John's Prison [*after
appearing to Magdalene*].
Here Jesus should disappear by the <u>secret</u> of the Flood or any other
suitable one [*after appearing to the Three Marys*].
Here Jesus enters the prison by the <u>secret</u> and brings Joseph [*of
Arimathea*] out, without breaking the prison.
Here let the devil, Fergalus, be warned to go via the secret ways
(<u>par les secretz</u>) and take up position underneath [*the place*] of the
Canaanite's daughter so as to make a great smoke and explosion (<u>ung
canon</u>) when he is cast out of her body hereafter [*two scenes
later*].

> Jesus: 'O woman, very great is your faith,
>   Be it as you will. Go forth!'

Here there comes a smoke and an explosion from under the girl and
Fergalus comes out. [*He speaks briefly.*] He goes to Hell.

Movement underground was also possible in the PARIS RESUR-
RECTION:
This being done, Jesus accompanied by these three angels shall walk
across the playing area (<u>parc</u>) and by a trick (<u>par engien</u>) pass underground (<u>aller par soubz terre</u>) to visit Our Lady, his mother, who
is alone in the meeting house (<u>cenacle</u>), and should show himself
risen, when the time comes.

The same play shows that in some cases trapdoors were self-closing:
And Jesus, clad in white or quite naked, accompanied by the angels
Michael, Raphael, and Uriel, shall cunningly (<u>subtillement</u>) and suddenly rise up from the tomb through a wooden trapdoor (<u>trappe de
boys colleysse</u>) which will close itself again as soon as he has risen,
and our Lord shall sit down on the tomb without touching or knock-
ing it (<u>sans le froisser ne entamer</u>) in any way. And at that same
moment, Carinus and Leoncius shall also rise up in Jerusalem each
from his own tomb.

Such effects existed elsewhere, as at LUCERNE, *where a
trapdoor allowed Christ to disappear at Emmaus:*
Have the two pilgrims start out. Have the Savior's tomb removed
and the pilgrims' table placed over the hole, together with a chair,
and also the table laid and a split loaf placed on it.
After conversation the Savior comes to a halt downstage (<u>unden</u>)
near the stand (<u>an der brügi</u>). The Savior wants to leave them but
is invited to join them for food. They all three sit at table; the
Savior in the middle of them blesses the bread, breaks it, gives it to
them half each, speaks, and disappears.

At MONS *careful preparations were made to depict boats on the Sea of Galilee:*
To Jehan de Gravelle called the shipwright (bacqueteux) for his salary for the wooden boat (bacque = *a flat-bottomed ferry or canal boat*) which he had agreed to make for the said mystery at the cost of £20, including delivery, has so far been paid £8. [*Another two payments are listed.*]
To Jehan dele Fontaine, brewer, for the value (interest) of his beer delivery cart (chariot a mener cervoises par les rues) lent by him during the said mystery to bring the wooden boat (bacque) from the quay (au rivaige) to the said stage (hourt) on the market place, inside which was made the great sea, and which in the process was damaged, has been paid by order of the honorable organizers (eschevins) and entered here, 40s.
To Jehan Bracquet, boatman, for his salary for going by water to Jemappes to fetch a little wooden boat (bacque) to put on the water and bringing it to the quay [*of Mons*] to be used on the sea of the said stage (dudit hourt), 6s.
To Jehan Bouchart, carpenter, for a piece of wood 13 foot long and 6 inches square, which makes a supporting beam under the stage (hourt) to support the boat (bacque), 15s. [*This may be either the* mer *itself or the small* bacque *used on it.*] Item for 5 sheepskins . . . to make waves on the water, 29s. For another piece of leather for this purpose, 8s, and for the calfskin, 8s.
Stage directions show them in use: Here remind St. Peter and St. Andrew to approach the sea and go in and out of the boats (batelez) several times, pretending to be fishing and moving their nets about. [*Seven apostles, by the sea of Galilee*] enter the boat. . . . St. Peter steers the boat . . . then they prepare their trawls (saines) and their nets. Then St. John, after casting into the sea, says. . . . They pretend to draw it in.

In the BOURGES EFFECTS *there was equally careful preparation of the shipwreck:*
There must be a ship on the sea to take St. Paul to Rome.
For the said ship there must be a pulley on the mast and a peg in the ground and a rope passing through the said pulley to steer the said ship. There must be weights (poix) for the ship to be sunk and repaired (pour fondre et rabiller la navire) by the captain.
There must be chests and other gear (mesnage) to throw into the sea from the ship, and the ship's mast must break in two pieces. The ship must be repaired (rabiller) under pretense that it is broken (que l'on faindra estre froisee).

In the REVELLO *Passion the Magi return home by boat:*
Here let there be a ship (nave) in which is a captain and his sailors among whom is one on the poop deck of the ship. [*The kings take passage on the ship and it sets sail.*] When he [*Balthasar*] has

spoken, the ship moves off and Freberic begins to sing the song
written below. . . .
While the ship is moving Freberic sings. Two war ships (galeote)
shall come to attack the ship. And the latter does not pay attention to them and goes on its way. And Freberic continues singing.
And the warships shall come to the place where the ship was and
remain there broken (rotte). [Later Herod passes that way and sees
the war ships; believing them to be those of the kings, he orders
them to be burnt.] Then Herod's followers kindle and set fire to
the war ships and burn them. Meanwhile, Herod goes on his way.

A considerable series of entries in the MONS *accounts refers to*
items for the waters of the Flood:
Paid out on 19 June: to Jehan Horion called Ninchon . . . item
for four ashwood handles to turn some of the said effects
(secrés), 4s; and for two wooden vertical pulleys (moulettes)
used for the Flood, 2s.
To Williame Petit, cooper, for six large ashwood hoops at 2s 6d a
piece, 15s, and for a small barrel used in the machinery (secret) of
the cloud in the Flood, 10s; altogether, 25s.
To Master Jehan du Fayt . . . item for four round iron hoops each
two and a half feet long, and two pivots, each pivot bearing two
thin strips [of iron] (molles bendes), and two eyelets with double
strips (double bendes) to turn the barrel, and four other thin strips
(molles bendes) making five feet long altogether, these pieces being
used for the machinery (secret) of the cloud for the Flood: 28s . . .
and for two days employed by him in helping to prepare the effects
(secrés) and machinery (conduit) of the said stage (hourt) at 8s per
day: 16s.

Paid out on 3 July: to Hubert the Cooper for an empty cask of
Burgundian wine bought from him to be put in Paradise to be used
with the lead pipes of the Flood and also for having set it up in
the proper place (comme il appartenoit) etc.: 14s.
To Jaquemart Cambrelant, for three empty casks of French wine
used in Paradise to put the water for the Flood in, at 6s a piece:
18s.
To Pasquier Francquerier, rope maker . . . item, for a hempen rope
used to draw (thirer) the waters in Paradise, weighing eleven pounds
at 3s a pound: 33s.

Paid out on 24 July: to Master Jehan de Fayt . . . item, for four
thin strips [of iron] (molles bendes) used for the Cloud, 9s . . .
item, for two eyelets used in the machine (engien) set in the Maison
d'Allemaigne [house on the Grand Place in Mons] to lower the cloud
for the Flood, 8s.
To Aubert de Guyse, plumber, for 708 lbs. of lead pipes delivered to
the said stage both for the Flood and otherwise, at 2s the lb.,
£70 16s T, and for 23½ lbs. of solder at 5s the lb., 117s 6d; making

in all £76 13s 6d T.

*A machine to raise Simon Magus to the top of the tower was
also among the* BOURGES EFFECTS:
There must be a tall tower in the form of the Capitol which Simon
Magus will climb in order to fly, and a semi-circular cloud (nue col-
lisse) should come and raise him in the air, then the said cloud
should be removed revealing the body of the said Simon.

*The contract for preparing the staging of the Provençal play
of SS. Peter and Paul at* AIX-EN-PROVENCE *in 1444 also specified
a device for Simon Magus:*
Item: within the auditorium (las lissas) the machine (engienh) for
Simon Magus which can lift up three people, secretly, all belted
safely (ambe talholas, segur), and then descend again equally secretly
in such a way that it is not seen (que non so veia).

The FRENCH SS. PETER AND PAUL *play merely utilized
manpower (or rather devil-power):*
Then he climbs on them and they [*the devils*] carry him on their
shoulders in style (bellement).

*The tower prison of Joseph of Arimathea was raised with the
help of brass wire in the* PARIS RESURRECTION:
Here Jesus appears to Joseph of Arimathea in the tower where he is
imprisoned, the doors being shut. . . . Here the tower shall rise in
the air by a device of brass wire (par engin de fil d'archal) cunningly
made, and Jesus takes Joseph by the hand and leads him to his city
of Arimathea, the angels singing melodiously. . . .

4. SPECIAL EFFECTS

The full list of EFFECTS *required at* BOURGES *runs into
many pages and includes the following entries:*
List of effects and properties (faínctes) which must be made for the
Mystery of the Acts of the Apostles.

BOOK ONE [*the printed text was divided thus*]
The Godhead (divinité), having decided at the prayer of Mary and
the apostles to confirm by the Holy Spirit the converts to the faith,
there should be a great earthquake. Fergalus [*a devil*] should come
out from the body of the demoniac child.

The angels shall go to set free from prison St. Peter and St. Paul,
and in the said prison should appear a great light and they must
come out without opening or breaking it.

BOOK TWO
The face of St. Stephen must appear radiant as the sun to terrify
(exterrir) the false witnesses who testify against him, at which
Manasses and the others expressed great wonder and continued until
he had returned to his former appearance.
There must be a court (parquet) where the king, queen, Denis,
Pelagia, and all the household are baptized. This being done, St.
Thomas must vanish under the stage (par soubz terre) and return to
where Abanes is.
Having done this [*freed St. Peter*], Gabriel must vanish and go
under the stage (par soubz terre) to give the news to the Virgin
Mary.

BOOK FIVE
This must be a bronze serpent on the ground which will move along
(cheminera) at the command of Simon Magus.

There must be a dog which will sing at the command of the aforesaid [*Simon Magus*]. There must be in the temple an idol which
will laugh at the command of the said Simon. [*There is a reference
to a similar idol in the* Jeu de St. Nicholas *but only in the dialogue.*]

The Jews try to get hold of the Virgin Mary's body to take it from
the apostles, and immediately their hands wither and they are
blinded by the fire the angels throw (gectent) at them. Belzeray [*a
Jewish prince*] puts his hands on the litter on which the Virgin Mary
is being carried, and his hands remain attached to the said litter and
much fire in the form of lightning (fouldre) is thrown at them, and
the Jews must fall to the ground, blinded. Belzeray's hands must be
detached and joined back onto his arms. Then he is given the palm
which he carries to the others, by which those who wanted to believe were enlightened (illuminez), then he brought back the said

palm.

The Godhead (divinité) determines to send to the tomb of Our Lady
to raise her and bring her up to Paradise, body and soul.

St. Michael must present the soul to Jesus Christ. Having done
this, they come down from Paradise accompanied by all the angelic
hierarchy, and as soon as Jesus Christ reaches the monument there
must be a great light at which the apostles are amazed.

Gabriel must raise the stone on the tomb and the soul be put within
so that it is not seen again.

The soul is reunited with the body, and Mary rises up with her face
bright as the sun and bows herself down to Jesus Christ. Jesus,
Mary, and all the angels must go up, and as they rise (en montant)
they stop from time to time as the orders [of angels] speak. A
cloud must cover the apostles, then they must go under the stage
(par soubz terre) each one to his place (region).

BOOK SIX
Zazoes and Arphasac, magicians, must go and fetch two wonderful
dragons, spouting fire from their eyes, nose, mouth, and ears, and
[St. Matthew must go] to a prescribed place over a trapdoor (sur
une trappe), and there the said dragons must [lie down] at his feet.

From the said trapdoor (trappe) must come forth another dragon, the
most horrible that can be made, which also will lie down at St.
Matthew's feet as soon as he has spoken.

Seven devils must come from under the stage (de dessoubz terre) in
the form of dogs, and they must come from seven different places.

There must be wood to burn St. Barnabas who will be bound to a
cartwheel (une roe de chareste), and there must be a dummy corpse
full of bones and entrails.

There must be a small child, aged eight, the son of the satrap, who
will be put on a trapdoor (une trappe coulouere) through which
someone else will speak.

There must be a nude (ung nud) or a body (une carnacion) for the
flaying of St. Bartholomew.

St. Bartholomew shall be placed on a revolving table (une table tor-
nisse) with a nude (ung nud) underneath, and when he is covered with
a cloth the table must be turned secretly.

BOOK SEVEN
There must be iron bars for St. Thomas. St. Thomas must walk on
the said red-hot (ardentes) bars, and immediately water must rise up
to make them steam and extinguish them.

There must be a fake (faincte) knife for the bishop of India with
which he shall strike St. Thomas in the stomach and kill him.

There must be a coffin to put St. Matthew in, and it must be put
on a trapdoor (trappe coulouere) so that he can go away under the
stage (par soubz terre).

There must be a device (faincte) which gives blood (qui rende sang)
for the child's wound.

There must be a great serpent which shall move through the playing
area (le parc) whistling and blowing fire, coming towards St. Andrew.

There must be a body moving in the sea near where St. Andrew is
preaching.

Several other dead bodies should appear in the water (venir sur
l'eaue) moved by the waves, which can then disappear under the
stage (retirer soubz terre) when it is time.

There must be a pillar near Paradise to which Cidrat, Titon, and
Aristarcus will be fastened to be burnt, and the said pillar shall be
sited over a trapdoor (sur une trappe) and three dummy bodies fastened to the pillar in their place, surrounded by faggots.

St. Paul shall be beheaded, and the head will bounce three times,
and from each bounce will spring up a fountain from which will flow
milk, blood, and water.

*The importance of painters in the construction of effects is
clearly seen in the following two contracts:*
ATHIS-SUR-ORGE, 1542:
Christofle Loyson, painter, living at St. Marcel vez Paris, promises
Maitre Jehan Vinot, clerk, of the Church of Athis-sur-Orge and
Nicholas Temponnet, merchant and innkeeper, living in the said
Athis, by these presents (a ce present) to furnish and hire three
devil's costumes, a mask for Death and Envy [*separate characters*],
four crowns, four scepters for the kings, a wig, beard, and mitre for
God the Father, two heads of angels supplied with wings (deux chefs
d'anges garniz d'ailles), a device (faincte) for the Judgment of Solomon; to equip (accoustrer) and paint the cart to transport Joseph
and, following his trade of painter (de son mestier de peintre), all
the other devices (fainctes) necessary for   the Selling of Joseph, the

Judgment of Solomon, and the Rich Sinner [*morality play*] which the
said Vinot and Temponnet are putting on (font jouer) this current
year in the village of Athis for a period of eight days and a day for
the parade (monstre). And also to provide the cannons and flaming
fireworks (fusees flambeaux) necessary for the said devil-scene
(diablerie), all according to his said trade of painter (mestier
de paintre), and to provide the materials necessary to make everything as the painters are accustomed to do in such a case, all properly according to the direction (dit) of those knowledgeable in
these things (a ceux cognoissant), and also to provide on the day
of the parade (monstre) two Swiss drums, and on each of the other
eight days of the performance one Swiss drum for the said painter
to play or have played at his expense. This contract is made for
the sum of £7 T for all that is said which the said Vinot and
Temponnet promise him and guarantee to supply and pay each
for all of it without division or discussion or to the bearer etc. (?ou
au porteur) . . . one gold ecu (escu d'or soleil) next Sunday and the
rest by degrees as he makes the aforesaid devices (fainctes) and
things, which he contracts to do well and truly as directed (ainsy
que dict est) so that there is no need to stop the performance for
lack of the said things. And they promise to feed during the said
nine days the said painter and his servant, who will play the said
drum, well and truly at his proper cost and expense without reduc-
tion of the price of the said day . . . [*legal formula of ending*].

MODANE, *1580:*
In the name of God. Amen. Be it known to all that on 24 January
1580 master Thomas Mellurin senior (l'ancien) of Oulx in Dauphiné
and master Thomas Mellurin, inhabitant of Modane, being present in
person (personnellement establys), painters and experts in handling
fire with gunpowder (jouer du feu avec pouldre), who having been
required by the officers (syndics), dwellers, and inhabitants of
Modane to use their skill in the service of the public performance
which those of Modane intend to present, with the help of God, of
the Mystery of the great Judgment of God at the feast of Whitsun
next, have of their own good will promised and agreed the two of
them together without division but guaranteeing each other, and each
of them alone principally and for the whole to the worthy persons . . . [*legal formulae of the contracting parties*].
That is to say to serve them in the art of painting and skill with
fire necessary to the said representation. [*More legalities.*] These
master painters . . . have promised and promise to toil and continue
hereafter in the service of the said mystery and to prepare advan-
tageously and in good order all that it will be necessary to do in the
said service for the honor of the said parish and the performers
(istoriens) doing first the first things needed and continuing until all
shall be done and finally accomplished and to use them in the said
performance, for which they shall do the painting and things here
designated and written down.

Firstly they undertake to paint Hell and the sea on cloth or heavy
fabric (?triolles) of such size as they are instructed.
To paint the sky with stars, the sun, and the moon with such skill
(industrie) that the said sun shall appear black to those watching and
the moon red when they are acting at the appropriate times (aux
heures que requis sers) . . . and to make the stars with such skill
that they can fall to the ground when necessary (lorsque requis
sera).

Item. They shall make and paint an image looking like Antichrist
which by skill they shall make move and alter its lips as a sign it is
speaking.
Item. They shall by a device (par engin) make an earthquake when
necessary with everything possible to make it convincing (pour lui
ressembler).

They shall make and supply fireworks for the costume of the play
(?des istoires) for each of the devils every time they emerge from
Hell and for Lucifer each time he speaks, each day.

Then they shall project fireworks in the air and along the cord (par
la corde) whenever necessary for the said mystery and shall make a
great blaze of fire and noise every time the devils take some dead
to Hell, every day.

They shall fire cannons and bombards when Gog and Magog greet
Antichrist and for the war which is enacted both on the first day
with the Kings as on the second against the emperor, with smoke in
front (par devant), in the most skillful way (le plus dextrement) possible. Also, they will make several limbs that look like the limbs of
people killed in the battle with the semblance of blood on those thus
killed and wounded.

They shall paint five or six souls, and they shall find some means by
skill and cunning (par engin et industrie) to put out the eyes of the
catholic with pointed skewers (brochettes poignantes), and to this end
they shall make the necessary eyes and false faces or some alter-
native as skillfully as they can.

Then they shall make a dagger with which someone can be struck in
the breast and die from the blow. And they will make blood issue
forth in the accustomed way (à la maniere accoutumée).
. . .
Then shall be made two dummy bodies to rip up or saw through the
middle, from which shall come out entrails and blood and which will
look as much as possible like the two Jesuits. And the officials
(syndics) will supply the flesh of the said bodies and the pig skins
and shall take back the said flesh afterwards.

Then they shall make water boil in the cauldron in which the
seneschal is put and do it with fireworks (fusées) without heating
the water in the best possible way.

. . .

They will paint the body of Jesus on pigskins with his wounds and
the marks of his having been flogged.

They will also paint the pigskins of the bodies of Elijah and Enoch
and the patriarch to put on over the flesh (vestir sur la chair).

. . .

Then they shall cunningly and skillfully make the cloud to raise up
Elijah and Enoch to Paradise. And also the cloud to bring Jesus
down to the throne, which throne shall be as richly painted as possible: also the seats of the twelve apostles. And the community
will supply the necessary wood and iron or bronze wire. They will
paint Antichrist's pavilion in which he tries to go up to Heaven and
will make various sorts of blazing fires when he falls to earth.

And the said painters will make all that is needful for their skill to
serve the Mystery in general, not including the painting of the
equipment of individual people (le paincteur des accoutrements des
particuliers), save that if the matters involved in this present article
should amount to more than five florins for the whole (sur le tout)
they shall not be held to them. For carrying out all this task, the
said painters will furnish the powder, colors, gold sequins (orpail),
glue, parsley (perrosyne), clove/carnation (garafoille), whips, blades,
daggers, rods, and all the material necessary to make fire and everything they will use for painting without them being obliged to do
anything else concerning the woodwork (chappuisement) of the scaffolds (chaffauds) and the buildings (bastiments) to be made on them,
which the community shall make at its own expense.

And all the tasks above mentioned and listed in the above articles,
master Thomas Mellurin the elder and master Thomas Mellurin the
younger have together promised without division and each one guaranteeing (cautionnant) the other and each of them principally and for
the whole as above to make and well complete all preparations a
week before the next approaching feast of Whitsun, to show and
display their said task completed to the said officials (syndics) and
worthy commissioners and to hear if they are satisfied with it . . .
[legal phrases].

And similarly the said master painters have promised to serve well
and truly in all things needful in the handling of fire (en l'art du
feu) and other necessities during the days of the public performance
of the said Mystery without failing in anything of the matters contained in the above written articles . . . and the said master painters have promised to do this for the sum of two hundred florins in
the currency of Savoy . . . as follows, one third at the feast of the
Purification next [2 February], another third at the feast of Easter

next, and the last third immediately after the said mystery has been performed . . . on condition that the said officials and community shall be obliged to have constructed (chappuyser) and made all that the said master painters need to paint before making the scaffold (chaffaut) and shall also have the said scaffold made in good time so that the said painters shall not be delayed by their failure. And they shall give them skilled men (homme experts) to help them and to guard their prepared items during the days of performance at the expense of the said community.

And they shall supply them and provide them with the large cannon and falconets with necessary petards (bosse = *bottle filled with powder which broke on landing and exploded from an attached slow match*) to make the earthquakes, and will supply them with containers (membres) that fasten securely (serrant et asseurés) on the scaffold to keep the said prepared items in.

From elsewhere we have information on a variety of individual effects. Burning spirit was used to create the tongues of fire at Whitsuntide in the PARIS RESURRECTION:
Here shall descend a fiery brand (brandon de feu) from Paradise that shall be round like a circle and shall be all soaked in burning spirit (eaue vive), and in the middle of this blazing circle should be a pigeon of white metal (fer blanc) surrounded by fire which does not burn it. And all round the circle should be tongues of fire (langues ardentes) which should fall on Our Lady, on the women, on the apostles and disciples.

Fireworks and gunpowder are frequently used for special fire effects, as in the MAJORCA SS. CRISPIN AND CRISPINIAN:
The official is to go away with two or three men, and they are to bring a piece of lead and a cauldron. They are to put the two youths into a cauldron and a little fire is to be made with straw. They are to put a firework (coet) beneath the cauldron, and when the youths have stopped singing, they are to set fire to the firework.
. . .
Now two devils are to come out of the cauldron, and they are to lay a trail of gunpowder up to Ractioner, and he is to be burned. Both servants are also to be killed, and the devils are to return to the cauldron. . . .

The Drapers at COVENTRY *paid for worlds to be made and then burnt in their pageant of the Last Judgment, besides creating an earthquake.*

1563:
Item: paid for a torch to set the worlds on fire, 6d;
. . .
Item: paid to Robert Croo for making the three worlds, 3s 8d.
And, possibly in the 1550's:
Item: paid for seven skins for God's tunic (cott) and the barrel for
the earthquake, 3s;
Item: paid for the pillar for the worlds and the barrel, 3s 4d.

At MONS, *pieces of cloth were painted to look like* Ecaus-
sine stone (pierre d'Ecaussines: *a blue stone from the Hainault
region, still highly valued*); pillars (ayant des pillers point
dedans); clouds (ainsi que nuées). *One piece was painted black
and white. According to the* VIEL TESTAMENT, *such a cloth
would be used to portray the separation of day from night; God
separates light from darkness:*
Then there should be displayed a painted cloth, that is to say, half
of it all white and the other all black.

The color red was used to simulate red-hot metal in the
MAJORCA ST. CHRISTOPHER *play:*
Now they are to take St. Christopher away from the tree and make
him sit on a piece of red iron shaped like a grid-iron, and they shall
put a helmet, which is to be red, on his head.

*Paint is also used for the bloody sweat in the Agony in the
Garden at* REVELLO *and* LUCERNE:
REVELLO:
And when he [*Christ*] is praying, the angel Uriel shall come and
show him the Passion painted on a cloth. Then he shall stretch out
on the stage (zafaldo) on his face, and underneath there shall be
someone who shall paint his face and hands with crimson paint as if
he were sweating. And when he has been like this for a time he
shall rise. And one of the angels shall come and without speaking
wipe away the sweat.

LUCERNE:
At these words they awake and start up as if they want to pray,
then the Savior goes for a third time to the mount and falls down.
Then the painter inside the mount is to splash him with the blood,
and when he has splashed him he is to arise with difficulty and say
the following with a trembling voice. . . .

In the ADMONT *Passion Play red paint is used for blood at
several points in the action.*

At the Flagellation:
A servant brings whips and rods dipped in red paint. When they
strike Christ's body it becomes bloody.

When the soldiers crown Christ with a crown of thorns:
They press the crown onto his head together with a small sponge
dipped in red paint, so that the blood runs down over his face.

At the Deposition:
The servants go along and break the thieves' legs with a club
(<u>kholben</u>) wound round with sponges dipped in red paint. . . .

*But no explanation is included to show how the Longinus episode
worked:*
Longinus rests his spear against Christ, opens up his right side, and
out flows blood and water.

At MONS *red paint was used for the face of Raphael at the
Resurrection:*
Note to warn the painter at this point to go to Paradise to paint
Raphael's face red.
Then they [*the archangels*] go to the sepulcher, and after Jesus has
risen they place themselves one at the head [<u>piet</u>, *which is obviously
an error here*] and the other at the feet (<u>pieds</u>), and Raphael should
have his face all red with paint put on it by a painter.

Red-faced angels are also mentioned in the PARIS RESUR-
RECTION:
Here Seraph, the keeper of the Earthly Paradise, having red clothing
and face, holding a white, naked sword in his hand, shall speak.
. . .
while God the Father speaks to Gabriel, dressed in white with a
crimson face, as follows. . . .

At CHESTER *both the Smiths and the Cordwainers paid for
gilding the face of the actor who played God. In the Cordwainers'
accounts it is combined with painting the faces of other characters.
Cordwainers etc., 1550.*
Item, paid for gilding God's face and for painting the jailers' faces,
12d. [*Christ's Ministry*]

Smiths etc., 1561:
For gilding little God's face, 12d. [*Purification and Doctors in the
Temple*]

Simple concealment was used for some special effects, as in the receiving of the stigmata from the MAJORCA ST. FRANCIS *play:*
Now he is to be raised and, after he has been raised a little, they shall cover him with the curtain, and he shall stand up and walk towards the Christ (el Christo) which is also to be behind the curtain; and when the curtain is opened, St. Francis shall be revealed with the stigmata on his hands, feet, and side. And after he has stood like that for a little while, they shall close the curtain again, and St. Francis shall return to his little platform (cadefalet) from which he was raised, and he shall say: [*Thanks Christ for his mercy*].
Descending slowly from there to the main scaffold (el cadefal major). . . .

Dummy bodies were commonly required for executions and martyrdoms. The MAJORCA JUDITH:
She is to enter the chamber. And Holofernes is to be sleeping in his bed; and there is to be made a head like his, so that it can be held and cut from a dummy body (una stàtua).
And kneeling, she says: [*prays to God*].

Now she shall get up, take his knife, which is to be on the bolster, and taking the head by its hair, she says: [*prays to God*].
After these words, she is to cut off Holofernes' head and take it to the servant.

The MAJORCA SS. CRISPIN AND CRISPINIAN:
They are to be beheaded. Where they are standing, there are to be two dead bodies which are to be dummies filled with straw, and the heads are to be made with masks with calm expressions (màscaras molt gentils).

BOURGES EFFECTS, *1536:*
There must be two severed heads (decolacions), one [*each*] for St. James and Josias.
There must be a well (puys) to throw the dead bodies into.

The FRENCH ST. LAWRENCE *play of 1499 has a detailed account of such a martyrdom:*
Then they attach two horses to the hands in addition to the two which are at Ypolite's feet. And after he has been dragged on a hurdle across the playing area (champ) by the first two horses, he speaks what follows. And then when he has spoken, the torturers put a dummy, similar to him, in his place, to which they attach the four horses, one to each limb.
[*Speech by Ypolite*]

Then the torturers exchange and put a dummy in the place of Ypolite under the protection (?custodes) of the scaffold (eschaffault), and
then they harness the other two horses as well as the first two and
do not move. . . .
[Dialogue in Paradise. The torturers each mount a horse.]
Then each one individually spurs his horse and each drags away his
limb of the dummy.
[Dialogue.] Then they untie the pieces and leave them in the playing area (place), and when they have done it they go away, and the
angels come to look for the soul among the pieces.

The ROUERGUE Judgment play uses dummies for the tortures
of the damned:
Then shall be prepared the throne (cadieyra) of Pride, and the devils
come out of Hell leading Pride all dressed in fine clothes and a
collar round the neck. And they set her on the throne and secretly
they must put there a dummy figure made to look like her. And let
him who plays Pride position himself behind the throne, and the
devils shall torture the said person in silence, and when they have
done so Pride shall speak thus . . . [dialogue between Pride and the
devils]. Then Pride shall be put in the pit (potz), and when that is
done they shall bring out Avarice. . . .
[All Seven Deadly Sins are tormented in turn, with minor variations
of arrangements. When all are in the pit, it is sealed, then the
devils assemble. . . .] Then, in the presence of Lucifer and the
others, the devils begin to turn the wheels [of the torments] and
bring iron pitchforks and gaffs to torment the souls inside when
anyone pokes his head out of the pit because of the pressure (es-
penge), and those within throw fire and smoke out of the hole when
it is time to speak.

Dummy bodies occur in other contexts as at MONS:
Then she [Herod's son's nurse] takes the baby-carriage (cariot) and
puts the artificial (futif) child in it.

The property list for the play of St. George performed in
1429, probably in TURIN, contains many details concerning dummy
bodies. It is in French:
Here follow the things necessary to perform the play of St. George,
for the two days. First, for the banner of the Emperor Diocletian
and the eagle above, in addition (par dessus), 1 florin.
Item: for red standards: 6 ells of red cloth, 2 florins 1 gros.
Item: for an idol made complete (?toute entyere comisse), three
feet long: 5 yards of coarse cloth, 7 gross.
Item: for St. Marcellin, St. Cladien, St. Cirin, St. Anthony, and for
the four martyrs whom Dacien first has beheaded, and for the wiz-
ard (?magence) Athainaise and St. George: 11 ells of cloth, for each

head one ell, for the said heads, 22 gross.

Item: for a pot of aquavita.

Item: for the wood of the stakes (rues) which will be broken, not including the tin foil put over them so that they look like swords, 2 florins.

Item: for the said tin foil, 6 gross.

Item: another idol in which is hidden a person who speaks: 3 ells of cloth, 5 gross.

Item: four lbs. of gold leaf to gild one of the idols, 16 gross.

Item: four lbs. of silver (?blanches) foil for the other idol, 1 florin.

Item: two lbs. of white paint (blanc de puillie) to do the flesh color (l'encarnacion) of those who are or appear to be naked and also for the faces of the [false] heads, 5 gross.

Item: to dye yellow the aforesaid banner: 2 lbs. of ochre (?archiole/argila) and 1 lb. of rock alum (?alon), 6 gross.

Item: 1 lb. of vermilion to cover (?escouffar) all the things necessary for the play, 10 gross.

Item: 6 lbs. strong glue, 9 Genoese (?gen) gross.

Item: at most one lb. of black earth, 1 gross.

Item: of rag (destraxe) paper to cover (?escouffer) the heads of the idols, the haloes, the crowns, the pinnacles of a castle (?d'un chastel), one ream, 6 gross.

Item: for the said crowns of God, the Pope, the emperors, and the twelve souls (armes) and for the king and the queen a hundred and a half of gold leaf (?or party), 1 flor.

Item: for the wigs of the heads of the angels and the souls, eighteen cloth bases (goiffes de toilles), and for eleven severed heads; for the wigs and beards, only for the cloth on which all this shall be set and for the said bases, four ells of cloth, 8 gross.

Item: for 6 pairs of wings for 6 angels both for the wood (fust) and everything else, 14 florins.

Item: for the herald of the emperors, for his emblazoned tabard, 2 ells of white cloth and 2 of red to make a tabard to match the banner and the standard, 2 gross and a half the ell and 4 gross an ell the red, in all 13 gross.

Item: for flax to make the hair of the angels and of the souls: 6 lbs., 6 gross.

Item: for 4 clean and large sheepskins to make the body of St. George, full length, to seem naked, and for the making (por la faczon) of the said body, 1 flor.

Item: 2 cartloads of wood to heat (?essuer) the things necessary and to melt the glue. Total, without the wood and the making (faczon), 30 florins 4d gross.

Given at Thonon on 8 April, the year of our Lord 1429.

The MERCADE VENGEANCE *has dummies for a battle scene, and also requires the actors to make the killing look convincing:*

Trumpets sound within and without [the city] and [the besiegers]

attack a second time for as long as they think fit, in order, as in
the first attack.

And they raise the siege ladders, and it shall last as long as seems
appropriate; and they throw [down] dummy bodies dressed like some
of those inside the town.   In addition, at the foot of the walls, the
besieged must pull inside the walls one or two of the attackers and
make a show of killing them: and then they must throw down dummy
bodies dressed like those who were dragged to their death.
. . .
Then Pilate stabs himself with a knife: and he must have something
on him which will spurt blood.   And he must so position himself for
the blow that it looks to the audience as if he had killed himself.

*Dolls or small images were apparently used for souls, as at
the raising of Lazarus at* SEMUR:
Here the soul descends and comes on a wire (filium) onto the body
in the tomb.

In MICHEL'S PASSION *Judas' soul appears from his belly, but
has to speak before it is led off to Hell:*
Here Judas bursts at the belly and the guts fall out and the soul
comes out.

In the MONS *Harrowing of Hell the Anima Christi is elaborately portrayed:*
Note that at this point there must be in the Limbo of the Patriarchs great brightness and melody, and the gates of Hell must fall
down and the Godhead, which is like a soul in a tent of fine gauze
(une ame en ung pavillion de vollette), must appear there with two
angels censing before it.

*Souls were sometimes represented by animals or birds: see
following section, B.5.*

*Holes in the ground are specified for the creation of Adam
and Eve in a number of plays.   At* LUCERNE *this hole was later to
serve as the Savior's grave:*
Adam is lying hidden under the stand on the fountain.   Eve is lying
hidden at the top of the square in Paradise in a ditch.

The serpent stays hidden in the Mount of Olives until its time [see
plan].   God the Father comes onto the scaffold on the fountain
under which Adam is hidden. This is in the hole which later is the
Savior's grave.   It should be covered with twigs or evergreen

branches and the lump of clay be beside it.

   At SEMUR *the ditch used for Eve seems to have been used*
later for Peter's lament:
Then [Adam] shall sleep, and next to him there must be a ditch in
which Eve is hidden.
. . .
Immediately the cock crows and Peter laments, saying: [speech]. He
goes into a ditch. [Speech continues.]

   In the ST. GENEVIEVE NATIVITY, *Adam and Eve were hidden*
by a cloth:
Here God shall take clay and pretend to fashion Adam, and let Adam
and Eve be covered by a covering (<u>couvertour</u>).

   Appearances and disappearances were sometimes emphasized
with special lighting, as at MONS:
And the two angels remove the stone, and Jesus rises and puts his
right leg out of the tomb first, and there should issue with him a
great brightness and smoke of incense and light.

   At REVELLO *in 1483 elaborate lighting was used for the*
Transfiguration:
When this has been said, Jesus shall go up on Mount Tabor, where
shall be God the Father, the archangel Michael, Moses, Elijah.   And
a short distance away from the mountain shall be Lucifer, showing
that he cannot look up at the mountain, but he shall be very eager
to hear what is done and said.   And when Jesus is on the mountain
let there be a polished bowl (<u>bacillo</u>) which makes the brightness of
the sun striking the bowl reflect on Jesus and towards his disciples.
Then Jesus shall let fall his crimson garment and appear in white
garments.   And if the sun is not shining, let there be torches and
some other lights.

   An especially elaborate set-piece of the Godhead accompanied
the pageant of Bethlehem at LINCOLN:
Item, a large head, gilded, set with seven beams and seven glasses
for the same, and one long beam for the mouth of the said head.
Item, three large stars for the same [pageant] with three glasses
and a cord for the same stars.

   The PARIS RESURRECTION *used a sunken hurdle for Peter's*
walking on the water:
Here St. Peter goes across the sea to Jesus, without wetting his

ankle, on a large hurdle (haies) cunningly set and dug in (mise . . .
et chevillee) in the water, and the apostles put their fish in another
net, still approaching the shore of the sea. Then they all kneel
before Our Lord without speaking and Jesus says. . . .

   The MAJORCA SS. CRISPIN AND CRISPINIAN *uses a fountain
from which St. Crispin pretends to take water:*
Crispin shall go to the fountain and pretend (farà sparas de) to
take water, and he shall take another pitcher similar to the one he
was carrying, and there will be wine in it. . . .

   *Moses' miracle of water from the rock was carefully prepared
at* LUCERNE:
Now the water comes with full force. They all run to drink, press-
ing forward in a throng. Note: the rock is to be made artificially,
namely a container (beheb) which will take a good amount of water
under a cover, arranged and made so that it looks like a rock with
at three or four places glass or brazen bungs (zapffen) sticking out
which Moses strikes out when the water is to flow.

   At DIEPPE, *in France, the raising of the English siege on the
Eve of the Assumption (14 August), 1443, was commemorated each
year with a play using mechanical puppets:*
. . . a religious and dramatic ceremony was celebrated in this town
in the Church of St. Jacques every year on 15 August. . . . Priests
and laymen played their parts in it assisted by a large number of
mechanical figures moved by springs (mues par des ressorts) which
were made to perform veritable marvels so as to represent (figurer)
in a sort of apotheosis . . . the Assumption of the Virgin Mary.

   *Somewhere between machinery and special effects come the
methods used for hanging people, in particular Judas:*
COVENTRY, *Smiths'* 1578:
. . . paid to Thomas Massy for a truss for Judas, 2s 8d; paid for a
new hook for hanging Judas, 6d.

CORNISH ORDINALIA:
A tree is prepared and a halter (capistrum) for hanging Judas. [*The
direction occurs 12 lines before the action is called for.*]

   *The hazards involved in taking part in such actions as the
Crucifixion and the hanging of Judas are shown at* SEURRE *in 1497
(see Section D) and at* METZ *in 1437:*
And the role of God was taken by a priest called lord Nicolle from
Neufchâteau in Lorraine who was at that time the parish priest of

St. Victor's Church in Metz. And this priest was in great danger of
his life and nearly died during the Crucifixion, for he fainted and
would have died had he not been rescued. And it was necessary for
another priest to take his place and finish playing the part of God,
which priest was one of the executioners and guards in the said
play. Nevertheless they gave his role to another and he played out
the Crucifixion for that day. And the following day, the said priest
from St. Victor was restored to health and played out the Resurrection and performed his part very nobly. And this play lasted four
days. And in this play was yet another priest called lord Jehan de
Missey who was chaplain of Mairange, who took the part of Judas;
and because he was left hanging too long, he also was unconscious
and seemed dead, for he had fainted; therefore he was swiftly taken
down and carried to a place nearby where he was rubbed with vinegar and things to restore him.

>   These considerations led the Lucerne director Cysat to note
> the need to rehearse such scenes in good time: see above p. 59.

5. ANIMALS: LIVING AND ARTIFICIAL

Live animals, especially donkeys, were used quite frequently in plays. The lists from LUCERNE *illustrate this especially well. The list for 1583 is relatively concise:*
Animals (vych) for the play.
A donkey. In the morning with Abraham. When Joseph and Mary go to Bethlehem for Christmas, he is to take the calf with it at once. When the child Jesus is taken away to Egypt and then back again. All this on the first day. Second day. Two donkeys are needed, an old one and a young one for the entry into Jerusalem.
The ten brothers should have: 1 calf, 3 sheep, 2 goats, 4 kids on the first day. On the second day the Traders in the Temple should have: Azor, a basket with doves; Sem, a calf; Cham, 2 kids; Japhet, 2 lambs. Likewise on the first day: the Virgin Mary, 2 doves in the Temple to sacrifice at Candlemas.

A list for 1597 shows greater detail:
Firstly, a donkey for Abraham's scene.
Likewise, in the Joseph scene the Egyptian merchants use the same donkey.
Likewise, for Christmas a calf besides the same donkey.
Likewise, after Christmas the same donkey serves also when Mary with the child goes to Egypt and then returns thence to Judea.
Likewise, for the Savior at Jerusalem on Palm Sunday, besides the preceding, another young donkey.

And elsewhere:
The donkeys for Palm Sunday are to be tied up downstage near the main stand (brügi) facing Pilate's stall when it is time.
These animals are to be provided by: Abraham, the Egyptian merchants, Joseph the husband of Mary, Azor, and Rehos.
Then in the scene with Israel and his 12 sons, again a calf, furthermore 2 sheep, 2 goats, 3 kids, 2 lambs.
These are to be provided by the 10 brothers who have them.
The 2 traders are also to have: 2 lambs, 1 calf, 2 kids, a basket of pigeons.

And elsewhere:
Arrange a stall for the animals which are required for the play at the top of the square near the Haus zur Sonne. In it there should be a calf, 2 donkeys, 2 sheep, 2 goats, 3 kids, 2 lambs.

The MONS *Creation scene requires extensive use of animals, some of which had to be fed:*
The waters produce fish and other reptiles; birds, some on the sea, others on land. The earth shall produce beasts: sheep, cows, horses, mares, and several other creatures (reptiles).

117

To Jehan Foucquart, called Docque Docque, for food for certain
birds of all kinds put in his charge, to be used for the Creation of
the World: 6s.
To Ghendart, official (sergent) at Nimy, for live rabbits this day on
the stage (hourt) at the Creation of the animals and birds: 5s.
To Brouillon and his companion, for several sorts of birds supplied by
him on this day, both for the Creation and for Noah's Ark, etc.:
12s.
For 1 goose, 2 ducks, and three live doves on this day for the stage
for the same: 12s.
For live fish on this day on the stage, at the said Creation: 16s.
For 2 live lambs on this day on the stage, both for the said Creation and for the Sacrifices of Abel and of Abraham: 32s.

   The killing of live animals on stage is shown at LUCERNE *in
the stage directions for the Jacob and Esau scene:*
Meanwhile Esau sets off hunting, that is, in the Garden of Eden, and
when he sees the rabbit (küngelin) he speaks to himself and shoots
it with a bow or crossbow, not with a gun (büchsen); and it can be
arranged so, for someone to be lying in the bushes who has a rabbit,
and as soon as Esau shoots the live rabbit which he is hunting in the
garden this person is to thrust an arrow through the rabbit he has
with him and throw it out quickly, as though it were the one Esau
shot.

*On the other hand, the ram which replaces Isaac as a sacrifice was
certainly artificial:*
Abraham sheathes his sword, looks around, and espies the ram, made
of wood, hanging from its horns on the bush.

   *In some scenes living and artificial animals were both used, as
in the following series of stage directions from the* MONS *Flood
scene:*
When he [Noah] has said, "The crow, to know what may be," then
he opens the window and, at the end of this phrase, lets go the crow
who flies away and does not return.
Then he sends out the dove, tied by a foot.
He pulls it in. Music (sillete).
Then shall Noah send out the live dove, which flies away; and an
artificial one (futif) shall return bearing the twig of olive and shall
come to rest on the ark.
When he has said, "Return, gracious dove," then the dove should
come from Paradise to Noah, and Noah should take this dove and
put it in his ark.
Then he sends out the living white dove which does not return.

   Specific instructions are given in the CHESTER *play for the*

return of the dove.
Then he [*Noah*] shall let the dove go; and there shall be in the boat
another dove carrying olive in its beak, which someone shall let
down from the mast by a cord into the hands of Noah.

From BARCELONA *in 1453 comes the record of a mechanical*
dove:
In addition it is agreed and understood that the said Johan Çalom is
to make or have made a dove with its mechanism (una coloma ab
son exercici) which is to issue from the mouth of God the Father in
the float of the Annunciation and descend with its wings extended
(ab les ales steses) until it reaches Mary. And it is to emit certain
rays of light or fire which are to do no damage when it is before
Mary. And afterwards it shall return to God, "flapping" its wings
(fahent exercici de les dites ales).

A white dove represents the soul of Christ in the SEMUR
Crucifixion:
. . . bowing his head, he gives up the spirit and a white dove shall
fly off (recedat).

Cysat's preliminary notes for the LUCERNE *performance of*
1583 contain the same idea:
Item: that a live dove is to be hidden in the cross, to fly out at
the death of Christ. *However, a marginal note no* (nüt) *makes it*
clear that this idea was not repeated in 1597.

The LUCERNE *list of properties for 1583 contains another*
example of the use of a bird, in a slightly different context; we are
told that the young man out of whom Christ drives an evil spirit is
to have a live black bird in his bosom, which he is to let fly off
when the evil spirit leaves him.

In this play a black squirrel, not a bird, represents the soul of
Gesmas, the thief hanged on Christ's left:
The one on the left is to have red hair and beard, also a black
squirrel on his neck or chest, as though it were his soul.

There is evidence of the use of a live camel at MODANE,
since we are told it cost 20 florins to bring it across the Alps. The
BOURGES EFFECTS *list calls for a camel and a dromedary with no*
indication of whether they are live or artificial:
There must be a camel and a dromedary for the said Abanes [*envoy*
of King Gondoforus] which shall be loaded with silver and other

necessities (besognes).

Since there are no supporting details for acquiring or feeding
exotic creatures, the mounts for the Magi at LUCERNE *were most*
probably disguised horses; this would fit the usage of the word
zuogerüst [= *'got ready'*] *elsewhere by Cysat:*
This is the order of the Three Kings' mounted entry. Each has a
specially-constructed (zuogerüstes) animal:

> A camel - Balthasar
> An elephant - Caspar
> A dromedary - Melchior

and on each animal a boy sitting. . . .

The TOLEDO *donkey was certainly artificial, as may be seen*
from the series of references in the accounts:
Two loads of clay (dos cargas de barro) to make the mold for the
donkey, eight maravedís.
. . .
Two journeymen painters came to mold the donkey and paint those
things which were necessary, and their wages were four rreales.
. . .
For hoops (aros) for the giants and for the donkey, twenty mrs.
. . .
A strap (correón) for the donkey and for the tomb (sepulcro), half a
rreal.
. . .
Five rreales were spent on some old sheets to mold the donkey and
other things.
For cork to swell out the hindquarters of the donkey, twenty mrs.
. . .
Four discs (rroldanas) of ashwood for the feet of the donkey, twelve
mrs.
. . .
For four Jews' masks (caras) and two devils' masks, the donkey's
head . . . ten rreales.
. . .
The donkey's pack-saddle cost three and a half rreales.
The rope headstall, girth, breeching, and the halter and bell cost one
and a half rreales.

At CHESTER *Balaam appears to be riding an ordinary ass*
until it kneels down and, eventually, speaks:
Then Balaam shall mount the ass and shall ride with the knight; and
an angel of the Lord shall come in the way with drawn sword; and
the ass shall see him, but not Balaam, and shall prostrate himself on

the earth. . . .
Then Balaam shall beat his ass. And it is necessary for someone to
be transformed into the likeness of an ass, and when Balaam beats
him, the ass shall say. . . .

> *Elsewhere at* CHESTER, *however, there is considerable evi-*
> *dence for the use of live horses:*
> Here Abraham offers to Melchisadek a laden horse. Melchisadek,
> receiving the horse from Abraham very gladly, says. . . .
> . . .
> . . . and King Balaak shall come riding by the mountain.
> . . .
> Here they [*the Magi*] dismount from the horses and shall go to the
> mountain.
> . . .
> Then they go down to the animals and ride about.

> *At Jaén in 1461 an indoor performance in the* IRANZO
> *household used an elaborate fire-breathing dragon:*
> In front of the place where the Countess was seated, there then
> appeared the head of this huge dragon (serpiente). It was made of
> painted wood, and a device inside it (su artificio) propelled the boys
> out through its mouth one by one, and it breathed huge flames at
> the same time. And the pages, whose tunics, sleeves, and hoods
> were soaked in spirits (aguardiente), came out on fire, and it seemed
> that they were really being burned up in flames.

> *The* VALENCIA CORPUS CHRISTI PROCESSION *made exten-*
> *sive use of animal "suits" with men inside them:*
> *1400:*
> And the salary of two men who were dressed as lions, and the pur-
> chase of eight skins (pells) for their costumes (vestes), and the cost
> of having the costumes made up and looked after throughout the
> year etc.

> *1404:*
> And the salary of the man who walked in the eagle, and to hire the
> men who walked in the dragons (los drachs), and for the purchase of
> the roe deer skins (les pells de cabirols).

> *1407:*
> For repairing (refer) the eagle which represents St. John the Evan-
> gelist.
> For repairing the wild beasts (les figures de les besties feres) of the
> blessed St. George, who walked in the procession as a knight with
> all his armor (guarnit a totes peses).
> . . .

And for having two new lions' heads made (per fer de nou dues
testes de leons) for the lions from which the prophet Daniel was
delivered.

. . .

And also the salary given in consideration of his work to the man
who walked inside the belly of the said eagle, and to those who
walked on all fours (qui a quatre peus per terra anaven) dressed in
skins as Daniel's lions, and to the man who walked inside St.
George's dragon.

1408:
And for the salary of the men who went dressed as lions.

. . .

And for the salary of those who walked inside the eagle and in St.
George's dragon (la cucha de sent Jordi).
And for mending and repairing the eagle and the dragons (les
cuques) of St. George and St. Margaret.

*There are records of dragons in England from many places.
They are mainly connected with St. George celebrations.*
NEWCASTLE UPON TYNE, *1510:*
Item, paid to George Howghell for 12 yards of canvas for the drag-
on, 3s;
Item, paid to John Dodes for nails for the dragon, 3d;

. . .

Item, paid to Roger Sewior for going with the dragon, 3s 6d;
Item, paid to Roger Sewior for making the dragon, 8d;
Item, paid to John Swynnow for painting the dragon, 2s 8d;
Item, paid to Edward Baxster for three spars for the dragon, 3d;
Item, paid for two girths for the dragon, 8d;
Item, paid for sail-twine and wax (candyll) for the dragon, 6d.

[*An eighteenth-century civic dragon still survives in Norwich Castle
museum.*]

See also the animals listed in the BOURGES EFFECTS *in the
previous section, B. 4.*

6. DECOR AND PROPERTIES

Hangings and curtains were used in many plays. At ROME *in
1498 painted hangings were used for the decor:*
The hanging with the painted angels, which is put behind the cross.
The other black hanging which is put at the front of the stage
(palco).
A large white hanging, torn and sewn, with ropes.
Eleven breadths of light-blue cloth (tela) painted with stars, sewn in
several places, each about two and a half rods [22 yards] (canne) in
length.

The 1433 inventory shows that this was also true of the YORK
*Mercers' pageant of the Last Judgment, with the addition of decora-
tive angels:*
A large backcloth (coster) of red damask, painted, for the back of
the pageant; two other smaller cloths (costers) for the two sides of
the pageant; three other cloths of broadcloth of Louvain for the
sides of the pageant; a little cloth, four-square, to hang behind God
. . . seven large angels holding the Passion [symbols] of God, one of
them has a brass emblem (a fane of laton) and an iron cross on its
head, gilt; four smaller gilt angels holding the Passion [symbols].

At MONS, *Paradise was enclosed by a curtain:*
To Jehan du Fayt: item for one iron upright (verge) supporting two
cross pieces (bendes) and a ring (cercle) used for hanging a curtain
to enclose God the Father on his throne in Paradise: 23s.
To Simon Maugart: item for sewing thread 18d and for curtain rings
4s.

The curtain round Paradise at SEMUR *could be opened and shut:*
God the Father is in Paradise on a throne and angels on each side,
and he says . . . and they shall draw back some curtain which was
before him so that he is clearly seen by the people and he shall say
. . . and sitting down on the throne he shall speak to the angels and
say. . . .

In the FRENCH ST. LOUIS *play the curtains were closed to
allow the actors to change costumes unseen:*
They draw the curtains of the bed and round the scaffolds
(eschauffas) for dinner and here ends the first half-day. . . . Let
each one dine and if any actors play two characters they should
change their clothes in curtained scaffolds (en eschauffaus encour-
tinez) without being seen and be in their chairs (sieges) all arrayed
(tous en estat) when they begin the scaffolds (on commencera les
eschauffaut).

At LUCERNE *the Nativity takes place behind drawn curtains,*

*in the Hut (see plan, Day 1) which otherwise consists only of a
framework:*
Now they [*Joseph and Mary*] go together up onto the stand and into
the Hut. Mary sits down, they pull the curtain in front, get the
Child ready, then they put the Child into the crib.

      *Portrayal of the Crucifixion involved the use of various pro-
perties. The* ROME *Passion Play lists a variety of instruments of the
Passion:*
The haloes (diademe) of pure gold (oro fino) for Christ and the
Apostles, of which there are twelve in all, are kept by Antonio de
Palitto, and two more, which makes it fourteen altogether.
Two crosses of gilded wood for the Resurrection and two banners of
white silk with red crosses for the aforesaid Resurrection.
The veil with the painted Veronica.
A box with all iron nails (ferri) of the cross for the hands and feet
etc.
Two copper lanterns (lumiere) on two poles (aste).
Items, there must be two more.
The iron lance for Longinus, joined and with a hollow shaft (con
l'asta busciata).
A thick rope (zaganella grossa) in two long pieces.
Item: another piece of thick, shorter rope (zaganella).
Item: two rope halters.
A jar to hold water.
Five wooden crosses including the one which stands on Mount Cal-
vary infra annum.

      At MONS *a fake cross was carried to Calvary, where the
crosses were hidden already:*
Then [*the carpenter*] shall pretend to shape (carpenter) a piece of
wood which shall be ready prepared there, for the crosses are hidden
in the secret (au secret), but the cross which Jesus is to carry shall
be there and the said carpenter shall show it to Pilate. . . . [*Mock-
ing and preparations.*] Here shall be brought out the small hollow
cross which Jesus is to carry, so that it shall be ready to give
him. . . . Here Griffon shall lift the said cross from the ground and
say to Jesus . . . then they load it on him and walk on their way to
Mount Calvary.

      At LUCERNE *a fake cross as well as a ready-painted "vero-
nica" were used:*
The light[-*weight*] cross quickly, secretly away, the heavy one forward in its place.
Then he takes from her hand the cloth, on which a "veronica" is to
be painted, presses it to his face, and gives it back to her. Then
Veronica lifts up the outspread cloth towards the people.

   Many plays contain references to meals on stage, some of
which are prepared as well as consumed. The Jewish priests in
SEMUR *kill and cook their Paschal lamb:*
Here Godibert and Malferas kill the lamb, and let them have another
lamb roasted on a spit (assatum in quodem veru).

At REVELLO *the Last Supper begins with a salad:*
And let Simon bring in first lettuces (latuce) with vinegar as a salad
(a modo d'insalata).

The CATALAN ST. EUDALT *play has only token eating:*
Now St. Prancaci and St. Eudalt are to begin to eat a small meal
(algunes viandes de poca importantia) so as to give the appearance
(solament per serimonies) of eating. . . .

   At LUCERNE, *stage directions for the Last Supper were fre-*
quently rewritten and are very detailed, as in the 1545 version:
They eat the Easter lamb. . . . The Savior cuts up (zerleyts) the
Easter lamb. . . . They are to stand girt (gegürttet), have staves in
their hands, and eat the lamb and leave nothing but the bones. And
when they eat they are also to eat wild lettuce (wilden lattich) and
blessed unleavened bread. Then, once they have eaten, they lay aside
their staves and sit down at the table, only the Savior and the
twelve apostles. They all drink out of the chalice (kelch). It is not
to be the cup out of which they subsequently drink the Lord's blood,
but another drinking vessel (trinkgschirr).

   There are also details of Christ eating a meal with the
apostles after the Resurrection in the FRANKFURT *Director's roll:*
Then the disciples are to have ready a table and a tablecloth, bread,
wine, and dried fish or alternatively eggs and cakes (tortas). While
they are sitting the Lord is to bless [*the food*], distribute it, and
eat it with them. And when the meal has been quickly finished they
are to stand up. . . .

   The Last Supper at MONS *is similar to Lucerne in the choice*
of food:
Then he [*the man carrying the water*] goes to fetch a roast lamb
and two or three plates of lettuce, with bread and wine. [*Dialogue.*]
And there is nothing on the table except small white wafers
(fouaces) with the others [*i.e., the lettuces?*] and the lamb, and
Jesus takes a loaf and breaks it in the middle.

   The full range of meals on stage in a long play is indicated

by the account entries for food bought for each day of the MONS
play, as in the following selected examples:
Tuesday, 6 July--Second Day.
For a piece of mutton on this day on the stage for the meal of the
Three Kings' servants: 4s.
For bread on this day on the stage, both for the said meal and for
the children in Heaven: 5s.
For three measures of wine on this day on the stage: 15s.
For two barrels of beer on this day on the stage: 40s.

Wednesday--*only entries for* bread, wine, and beer. *These occur
every day and will not be mentioned each time.*

Thursday, 8 July--Fourth Day.
For a shoulder of mutton, a breast of veal, and a chicken pie on
this day on the stage for the Marriage at Cana: 16s.

Friday, 9 July--Fifth Day.
For 5 large breadcakes on this day on the stage, to put with the
two fish hereafter, for the Feeding of the Five Thousand, etc.: 5s.
For carp and pike on this day on the stage, including the two fish
for the said Feeding of the Five Thousand as well as for the dinner
and banquet of Herod at the Decollation of John the Baptist and the
meal with Simon the Leper: 32s.

Saturday, 10 July--Sixth Day.
For a roast lamb on this day on the stage, for God keeping the
Passover with his apostles, etc.: 16s.
For another lamb of paste, covered with roast fish, eaten on this
day at the said Passover instead of the other [*mentioned*] above,
because it was Saturday: 3s. [*Saturday was a fast day.*]
For lettuces on this day on the stage, eaten at the said Passover
with the said lamb: 3d.   For roast fish on this day on the stage,
both to cover the said lamb made of paste and for the the meal and
supper taken on this day at the house of Simon the Leper: 30s.
To Maistre Guillaume for eels on this day, used in one of the stage
effects (secrés): 2s.
For 2 bundles of grass bought on this day for the ass and its colt to
eat when on the stage: 12d.

*The meals might be staged elaborately with borrowed furnishings as
at* MONS:
To a carter (broueteur) for the transport of a sideboard (buffet)
taken from the house of monseigneur de Chimay, which was used as
a dresser to put the plate (vaissel) on the stage: 12d.
To Anthoine Meurant, concierge of the house of monseigneur
d'Aymeries, who had been engaged to hang on the said stage (hourt)
the tapestry borrowed from the said seigneur d'Aymeries and afterwards for refolding it (reployet): 12s.
To a carter for the transport of a tapestry borrowed from the

Church of St. Nicholas: 12d.

Many properties were listed as part of a costume, as in the records of the BARCELONA *Corpus Christi procession for 1424:*
The following properties (arreus) are sent each year to the Monastery of Our Lady of Mercy or to the brother appointed there:
Firstly, one bear with all its equipment, and it is made of black lambskin.
Item, one halo (diadema) for St. Euphemia.
Item, the wheel of St. Catherine, and one halo.
Item, the torture "horse" and halo of St. Eulalia.
Item, one platter with two breasts, and the halo of St. Agatha.
Item, one platter with the two eyes of St. Lucy, and a halo.
Item, one rock with an arm, and a halo for St. Tecla.
Item, one dish, an image, and a halo for St. Faustina.
Item, an image and a halo for St. Antonina.
Item, two haloes and one head for St. Quiteria and St. Apollonia.
Item, one halo for St. Barbara.
Item, one halo for St. Ursula.
Item, one platter with a lamb, and a halo for St. Agnes.
Item, one platter with flames, and a halo for St. Cecilia.
Item, one wooden sword, a heart, and a halo for St. Bridget.
Item, one green branch and a halo for St. Petronilla.
Item, one lance and a halo for St. Digna.
Item, the dragon, cross, and halo of St. Margaret, together with the trousers of the said dragon.
Item, the halo, beard, and wig of Joseph.
Item, pincers and an ear for St. Veneranda.
Item, one platter with two sponges.
Item, two dresses, one for St. Mary and one for St. Margaret. One of them is white with a pattern of crowns and the other is blue.
Item, one dalmatic of white cloth (bordat blanch) embroidered with gold, and the halo of the infant Jesus.
Item, one halo for St. Marina.
Item, another halo for St. Eulalia of Mérida.
Item, another halo for St. Engracia.
Item, another halo for Sister Maria Saccó.

The properties listed below are delivered each year to the Monastery of St. Anne, or to the brother appointed by the said monastery.
Firstly, the beard, wig, and halo of Joachim.
Item, the Jewish head-dress and clasps of St. Anne.
Item, the halo for St. Elizabeth.
Item, the box of gilded wood for St. Mary Magdalene.
Item, a crown, a green cross, and three green nails for St. Helen, and also her halo.
Item, the hairy garment and halo of St. Mary the Egyptian.
Item, the lion, and two wild men's costumes with beards and wigs.
Item, two haloes, one for St. Paula and one for St. Perpetua.

Item, one wooden halo, carved and gilded, and a dress of cloth from Constance (drap de Constança), embroidered with gold and lined with blue cloth for the man taking the part of St. Mary.
Item, one halo for St. Samforiana [female saint].
Item, four pairs of red wings.
Item, a large halo, a beard, wig, a staff with white pennant, and one cloak of cloth from Constance embroidered with gold for Jesus when he rises from the dead or leaves the tomb (sepulcre).
Item, one complete outfit of soft leather and one pair of gloves for the said Jesus.
Item, one shroud of burdet (drap de bordat).
Item, two pairs of silvered wings for the two angels at the tomb (monument).
Item, six haloes for six apostles--that is, one for St. P[eter?] together with a mask (testa), beard, and curled wig; another for St. John; another for St. James the Greater; another for St. James the Less; another for St. Simon; and another for St. Thaddeus, with beards and wigs.
Item, one scepter and one orb of gilded wood and one crown for the Emperor Constantine.
Item, one mask (testa) for St. Zosimus the monk, with a halo and one black habit.
Item, one dress of fine red cloth (bocaram) embroidered with gold and lined with green cloth from Constance for the Magdalene.
Item, a wooden monstrance with its base, gilded with fine gold.

The following properties are now delivered each year to the said Monastery of St. Anne instead of the monastery of the Friars of the Sack to which they used to be sent.
Firstly, seven croziers and three mitres.
Item, the "seraph" (saraphff) of St. Francis, an iron rod, two gloves of fine tanned leather, one habit of coarse woolen cloth (burell de bordat), one pensera [?an object made of metal], one pair of sandals, and one corded belt.
Item, three balls of gilded wood for St. Nicholas.
Item, the leather garment, with trousers [hose?], halo, beard, wig, and one pair of gloves for Jesus, who in the guise of a poor man appeared to St. Martin.
Item, six monks' habits of black hempen cloth, and six amices.
Item, eleven haloes and eight masks (testeres), together with the ones for St. Francis and St. Benedict.
Item, a rod of gilded iron, to be carried by the man taking the part of St. Benedict. And one pensera. And the raising and lowering machinery (la Ara Celi). And one white habit and one pair of gloves.
Item, the sol [?sun] of St. Benedict.
Item, two costumes with hempen trousers, and two masks (testes) for the two devils.
Item, one cloak of blue cloth on which there are divers gold leaves for St. Martin, and it is lined with vair (vays).

Item, three wigs of short golden hair, that is, one for St. Martin, another for St. Julian, another for St. Elzear, and a gilded feather.
Item, a triple crown for St. Gregory.
Item, two mitres of paper for St. Augustine and St. Ambrose.
Item, one hat of red leather for St. Jerome.
Item, the church of St. Augustine.
Item, the oven and its shovel for St. William.
Item: one pair of green wings and a sword for the angel of St. Julian.

The properties that occur in English guild records are mainly either consumable, in which case it is often difficult to tell whether they are props or food for guild feasts, or in need of repair. Occasionally other types of entry occur. NORWICH, *Grocers'* 1557:
For oranges, figs, almonds, dates, raisins, prunes, and apples to decorate the tree with, 10d. [*The Grocers' pageant was the Creation and Fall.*]
1563 inventory:
A rib colored red.

YORK, *Bakers'* 1553:
Item, for mending the lamb and painting the haloes (dyadems). [*The Last Supper.*]

COVENTRY, *Cappers'* 1567 *inventory:*
Item, God's cross and the Spirit's cross;
Item, Pilate's mace and his club;
Item a distaff and a spade.
. . .
Item, a basket and a box;
. . .
Item, 4 boxes (cofferes);
. . .
Item, 3 more Marys' boxes. [*The Resurrection and Harrowing of Hell.*]

Earlier producers at LUCERNE *tried to keep separate lists of properties and costumes, but Cysat conflated them into one detailed inventory: see below Section B.7.*

7. COSTUME

The most detailed extant lists of costumes are those from
LUCERNE; *the following is the greater part of the list for the First
Day of the 1583 performance, to which have been added some ad-
ditional items of information from 1583 and 1597:*
God the Father
Is to have the usual halo (Diadema).
Handsome, like an old man with gray beard and hair.
An orb in his hand (Rychs öpffel).
A lump of clay should be lying ready down on the stand (brügi)
where Adam is.
A white rib in his sleeve.
Further, the tablets for the Ten Commandments and the manna.
He should be dressed in an alb and over it a costly choir cope (Chor
Cappen).
He and the angels should set up and decorate Heaven; further,
Heaven should be fitted with a roof (Oberdeckel) and curtains which
can be pulled round in front.
He should also have two tunics (Röcklin) of raw sheepskin together
with the girdles, to put on Adam and Eve.
He should also organize the people who are to spread the manna
over the square from the top of two houses.

Adam, Eve
Adam is to have fairly long hair, neither black nor gray; a short
beard; the appearance of a man of thirty; Eve as a young woman
with beautiful long loose woman's hair. Both are to appear naked in
body stockings (lybkleidern) over their bare bodies. The two of them
are to prepare Paradise, including the tree with the apples in the
middle of Paradise. Likewise the pit in Paradise, in which Eve is to
lie hidden, covered with a lid (laden) or with branches.
They do not join in the entry procession, but early in the morning,
before the entry procession, they hide themselves in their positions,
Eve in the pit in Paradise and Adam beneath the stand beside the
fountain in the place where later the Savior will be buried.
When they are expelled from Paradise, Adam is to have a spade
made of wood with no iron in it and Eve a distaff.
They should also have two pieces of woven green branches to cover
themselves in Paradise.

Serpent
As a venomous four-footed serpent, with female face and voice. A
veil and a crown on its head.
It does not join in the entry procession but hides early in the morning in the Mount of Olives until it is its turn to speak [*Elsewhere:*
it gets up into the tree], and when it is cursed it crawls away on
all fours through Hell.

Angels
The angels are seven in number.
Namely, the four archangels; they should be dressed and attired in
the most costly manner in the clothing and decoration of angels,
white, with beautiful hair, crucifix, garlands of pearls on their
heads, beneath their feet painted stockings with soles, as if they
were barefoot, since they indeed do not have far to walk (die doch
nit wytt für gangent). [Elsewhere: tights (lybstrümpff) with soles,
painted.]
Gabriel is to have a scepter with the text or proverb Ave Maria
etc. wound around it and also the wooden ram to give to Abraham.
Uriel is to have the fiery or burning sword.
Michael is to have the chalice with the crucifix on the Mount of
Olives and is to sing this song: Constans esto etc.
Raphael, a scepter.
The four archangels are to carry scepters in their hands whenever
they have anything to do. Gabriel has the text of the greeting on
his scepter only when he greets Mary. [Elsewhere: the angels' scepters differentiated.]
The three other angels--namely first, second, and third--are also to
be dressed well and finely as angels. They should all know how to
sing (dess gesangs bericht sin). [Elsewhere: that the angels shall all
see about wings, and that these shall not be too big, pliable
(gschmydig) yet fine.]

Doctors (Leerer)
Gregory is to be dressed as a Pope.
Jerome as a cardinal.
Ambrose as an archbishop.
Augustine as a bishop.
Chrysostom--is omitted in the revision of 1597.
They are also to have their crucifixes and to bear staffs in their
hands, each according to his rank.
Also a book each and a boy to hold his staff when he has to speak.
They do not walk about the square when they are speaking, but they
have a low pulpit placed for them on the square at the top of the
square out in front of their place (stand). This they stand in when
they want to speak; they are to equip and decorate this pulpit.

Prophets--beside the Doctors
Jacob the Patriarch. Should be dressed in a somewhat different
manner from the prophets, as an old patriarch, yet honorable and
wealthy, in a quite old-fashioned way, the stranger the better.
The remaining prophets as prophets, almost identical in a strange
way, as far as the over-capes (ÿber cappen) and hats are concerned; underneath long priests' robes, at the waist (?in der Weiche)
gathered in with broad belts or other strips. Each is to have a book
and a staff in his hand, likewise boots, also long gray hair and a
beard.

[*In the left-hand margin of MS.:* are abolished in the revision of 1597.]

The Director (<u>Rector oder Regens</u>)
Is to be alone with a fine-looking boy, dressed in costly fashion to his own taste.

Herald (<u>Proclamator</u>)
Should be mounted on horseback, fully armed with a breastplate; over it on the first day in white, the second day in red a slashed silk surcoat (<u>sydin zerhouwen wapen Röcklin</u>), a white velvet cap with feathers (<u>sammatin paret mit fädern</u>), and otherwise expensively dressed in white on the first day, the second day in similar fashion but in red.
On both days he should also have four footsoldiers, two going in front of him and two behind, dressed in the same color, their velvet caps also with feathers.

Herald's Cornet
Should also on both days be clad like the Herald. He is also to have the two small banners made of taffeta (<u>daffet</u>) on which are painted the emblems of Christ's Passion, one white on the first day, the second red on the second day; these the Herald has made.

Herald's Squire
Is also to be dressed like the Herald and his Cornet on both days. He is also to have a shield or round shield (<u>rodellen oder schillt</u>) of a fair size, on which are painted as on the small banners the signs of Christ's Passion, the first day on a white, the second day on a red background, the outline, however, in the opposite color, white and red. [*And from elsewhere:* the squires are to have shields and in their right hands short, thick, painted staffs, thicker than scepters but different from the latter, silvered, with a gilt knob. The Herald's squire *has* the arms of Lucerne on his shield.]

Cain, Abel
Are to be dressed as shepherds and farmers in tunics (<u>lybröcken</u>) made from rough sheepskins, belted, with long hair, a fair amount of beard, not too old, the tunics (<u>lybröck</u>) over body stockings (<u>lyb-kleider</u>) only.
Cain is to have a hoe, prepared in such a way that in the front is a hole containing blood or blood coloring, but everything the color of wood, not of iron, and easily broken; he is also to have a sheaf of corn which has been lying in water for some time and is wet.
Abel is to have a mattock, but there is to be nothing about it too which is like iron; a hollow wooden lamb filled with wood shavings, which burns well.
The two of them together are to prepare the table or altar.
Abel is to have an iron skull-cap (<u>ysin beckelhüblin</u>) on his head

under his hair to protect him from the blow from the hoe.

Abraham
Is to be dressed as a rich old patriarch in an expensive and strange
style (manier), the stranger the more worth looking at, with boots
and a saber at his side. He is to prepare the altar for the sacrifice, also see about the donkey, likewise have a flint and steel
(füwrzüg) and a small bundle of dry wood. [And elsewhere: have
a flint and steel ready and also, as a precaution, a small amount of
red hot coals covered over in a pot.]
Also, a wooden ram for the sacrifice, to be provided by Gabriel.

Young Isaac and the Two Boys
Is to be with his father, also dressed in a costly manner in a strange
old fashion.
He is to have with him two boys, also strangely dressed, but not so
richly as he.
Isaac is to have a coat of blue with wide sleeves, open at the front,
with buttons the same as the material, large, lined (?yngethan),
reaching down to his knees, belted at the waist, with a yellow or
green silk strip, a fine hat, but not with a hood like the Jews, and
then boots to his calves but not pointed, yellow.
The two boys can also be dressed like this, but in a different color.

Isaac as an Old Man
Is to lie as a sick old man on a low bed with curtains, with a long
old garment and a lace cap with lappets (?widerlitzen).

Rebecca his Wife
Is to be dressed in an honorable, costly, and rich manner, but in the
Jewish and old-fashioned style, also with proud arrogant gestures. She
is to have kidskin gloves and also a kidskin with which to wrap up
Jacob's hands and neck. Also a drinking vessel with wine to give
Jacob.

Esau
Is to be attired expensively, but fitted out and dressed as a hunts-
man in an old-fashioned and strange manner, also with hair and
beard. He is to have hunting and shooting equipment (however, not
a gun, but bow and arrows). [Elsewhere: crossbow (flitschbogen).]
Two hounds, a boy (jegerknaben), two rabbits, one of which he lets
run loose in the garden and in the hunting episode, the other to
skewer (zestechen) in the thicket. He should also have a cooked
meal in a bowl to bring his father.

Jacob
Is to be younger than Esau, also strangely dressed. He should also
have two kids ready from which to prepare his father the food.
Likewise cooked food and an expensive garment like Esau's garment
to put on over his other clothing.

Israel as an Old Man
Is also to be dressed as an honorable and wealthy man, like an old
patriarch, in a strange fashion.
He is also to have the parti-colored (getheilten) silk coat to put on
Joseph.
[*Elsewhere:* there are to be two of Joseph's coats. The first silk-
en, parti-colored one side all purple or red, the other side divided
otherwise, white, yellow, or blue. The other coat of linen but like
the first in colors. Dan is to have this one and wet it in the kid's
blood. Under the coat Joseph is to wear a clean shirt with broad
sleeves and a flat collar in the old manner.]
[*And for 1597:* there are to be two of these coats, one of good
material with one side red or brown, the other yellow and blue. The
second, which is messed up (besudlet) in the blood, also in these colors but made of linen.]
Joseph and Benjamin, his two youngest sons, as two very young boys,
almost identical, except that Benjamin as the youngest is to be
dressed in a somewhat differentiated manner, also in a strange, alien
style.
Dan is to have a kid to butcher in order to wet Joseph's coat in the
blood.

The Twelve Brothers, or the Sons of Israel in general
Together they are to equip the Valley of Hebron or the place to
which they go for pasture for their sheep for the second time; firstly they are in the Valley of Hebron, secondly in Sichem. [*Elsewhere:* the Valley of Hebron, to which they go the first time for
pasture, is in the middle of the square; Sichem, to which they go
the second time, is near the top of the square, in front of Paradise.]
They are also to equip the well or cistern (sodbrunnen oder cistern)
into which they throw Joseph; this well is to be down at the foot of
the square towards the fountain, and they are to decorate it with
ivy or green branches. But it is not to have a superstructure (gal-
gen), bucket, or anything else over it. The ten eldest are to be
dressed as cow-herds (vychhirten), not alike and in a strange style,
with hats, staffs, leather pouches or food bags, no two alike, the
stranger the better, and each is to have one head of small beasts--
sheep, goat, kid, and the like. [*Elsewhere:* the beasts are to be one
calf, two sheep, two goats, three kids, two lambs; also each his
particular musical instrument, such as fiddle (gygen), tromba marina
(trumschytt), bagpipes (sackpfyffen), xylophone (höltzin gelechter),
flute (flöutten), pipes (pfyffen), and other such like, no two the
same.]

Joram
As a vagabond (landfarer) in a poor Jewish style (Jüdischer
schechter Manier).

Putiphar and Sother, the Ismaelite or Egyptian Merchants
Are to be dressed in long robes with curved sabers, also tall hats
with feathers, veils, as Arab (Heydnische) or Turkish merchants.
They are also to have a donkey.

Moses
Is to be dressed in a soldierly manner (harstlich), something different, between a patriarch and a prophet. Underneath a long coat,
belted, an overcoat, long hair and a beard, in his hair two curls like
two horns. A staff in his hand, two tablets on which the Ten Commandments are written. [*Elsewhere:* is to have two tablets of the
Commandments, one made of earthenware (von Herd gebrennt) which
he throws down and breaks (zerwirfft).]
He is also to provide and look after the brazen serpent together
with the cross on which to hang the serpent, likewise the Rock from
which water flows. [*Elsewhere, 1597:* likewise, let a piece of piping
(tünckel stücki) into the surface of the square into which can be
slotted the pole for the brazen serpent; likewise, the Holy Spirit at
Pentecost can be the same thing; likewise the Holy Spirit at the
Baptism of Christ.]

Jethro
In long, clean, honorable, and almost priestly clothing, but different
from Moses and Aaron, yet Jewish.

Aaron
Is to come dressed like an Old Testament priest with the alb, "Le-
vite's Coat" or cape round his shoulders (leviten Rock oder ÿberkleid
umbhenckt), with bells at the bottom (unden mitt Cimbalen), also the
breastplate (brusttafel), mitre (yffeln), and other things.
He is also to provide the pillar for the golden calf and the altar for
the sacrifice at the pillar and an axe beneath the altar with which
Moses knocks down the pillar, and two earthenware candlesticks for
on the altar, hollowed out at the top and containing brandy to light.
He and the goldsmith are also to get ready the golden calf and the
pit in which it lies hidden, also to have a guard there to stop anyone from falling in.

Goldsmith
Is to be dressed in Jewish fashion like the traders, but not too long
and when he is to pour the calf he is to have his equipment with
him: furnace, fire, and bellows as well as a boy to operate them.
He is to help Aaron prepare the calf.

The Jews with Moses and in the Synagogue
Are all to be dressed in good Jewish style, in long clothes, or else
priestly clothing inside and then outside over it capes with hoods
(guglen), also their Jewish hats with buttons and tassles, but some
flat with turned-up brims (überlitzen); they should have their clothing covered all over with Jewish letters, likewise also on the hats

and brims (ü̲b̲e̲r̲l̲i̲t̲z̲e̲n̲), sun, moon, stars, and other things painted
on, everything as diverse as possible. The old ones can have short
sabers, wooden and painted or otherwise, and in general they are to
be all different from one another, some young, some old.
They are also to have imitation serpents or worms with bent pins or
fasteners (g̲e̲k̲r̲ü̲m̲p̲t̲e̲n̲ ̲g̲u̲f̲f̲e̲n̲ ̲o̲d̲e̲r̲ ̲h̲e̲f̲f̲t̲l̲i̲n̲e̲n̲) in the heads, one or
two each, fewer or more according to individual taste, to be able to
attach them quickly in the attack by the plague of worms.
And the grumblers are to have strange woven baskets, all of different styles, no two the same, to collect the manna from heaven.
And when the procession of Israelites and the scene with Moses is
over, the grumblers, both young and old, depart; they have nothing
more to do, and only the people in the Temple (T̲e̲m̲p̲e̲l̲h̲e̲r̲r̲e̲n̲) and
the Synagogue remain.
In the procession of Israelites with Moses, all of them, both young
and old, are to have brass rings or clasps hanging from their ears,
and further they are to wear all the time on both days short boots
in the Jewish style, yellow or blue.

Caiaphas, Annas

Are dressed in a soldierly manner (h̲a̲r̲s̲t̲l̲i̲c̲h̲) as Jewish princes and
heads of the priesthood, but differentiated from the rest of those in
the Temple, most magnificently or most elaborately.
But whenever Caiaphas is in the Temple he is to have on the episcopal mitre and ornaments.

Raabod or Chief Rabbi (A̲r̲c̲h̲i̲s̲y̲n̲a̲g̲o̲g̲a̲)

He is the Chief Rabbi in the synagogue or amongst the Jews, he is
to be dressed in a rather more costly fashion than the remaining
Jews in the Temple to stand out amongst them.
He is to have a small sponge with blood and a stone razor for the
Circumcision.
He circumcises the child Jesus.

Laban

He too should be dressed somewhat differently from the rest, like an
old Jewish priest, but in less costly fashion than Zacharias.

Zacharias

Is to have the same clothing as Aaron until the Old Testament is
ended, for at the beginning in the procession of Israelites he is
dressed like any other Jew.
But when the New Testament starts he is a priest and the father of
John the Baptist, keeping the same clothing until he comes to John
the Baptist asking who he is; thereafter he puts on again his original
clothing which he retains to the end.
He is also to have the censer and other equipment for the sacrifice
and ceremonial in the Temple.

Urias
After Raabod he is the foremost of the Jews in the Temple and
should also be dressed in costly fashion.
He is to have a small tin with chalk powder, like a salt tin, for the
Circumcision.
He is also to have a fine large book fastened with clasps to carry
before Herod.

Chore, Mosse
These two are to be dressed the same, as two old Rabbis, with gray
hair and beards and yellow capes or hoods with ribbons down the
back to the waist, and both the same.
With Moses, on setting out, and in the Temple, they are to have a
book each.

Jews in the Temple (Tempelherren)
The remaining Jews in the Temple can dress themselves the same as
is said above about the Jews. The Hebrew letters they can attach
to their clothing on metal foil (uff stangiöl) or the like, somewhat
broader and more visible than the Pharisees or other Jews; they
should belt themselves with yellow bands, some with blue, the metal
foil letters painted on blue paper. [Elsewhere: these of the Jews in
the Temple are to have books: Raabod, Urias, Zacharias, Sedechias,
Laban, Lamech, Amalech, Zorobabel, Magog, Aomar, Chore, Mosse.
Elsewhere, 1597: When the Savior is put on the cross, the youngest
of the Jews in the Temple is to pull the curtain round the Temple
and, when he has died, is to pull it quickly apart.]

Pharisees and ordinary Jews (gmeinen Juden)
They too are to be dressed in long garments as was said above
about the Jews, but somewhat more differentiated and with narrower
letters around their clothes, also not as costly as the Jews in the
Temple, just black on yellow paper, but the more eminent to have
them broader than the other ordinary Jews. The latter should also
not have long garments but tunics (Röck) to or over the knees,
short sabers, boots, and hats in Jewish style.

Salmon
Is to have a fine water beaker and a fine towel over his shoulder in
the Temple for the Circumcision. When the procession of Israelites
is over he is to go to King Saul's stall, put on his armor, and when
this scene is over return to the Jews in the Temple in his original
clothing.

Goliath
As a giant, got up and armed in a strange and heathen manner, in
full armor with shield and stave.
He is also to have a dummy head (ein Contrafeteten kopff) made as
much like himself as possible.

[*Elsewhere:* a copied, painted head (?ein abgetruckten gemalten kopf).]

David
Is to be dressed as a shepherd, a green garland on his head, a shepherd's staff in his hand, a leather pouch (carnier) slung across (überzwerch) at his side containing bread and cheese, a sling and a hollow egg painted the color of stone, filled with blood, which he casts at Goliath's head. He is also to arrange for several stones to be placed in his way, the size of eggs.

King Saul
Is to be dressed as a Jewish King, in a costly fashion. He is also to have a suit of armor ready to give David.

Abner
Is King Saul's captain in the field, is to be in armor and equipped as a captain.
[*Added for 1597:* very powerful. He is also to have a shield-bearer.]

Eliab
Is also to be in armor as a soldier of stature.
[*Elsewhere:* should the Jews who are soldiers not also have some indication with letters on their armor? Likewise boots, round shields, short weapons (?wör)].

Mary, the Mother of Christ
Initially as a most virtuous virgin, humble in manner.
Her costume is a white underskirt or nun's skirt and over it a blue silk coat. A beautiful spread-out woman's hairstyle with a halo (schyn) above it, white hose and shoes, honorable.
She is to arrange the place of the Annunciation: a prie-dieu (Pulltpret) standing upright with a crosspiece and a small stall in front of it, so that she can kneel, with a book on it, a jug beside it containing flowers and white lilies on stalks (gilgen stengel).
For the Nativity she should have a clean little boy about six months old in a beautiful little shirt and a tiny halo with three gilt lilies on his head, also swaddling clothes.
She is also to prepare the crib, with hay in it, likewise a pair of turtle doves in a clean cage, to offer in the Temple.
From the Nativity onwards she is then to have a pure, sweet cloth over her hair, but which is not to cover her hair completely.

Various kinds of information about costumes have survived in documents from different countries:
Saragossa, 1414; a costume for Death at the CORONATION OF FERDINAND OF ARAGON:
A man dressed in tight-fitting yellow leather so that his body and

head looked like those of a skeleton, quite cadaverous, without sub-
stance, without eyes--he looked so ugly and terrifying--and with his
hands he gestured in every direction, beckoning now to some, now to
others to come.

ROME, *1498:*
A cloak of light-blue cloth for Our Lady adorned with tinsel and
little stars of batiste (?<u>battita</u>).
Item: another pinkish cloak (<u>de rosino</u>) with a ribbon of gold (<u>de ora</u>)
for the Magdalene.
Item: another cloak of black mourning cloth for Our Lady.
A widow's skirt (<u>bonna vedovile</u>) of black cloth.
A Turkish dress (<u>turca</u>) of silk of different colors, worn, lined with
yellow shot silk (<u>cagnante</u>).
Four little silk tunics in different colors for the Pharisees.
A rough tunic (<u>saltaimbarca</u>) of woolen mixture bordered with black,
white, and red.
A silk standard for Pilate, with the black scorpion on a yellow field.
Two banners for trumpets (<u>pendoni da tromette</u>) of red sendal (<u>zan-
nato</u>) with S.P.Q.R. on them, and silk fringes of various colors and
four buttons for each banner.
A skull-cap (<u>cacamauro</u>) of brocade for Caiaphas.
Two sheets (<u>traverse</u>) of red sendal (<u>zannato</u>).
Item: one of deep-blue sendal.
Item: two more of gold sendal.
Item: another of yellow sendal.
Item: another of yellow shot sendal (<u>zannato cangiante</u>).
Item: another large one of faded purple sendal.
Seven girdles of striped light-blue sendal.
Two pieces of girdle of deep-blue sendal (<u>zanzile</u>).
Four more girdles of faded old sendal.
Two cloths of buckram (<u>vocarame</u>) with red and light-blue roses for
Christ at the Resurrection.

PERUGIA, *1426:*
These are the objects lent to the confraternity of St. Dominic for
the play (<u>devotione overo representatione</u>) of the dead of Francesco
and Biagiuolo. Pietro Pavolo de Francesco and Bartolomeo de Pavolo
de Nato came to fetch them.

First
The cloak
scythe
hour-glass ———————— of the dead
the hands

And for the play of the Passion:
4 short surplices (<u>tonecelle</u>)
1 yellow cope
2 shirts without tails (<u>fondo</u>) with the amice (<u>amitto</u>)--re-

turned but torn (<u>schagnate</u>)
10 wigs, five in good condition and five middling--returned the
five good ones and three middling
7 beards
1 flesh-colored garment with stockings
Another pair of flesh-colored leather stockings
7 yellow angels' crowns

PALERMO, *1581:*
And forthwith Human Nature shall appear, dressed in garments on
which the four elements shall be painted, with a veil over her head
which shall cover her to the waist.

When the queens have finished [*their songs*], eight prophets and
eight sibyls shall enter (<u>verranno</u>) in the following order: namely,
from the right-hand side of the nave, which faces east, the Prophet
Isaiah shall appear and recite his verse, and after him the Persian
sibyl shall enter from that same side, and after she has spoken,
another prophet and another sibyl shall speak on the opposite side,
and so they shall continue every time, two on one side and two on
the other.

When Isaiah has finished, the Persian sibyl shall come (<u>uscira</u>) from
her cave, dressed in a golden dress with a white veil, singing the
following verse. . . .

Immediately the Phrygian sibyl shall come forth in a purple garment,
with naked arms, her hair flowing; and pointing her finger she shall
sing. . . .

Then the Hellespont sibyl shall come forth, old, wearing a peasant-
like garment, with a veil arranged according to the ancient custom,
and she shall sing. . . .

Afterwards the Samian sibyl shall come forth with an unsheathed
sword under her feet (<u>con una spada ignuda sotto i piedi</u>), with a
delicate veil over her head, and richly dressed.

Afterwards the Delphic sibyl shall enter (<u>venirà</u>), dressed in a
black garment, with her hair rolled up and plaited, with a horn in
her hand.

Then the Tiburtine sibyl shall come forth, not very old, dressed in a
pink-colored garment, with a goatskin over her shoulders, her hair
flowing, and a book in her hand.

Then the European sibyl shall come forth, young and beautiful, with
a resplendent face, a very thin veil over her head, dressed in a
garment sprinkled (?<u>toccata</u>) with gold.

The VALENCIA ST. CHRISTOPHER *play, which may go back
to the end of the fifteenth century, has survived only in a
seventeenth-century version:*
For the play (<u>misteri</u>) of St. Christopher: for St. Christopher, a blue
tunic to be worn underneath. Another one, with fish painted on it
(<u>pintada ab pexos</u>). A rochet, thick-soled shoes (<u>tapins</u>), palm, halo,
and red gloves. Two hermits' costumes, two albs, two scapulars, two
hoods, three masks (<u>caretes</u>) for the three pilgrims; three tunics,
three short capes, three staffs, two dozen shells for the said pilgrims; two trumpets for the said play; two dead men (<u>morts</u>) with
their hoods and masks.

*There are few full descriptions of costumes from the English
plays. Some of the most informative are in the* N. TOWN PASSION
plays:
Here Annas shall show himself on his stage appearing like a bishop
of the Old Law in a scarlet gown and over that a blue tabard furred
with white and a mitre on his head in the style of the Old Law; two
doctors standing by him in furred hoods, and one in front of them
with his staff of office; and each one of them with a furred cap on
his head with a large knob on the crown; and one standing in front
like a Saracen, who shall be his messenger.
. . .
Here the four citizens make themselves ready to meet Our Lord,
going barefoot and barelegged and in their shirts, except that they
shall have gowns thrown around themselves. And when they see
Our Lord they shall spread their clothes in front of him.

The information mainly comes piecemeal from accounts.
COVENTRY, Drapers' ?1557:
Item, paid for canvas for the souls' tunics (<u>cottys</u>), 19 ells, 24s
3d;
Item, paid for 4 ells of linen cloth for the players' gowns, 3s 8d;
Item, paid for [*dyeing*] 9 ells of canvas yellow, 12d;
Item, paid for 10 ells of canvas made black, 10d;
Item, paid for four pairs of angels' wings, 2s 8d;
. . .
Item, paid for three wigs (<u>chefferellys</u>) and a beard of hair, 3s 10d;
Item, paid for four haloes (<u>dyadynnes</u>), 2s 8d;
Item, paid for six golden skins, 5s;
Item, paid for seven skins for God's tunic. . . .
Item, paid for two pieces of yellow buckram, 7s 6d;
Item, paid for 4 yards of red buckram, 2s 8d;
Item, paid for a demon's mask (<u>face</u>), 2s;
Item, paid to Francis Tayller for making the souls' tunics, 6s 8d;
Item, paid for making three gowns and a tunic, 6s;
. . .
Item, paid for blacking the souls' faces. . . .

Earlier in the century the souls' costumes are described as shirts and hose, as the souls' costumes from the YORK *Mercers' pageant in 1433 also are. At York however, the souls also wore masks* (vesernes) *and wigs* (chevelers).

      Though God in the YORK *Mercers' pageant has only a* "wounded" *shirt and a halo and mask, he is elsewhere dressed in a costume of leather.*

COVENTRY, *Smiths' 1452:*
Item: paid for six skins of tawed leather for God's costume (garment), 18d;
Item: paid for making the same costume, 10d.
1499:
Item: paid for mending a wig (cheverel) for God, and for sewing God's tunic (kote) of leather and for making hands for the same tunic, 12d.

NEW ROMNEY, *1560:*
Item: paid for half a dozen sheepskins for the Godhead's coat for the fourth play, 2s.

      Adam and Eve, and occasionally the devil too, are clad in leather:
CORNISH CREATION:
Adam and Eve, dressed in tawed leather, in a place arranged by the director (conveyour) and not to be seen until they are called for, and then kneel and rise.

COVENTRY, *Smiths' 1477:*
Item: for mending the demon's costume (Garment). . . .
Item: for new leather for the same costume, 22d.

      The TOLEDO *accounts include a variety of items connected with costumes, as in the following extract:*
The rough woolen cloth (sayal) for making the hermit's cape and scapular cost three rreales.
For some sandals, twelve mrs.
The two strings of beads for the hermit cost twelve mrs.
. . .
Three and a half yards of Brittany cloth for the shift of Our Lady's soul, three and a half rreales.
For making it up, and for silk, half a rreal.
Four yards of rough white woolen cloth for the gown of the man who exploded (el rrebentado) at half a rreal the yard.
Three yards of ribbons (çintas) for a girdle for the soul of Our

Lady, six <u>mrs</u>.

The CASTILIAN TRIAL IN HEAVEN AND NATIVITY:
For Man, clothes which are neither typically those of a man or a
woman; he should look very old, have a white beard and a head-
dress (<u>tocador</u>).
Desire to be dressed as a shepherd, in green.
The Godhead, very richly dressed, with a crown and a branch of
laurel in the hand.

Justice, dressed in blue with a drawn sword in her hand.
Peace, dressed in purple, carrying a crook (<u>un cayado</u>).
Mercy, in red, carrying an olive branch.
Truth, in white, with a ruler in her hand.

The Eternal Word, in red, dressed in clothes typical neither of men
nor women; tightly girded like a wrestler (<u>muy cenido como lucha-
dor</u>); a crook in the hand and a halo on the head.
Love, in a purple costume with hearts painted on it; a garland on
his head. He is to be very small and pretty.

The angel of course with alb, stole, and halo.
Our Lady, dressed in traveling clothes.
Joseph, as an old honorable man, dressed for a journey.
The shepherds, dressed as such.

*For French plays the actors normally provided their own cos-
tumes. Evidence about them is available in eye-witness descriptions
(see below Bourges in Section D), or in individual references often
associated with a change of costume, as in the following:*
BOURGES EFFECTS:
There must be a white robe for the Virgin Mary to wear when dying.
. . .
There must be a mask (<u>visaige fainct</u>) for Simon Magus which can be
put on and taken off at will (<u>quant on vouldra</u>) by which he can
appear in another form than his own.

The Last Supper at MONS:
The Apostles should here be wearing white shoes (<u>sorles</u>) on their
feet and be girt with leather belts (<u>coroyes</u>) or sashes (<u>tarelles</u>) over
their robes, their mantles taken off, and with a white staff in their
hands like a pilgrim's staff.

The PARIS RESURRECTION:
Here the holy souls sing this hymn sweetly: <u>Jhesus Noster Redemptor, amor desideratio</u>. And Jesus should be wearing the robe in
which he appeared to Our Lady after the Resurrection, and his five

wounds should be gaping (ouvertes) and red. And with him should be
Gabriel and Michael, Carinus and Leoncius.

*A warning against wearing unsuitable costumes was given to
the people of* ISSOUDUN *in 1535:*
I implore you to allocate the parts to the actors according to their
age and not to use borrowed costumes (though they be of gold) unless they are truly appropriate to the roles of their wearers. It is
not good that the learned doctors, the Pharisees, or the councillors
should have clothes similar to those of Pilate.

*The minutes of the first general meeting preceding the 1597
performance in* LUCERNE *include an exhortation to take good care
of borrowed items:*
Item, that everyone should take the best possible care of borrowed
items and costumes and treat them most carefully, so that no cause
for complaint is given and in future they are not found to be un-
available for borrowing. Also that everyone should return such items
immediately after the performance with thanks, clean and in good
condition. But what anyone has had made at his own expense he is
to keep in good conditon so that it can be used again in the future
to the praise and glory of God.

Change of costume is recorded in the MAJORCA JUDITH:
Now Judith goes into her house and puts on a hair shirt and puts
ashes on her head and says: [*prayer*].
Then she gets up, takes off the hair shirt and puts on fine clothes,
goes to the city gate and addresses the magnates of the city.

In the ANGLO-NORMAN ADAM, *Adam symbolically changes
clothes when he sins, hidden by the chest-high walls of Paradise:*
Then let Adam eat part of the apple. Having eaten it he shall
immediately recognize his sin and shall bend down so that it may
not be possible for him to be seen by the people, and he shall take
off his dignified clothes (sollempnes vestes) and put on poor garments sewn with fig leaves.

In the MAJORCA LAST JUDGMENT, *music sounds while the
souls change their costumes behind the scenes:*
Now the saved and the damned shall fall down dead and enter behind
the scaffold, and shall change into the following costumes: the saved
shall wear an alb (camis) and over it a light-colored cape (capotín),
on their heads black wigs, strips of cloth round the forehead with a
red cross on them. The damned are to wear black cassocks
(sotanes), and on their heads white, black, or reddish wigs. While

they are changing the angels are to blow their trumpets, and when they get word that the actors have finished changing, St. Michael shall sing his words to the melody of Vexilla.

At LUCERNE *the actors changed in the houses round the square:*
[1583] Chore, Mosse are to exchange clothing on the second day.
[1597] Aaron: like a high priest. When he departs, Zacharias puts his clothing on, but he does not remain (halt sich nit) with these Jews.
When his scene is over, Raabod puts it on.
John, son of Zebedee, changes his clothing (verkleidt sich) for the Marriage at Cana [*where he was the bridegroom*].
[1597] Those who have to change parts or clothing (sich verendern . . . oder verkleidern) go out for this purpose to suitable places in the houses around the square.

Wigs were often worn, sometimes of horsehair, as in the SARAGOSSA *Nativity of 1487:*
Some horsehair wigs (unas cabelleras de cerda) for the prophets, 4s 6d.
For the hire of seven women's wigs [*or* wigs of women's hair] (cabelleras de muger) for the angels, 6s.

LUCERNE *took the trouble to collect women's hair for future use:*
From time to time enquiry should be made in the country for beautiful women's hair, for future use.

Wigs and also masks are common in the records of the English plays.   The serpent at Norwich had both wig and mask.   There is also the occasional reference to face painting.
NORWICH, *Grocers'* 1534:
Item: a new wig (heer) with a crown for the serpent, 6d.
1563:
A coat with hose and tail for the serpent, painted, with a white wig (heare);
. . .
A mask (face) and wig for the Father;
Two wigs for Adam and Eve.

CHELMSFORD, *Essex, 1562 inventory of properties for the town plays:*
Item: 23 beards and 21 wigs (hares).

COVENTRY, *Smiths'* 1502:
Item: paid for painting their [*the players'*] faces, 2d.

*Nudity on the stage was dealt with in a variety of ways.   In
France the stage directions demanded nudity at the Crucifixion, as in*
MICHEL'S PASSION then they strip him naked.   *The* MONS *stage
directions show how this could be done:*
Then [*the soldiers*] pretend to strip him naked and lay him on the
ground.
[*Short scene with Pilate, then Virgin Mary approaches.*]   Then Our
Lady passes right through them and goes to Jesus and pretends to
fasten her wimple round him, but there is one already there.

For the treatment of nudity in other plays see also the
LUCERNE *list and the* TURIN St. George *play quoted above, Section*
B.4.

A further reference to a "naked costume" occurs in the
LUCERNE *play at the moment of Christ's betrayal:*
The formerly blind Marcellus is naked in a garment (cleyd), with a
white cloak over it.   When Malchus reaches up and grabs him by the
cloak, he leaves him the cloak and runs off in the naked garment (im
nacketten cleyd).

8. STAGE STAFF

*From early liturgical drama onwards references are usually
not to stage staff but to having properties or scenery ready.
There are, however, references in later periods from various
countries specifically to stage staff.* The records of the 1583
performance in LUCERNE *mention at various points those assigned the duties of stage hands:*
At each barrier (gatter) the foremen are to detail two strong men
from the works department to hold back the crowd and to let out
and in those who belong to the play.
. . . of the men from the works department ordered to be in the
square, two are to have their light staffs in order to keep the press
of the people behind them.
. . . men from works department to prevent anyone from entering
the stalls apart from those who belong there.
Assign guards for the entrances. Guards for Paradise and Adam's pit
[*where the actor hides before creation of Adam*]. A guard for the
golden calf.
There are to be several men from the works department in the
square at the ready, when the scene is finished to move the properties (Rüstungen) in and out.
The director of works (Herr Buwmeister)--or, if he were to be in the
play, his deputy until he is free again--together with four men from
that department and also both foremen, to be in the square and if
the Director requires anything or anything occurs requiring doing, or
orders being given in which the men and the foremen are required,
then the director of works at the Director's request shall order the
foremen and men to do that same on the spot.

Their duties are enumerated in even greater detail for the
1597 *performance, where their title* platz diener *brings out explicitly
in the word* platz *the association with "acting area":*
The master carpenter is to assign people as stage staff (platz
diener) to perform duties as required, and they must be strong and
powerful, namely two for each of the three gateways, in armor with
good staffs (knebelspiessen); one guard for the rock from which the
water flows; one guard for the pit in which Eve lies hidden in Paradise; one guard to guard Paradise on the first day and on the second
day the Mount of Olives; one guard for the golden calf; eight
guards to guard the square (platz) until the opening procession enters
so that nobody occupies the stalls.

*Some more specific details regarding their duties are also
recorded:*
The gatekeepers (portner) . . . immediately after the entry, close the
gates and keep good watch.

The stage hands. On the first day at the creation of Adam and Eve, shut up the pit in which Eve has been lying. Also, whenever anything is finished to remove the stage properties (rüstungen) and tidy up, clear away, clear up. When the scene (figur) with Adam and Eve is over, remove the tree and put the altar table (Opffer tisch) of Cain and Abel in place. Put the pulpit (Cantzel) of the doctors (Leerern) in position and remove it again. Immediately after Cain and Abel's scene is over, put the altar table in position for Abraham's scene, and when it is finished, take it away again and remove the donkey. For the scene with Jacob and Esau one of them should be hidden in the thicket (gstüd) to impale and throw out a rabbit.

The moving of Abraham's altar is even further specified in a stage direction:
Tell Abraham to get ready, and have the altar (Opfer Tisch) at which Abel sacrificed moved to the other side of the square well up-square in front of the Butchers' passage (Metzgergang) immediately in front of Paradise, and have a bush placed beside it, to which the angel is to attach the ram (daran hencke).

In addition there are other staff with specific duties:
Operator of Star and Holy Ghost [*elsewhere:* also Eclipse Maker]. He is to be in the topmost room of the Haus zur Sonne and have his equipment ready with strings reaching across down to the pillar of the fountain. [*Elsewhere:* the operator of the Star and Holy Ghost is to test his equipment. The Holy Ghost with a live dove onto Mary in the Annunciation and onto the Savior at the Baptism.]
He lowers the Holy Spirit over Mary at the Annunciation.
Later over the Savior when John baptizes him.
He lowers the star as far as the middle of the square when the Three Kings ride in, and when they set off for Jerusalem he draws it in again. Then when they have been with Herod and remount, he lowers the star again, right to the bottom over the Hut of the Nativity.

[*Elsewhere:* the doves for the Holy Ghost and for Pentecost; how are the fires to go rushing along in front of the Holy Ghost? (wie die Füwr rasen gan wöllent?).
And when the Savior has spoken the third of the Words from the Cross, he is to turn round the sun and the moon, turning the eclipsed part to the front.]

Thunderers. There are two of them in two places--namely, in the attic of the Butchers' Hall and on the Court House. They start the thunder when God the Father is about to give Moses the Ten Commandments on Mount Sinai. [*Elsewhere:* also, when the Savior on the Cross dies; also at Pentecost.]

Musketeers (<u>Schützen</u>). There are to be four of them with mus-
kets--one on the Court House, one on the Butchers' Hall, two in the
<u>Haus zur Sonne</u>, all at the top. They fire when God the Father is
about to give Moses the Ten Commandments on the mountain. Later
when the New Testament is about to start. [*Elsewhere:* on the
second day for Pentecost.]

Horn Blowers. [*Elsewhere called* Military Horn Blowers (<u>Harsthorn-</u>
<u>blasser</u>) and Smoke-Makers (<u>Roucker</u>). Each is to have his horn with
him.]
There are four of them.
They blow for the beginning, when the procession has entered the
square, a third time.
In Moses' scene, for the fourth time.
Also, when God the Father is about to give Moses the Ten Com-
mandments on the mountain, they are to set the smoke mechanism
working so that a cloud is produced.
[*Elsewhere:* here the horn blowers are to go secretly into the
mountain to get ready the smoke for the cloud.]
Also they blow too when the New Testament is to begin.
[*Elsewhere:* on the second day in the morning they again blow as
on the previous day.]
Later when the Savior is to be led out to Crucifixion.
And when the Savior has spoken the third of the Words from the
Cross, they are again to make black smoke in the Mount of Olives
for the eclipse.
Also, when the Savior has died on the Cross they are to make the
rock by the Mount of Olives split, that is, they are to turn the split
part to the front.
[*Elsewhere:* for the Ascension the smoke-makers are to make a
cloud; for Pentecost thunder, smoke, and shots. Note: In Milan
they have artificial fire in the plays which goes up quickly (<u>gäch</u>
<u>uffgat</u>), produces much smoke, and yet neither burns nor stinks.]
They are to be dressed in Jewish fashion as trumpeters on the first
day; on the second day the two who are in Pilate's stall are to be
dressed in heathen fashion.

Whereas the Lucerne stage staff were municipal employees,
elsewhere payments were made to stage staff. At MONS they were
paid for their work in Hell, for which protective clothing was also
provided:
To Maistre Jehan du Fayt and his companions to the number of 17
persons for having helped in Hell for nine days during the said mystery at 6s per day for each, £45 18s, from which must be deducted,
as one of them was only there for three days, 36s, remaining therefore £44 2s. To the said du Fayt, for having worked for the said
nine days at the said Hell and made the powders and crackers
(<u>fuzées</u>) used there, paid as agreed £6.

. . .
To Simon Maugart, tailor, for making three pairs of canvas hose
(cauches de cannevas), three doublets, worn by those helping in Hell.
. . .

*There are also payments to helpers in Hell on the pageant
wagons in* COVENTRY. *Drapers', 1562:*
Item: paid for looking after Hell-mouth and the fire, 12d;
. . .
Item: paid for looking after the windlass, 8d.

*The commonest appearance of stage staff in the English civic
plays is as pushers of the wagons.*

Records from VALENCIA *include payments to stage hands for
a* DEPOSITION *play performed in 1517:*
Item, to Joan Moliner, who helped with the ladders (les scales) and
other necessary things . . . two sous three diners.
Item, to Pere Sepulcre, for opening and shutting the tomb (lo sepulcre) . . . three diners.

*The producer's copy from Mons and the partial one which
survives from Lucerne contain frequent cues to stage staff as well
as actors.*
MONS:
Note that here the coal shall be prepared and lighted in front of
Adam's house so that it shall be glowing when Abel makes his sacrifice hereafter.
. . .
When he [*Noah*] has said: "Hast been in this mortal plight," he rises
and addresses his children who are in the ark and speaks. Here let
there be prepared the lamb which Noah will sacrifice. Then at the
end of the phrase, Noah pretends to build an altar which shall be
prepared beforehand and hidden. Meanwhile they come out of the
ark and there is music.

In the LUCERNE *text towards the end of the previous scene is
the instruction:*
At this point (hiemit) give the Three Kings their final signal and
have them ride in. . . . After that the Three Kings ride into the
square, each from a separate direction (ieder ein besondere
straß har). *See plan, Day 1. Also at the Annunciation:* have the Holy
Ghost operator get himself ready; *and at Peter's denial:* give the
cock the signal to crow.

Those who worked the thunder at MONS *had their own written
cue-sheet, which in the case of the calming of the lake was sup-
plemented by a direct reminder from the producer:*
Remind those who work the thunder effects to do their duty, following the contents of their cue-sheet (<u>billet de advertence</u>), and not
to forget to stop when God has said: "Cease and be still."

*Besides giving cues to others the Director sometimes cues
himself as one of the stage staff. In the* LUCERNE *text as the
devils prepare to drag Judas off to Hell occurs the marginal direction:* Director go to Hell (<u>Regent ganng zur hell</u>).

9. MUSIC AND SOUND EFFECTS

*Though it is generally recognized that music played an im-
portant part in many medieval plays, the amount of information
about the music contained in the extant texts and records, apart
from sung Church drama, is comparatively   slight.   There are numerous examples of vocal and instrumental music being used both to
create the right atmosphere (e.g., in Heaven) and to cover a break
in the action.   There are some instances, however, of musical effects being used within the action of the play.*

*The worldliness of Mary Magdalene may be indicated by music
and song.   In LUCERNE, for example, the text requires there to be
among the actors a lutenist and a good singer for the party held in
Magdalene's garden.*

In several German plays, including the VIENNA PASSION *Play
and the play on the Worldliness of Magdalene in the* ERLAU *collection, the same words are given for Magdalene's song.   In the
Vienna text, which also has the music, after* walking round
singing (circumeat cantando) in *Latin she then* repeats a German
version (in theutonico eadem sunt).

In MICHEL'S PASSION *the words but not the music are specified:*
Now begins the worldliness of Mary Magdalene and note that she can
sing to any music she likes (de choses faictes a plaisance) what follows, and after she can say it without singing [two stanzas with
refrain follow].
Later her attendants join her in singing an unspecified song:
Here Magdalene and her attendants sing some happy song, joyously
and suitably (en soy demenant joyeusement et honnestement).

In SEMUR *the choice of music for the song Eglantine
(= Salome) sings at Herod's feast is left open:*

"Lord, if God gives me health,
I will sing before you immediately."
At pleasure (ad placitum)

[*The song in French follows, written beneath blank music staves.*]

Also in SEMUR *we learn from the text that the smith's wife,
Grumaton, sings with the soldier who comes to collect the nails for*

the Crucifixion:

> "Let us sing high and low as we forge--
> It will not make us late at all."

[*Miroufflet, the soldier, agrees and apparently recommends a tune:*]

> "Now then, 'for a sheaf of barley'."

Then Grumaton sings, Miroufflet shall reply.
[*The words of the song follow under blank music staves.*]

At LUCERNE *the Crucifixion is proclaimed by the horn-*
blowers:
Pilate to the horn-blowers:

> "Blow your horns, so that everyone shall hear
> that Jesus Christ is to be crucified.
> You Jews, stand still for a while!
> Let the horns sound out
> To see whether his disciples will rescue him."

Tubal to his fellow horn-blower:

> "Fellow, you are to go with me.
> We must make the horns ring out
> In all the accustomed places in the town
> So that many of the people hear
> That Jesus Christ is to be crucified--
> Procurator Pilate has commanded it."

They go into the middle of the square and blow their horns:
then the other horn blower replies. . . .
They blow in two more places.

In the Ascension pageant at CHESTER *the action is continued*
by means of an elaborate set-piece with music:
Standing in the place where he ascends, Jesus shall say: <u>Data est</u>
<u>mihi omnis potestas in caelo et in terra</u>. . . . Then he shall ascend,
and in ascending he shall sing [*added later:* God sings alone]: <u>As-</u>
<u>cendo ad Patrem meum</u>. . . . When Jesus has finished this song, let
him stay half way up (<u>in medio</u>) as if above the clouds, and let the
greater angel speak to the lesser angel. The first angel sings: <u>Quis</u>
<u>est iste qui venit de Edom</u>. . . .

The lesser angel replying sings: <u>Iste formosus in stola sua</u>. . . .

Jesus sings alone: <u>Ego qui loquor justitiam</u>. . . .

The choir sings: Et vestimenta tua. . . .

Jesus sings alone: Torcular calcavi solus. . . .

The first angel says in the vernacular: [*The speeches are adaptations and extensions of the Latin*].

Jesus, pausing in the same place, shall say: [*Conversation between Jesus and a third angel*].

Then he shall ascend, and as he ascends let the angels sing the song written below. Let them sing: Exaltaremus, domine, in virtute tua. . . .

Then the angels shall descend, and let them sing: Viri Galilei, quid aspicitis in caelum.

A similarly elaborate musical set-piece appears in the YORK *pageant of the Assumption of Mary and her appearance to Thomas. For this the music appears to have been specially written and it survives in the fifteenth-century manuscript of the play.*

Songs with nonsense words are sometimes used to characterize the Jews. At SEMUR *the music for these songs is written in the manuscript:*

Modo veniant omnes Judei insimil

ad Templum cum magno gaudio.

OMNES JUDEI cantant:

A – bra – am, a – ta – ram, do – da – rem, na – ta – brom,

Sa – mu – el, Ge – re – om, Fa – nu – el

Gor - ga - tas, en - gro - te, fa - si - as, bar - bot - te.

In the ADMONT *Passion Play the nonsense words of the Jews'
song are included in the text, with music, in the same way as the
Latin words of the other serious songs.* This song also serves to
cover movement:
The Schola Judeorum (Juden Schuell) sings the song Schorbis.

Scorbis. Adonaÿ, zipfelraÿ schahor Machiami tripolim
Iericho tripolim schlericho Cados Cados Adonaÿ.
Cados Cados Cados
Adonaÿ Kirios Kos Kos melos Imbros telos procaÿ procae
    Aurecolare nas nas.
Nigeos Roseos und Ambos. Campadurna Machuj.

While the Jews are singing, Annas and the Scribes stand up and lead
the Lord slowly, with his hands bound, to Caiaphas the High Priest.
Peter and John follow at a distance.

In the VIENNA EASTER PLAY *the stage direction the Jews
dance to Pilate and sing in Hebrew (Jodisch) is not explained, although Latin incipits are given for other sung items in this play.*

At LUCERNE *the words and music for these Jews' songs are
preserved mounted on boards; for details see Bibliography, above.
This same group of Jews, functioning as one of the choirs, also sings
liturgical pieces--e.g., on Palm Sunday at the entry into Jerusalem:*
. . . and the Synagogue sing the Sanctus, Benedictus, and Agnus
Dei.

The LUCERNE *text also uses liturgical pieces more centrally in
the action when the three Marys come to the sepulcher on Easter
morning.*
Then each of them takes a box of ointment. They go towards the
tomb beside which are the two angels, First and Second. The three

Marys sing:

> Jesu nostra redemptio, amor et desiderium etc.

As they approach the tomb, the two angels sing:

> Quem queritis, o tremule mulieres?

Then the First Angel speaks to the Marys. . . .

In the sixteenth-century BODLEY RESURRECTION, *otherwise solely in English, part of the action is first presented by means of a liturgical piece sung in Latin:*
Victime paschali laudes immolant Christiani. Then the three Marys sing it, that is, Victime paschali, all, as far as Dic nobis, in parts or at least antiphonally (in cantifracto vel saltum in pallinodio). Then the apostles run to them, namely Peter, Andrew, and John, singing this, namely, Dic nobis Maria; quid vidisti in via? The women reply singing: Sepulcrum Christi viventis etc. as far as: Credendum est. The apostles replying sing: Credendum est magis soli Marie veraci, quam Judeorum turbe fallaci. The women sing again: Scimus Christum surrexisse vere. The apostles and the three women sing together as if believing: Tu nobis Christe rex miserere. Amen. It will suffice if it is sung with the same notes and music (eisdem notis et cantibus) as are used for the aforesaid sequence. After the song Peter says:

> "How is it now, Mary? Can you tell
> Any news which may please us well?"

The Victimae Paschali *is similarly performed at* SEMUR, *with the same division between the Marys and the apostles.*

Sometimes singers are sent to a specific part of the stage to perform, as at MONS:
Here warn those who sing the motets in Paradise to come down from Paradise and go towards Limbo to sing a motet when they are told to.

Music might also be used to cover a delay in the action as at LUCERNE:
Note: the angels sing until Joseph has got ready for the Purification of Mary to go into the temple with her, according to the law, with Jesus.
Item: the music is to be assigned to the scenes (Actus), and there are also to be several short songs, so that on any occasion when

pauses occur unexpectedly, there will be something to sing.

Similarly at MONS:
When God has said, "And we shall go down to earth," he comes down
and goes to the field of Damascus. If he is too far away, music
(silete).

*To create the greatest possible effect, musicians and others
might be located in various places around the playing-area, as at the
point in the* LUCERNE *text where the New Testament action begins:*
The thunder is to be in the attic (uff dem Estrich) of the Butchers,
the horns and trumpets beneath Heaven.
The musketeers, two at the very top in the Haus zur Sonne, one in
the attic of the Butchers, and one in the attic of the Court House.

*Musical instruments can be used to create the effect of a
battle, as in the* CHRISTMAS PLAY *by Diego* SÁNCHEZ DE
BADAJOZ:
Trumpets are heard in the choir, and they shall make a din with
harness bells and by dashing from one end to the other. [*The Sibyl
is describing a tournament between the Virtues and Vices.*]

*Sound effects on a smaller scale seem called for by the re-
quirement for the early sixteenth-century liturgical* EASTER CERE-
MONY *from* GRANADA: to find some people who can do bird song
(música de aves).

*The sound effects for Hell used a variety of drums, fireworks,
and cannon.*
In ROUEN *in 1474:*
Then all the devils cry out together with the drums and other thun-
derings made by machines (engins), and the cannon (couleuvrines)
are shot off and flames of fire are thrown out from the nostrils, the
eyes, and the ears [*of the Hell's mouth*].

In MONS *there are entries in the accounts for making the thun-
der-machine:*
To Anthonne de Vricourt called Fagho for two large vellum skins
used for a cask of fir wood (thonneau de sapin) and a skin of parchment used to cover a cauldron; all this for Hell: 36s.
To Pierre Viscave, cauldron-maker (caudrelier) for the depreciation
(amenrissement) of two large, flat bronze basins (bachins d'airain)
lent by him for the said Mystery and which were put in Hell to
make thunder.
To Alixandre Macquet, cauldron-maker (caudrelier), for a pound of

brass used both for the Pinnacle (Pinacle) and for joining together
two copper basins (bachins de keuvre) for some effect (secres) in
Hell, 14s.
Item: for a pivot of iron and for four pieces of iron and four eyelets to turn on it and two handles (manevelles), 16 fasteners (cram-
pons) to attach them to two great vats (keuvres) to make thunder in
Hell, weighing 24 lbs. at 2s the l lb., 48s.

   *Comparable account entries for the thunder-making machinery
at* LUCERNE *are included in Section C below.*

   Precise instructions are given in the ROUEN *Nativity for the
performance of a song of rejoicing in Heaven with mimed instrumental accompaniment:*
Then they sing the first line of the song following. Then the instrumentalists behind the angels repeat the line while the angels who are
holding instruments pretend to play them. Then the angels sing the
second line, and then the instrumentalists repeat three lines. After
that the angels sing the third line, and then the instruments repeat
the first and then the end. [*The MS. does not specify the musical
setting, though the song is vernacular, not in Latin.*]

*For King David, however, a hidden instrumentalist is not considered
practical:*
Then let him play the harp if he is a harper, and if not let him
omit this last section [*of the speech announcing his intention of
playing the harp*].

   *Hidden music and quiet sound effects are used for the coming
of the Holy Spirit in the* PARIS RESURRECTION:
And at the coming of the Holy Spirit upon them, there should be a
very soft peal of thunder over the meeting room (cenacle). Meanwhile instruments should sound softly in Paradise and in the meeting
room without being seen by those in the audience (ceux du parc).

   Large numbers of musicians came to LUCERNE *for the play at the
city's expense. The director, Cysat, observed in 1597:*
One ought to make a list of what musicians are wanted, and all the
rest should be sent away. This saves much expense; one thinks the
usual city musicians ought to suffice, except perhaps one or two who
would be good for the choir (Cantory).

Somewhat later: Make a list of the number of musicians needed
dealing exclusively with those in the square (platz). The choir
[*which was not at ground level 'in the square' but on the front of
the* Haus zur Sonne *below Heaven*] is entrusted to the schoolmaster

(h. Schuolmeister). We need two drummers (2 Trommen schlaher),
two fife players (2 pfyffer), five trumpet players (5 Trommeter).
Item: lutenists (Lutanisten), zithers (Zittern), viols (Vyolen), etc.,
krummhorns (krumm hörner).

10. MOVEMENT

*The eyewitness accounts and extended descriptions which con-
stitute Section D are, because of their fullness, among the most
informative sources regarding movement in the plays. The entries in
this section generally deal with movement in a more limited way,
though some more extensive directions are included.*

*Sometimes by taking a number of stage directions together a
fuller picture of the action within an episode can be gained. This is
especially true of* LUCERNE *where the stage directions and the
plans are mutually enlightening:*
Nativity:
Now they [*Joseph and Mary*] go together up onto the stand and into
the Hut. Mary sits down, they pull the curtain in front, get the
Child ready, then they put the Child into the crib. Then the trumpeters blow magnificently (ein herrlich uffblasen) and the prophet
Isaiah comes [*speaks*] to the people from the middle of the square
[*eight lines*]. Now the angels next to the hut sing Puer natus etc.,
thereafter go on from the stand into the square, except Gabriel and
Raphael who remain with Mary and the Child beside the Hut. Then
the First Angel from the middle of the square addresses everyone.
. . .
Here Joseph gives Mary swaddling clothes (ein windlen) with the
words

> "Wrap the child in these swaddling clothes,
> I tell you, so that it does not feel the cold."

He then goes off to the side and pretends to cook (gat nebent sich,
alls ob er kochete).

The Second and Third Angels, accompanied by the First Angel and
Uriel and Michael, go to the shepherds in the square and speak to
them.

Meanwhile Joseph returns with a small pot of baby food (pfendlin
kinds muß). Mary feeds the Child, and meanwhile the Second Angel
addresses the shepherds in the square. [*In margin to this speech:*]
The shepherds look around, are afraid, soon they get up and kneel,
listen to the angels with folded hands.
. . .

After the adoration:
The Shepherds now depart and are not seen any more.

Circumcision:
Joseph takes the Child on his arm, carries it into the Temple, and
speaks to Zacharias. He is standing at the entrance to the Temple,
the other five [*Raabod, Urias, Salmon, Josaphat, Amalech*] are
standing by the altar. Now Zacharias puts the Child on the altar,
has it in his arms. Salmon lifts up the basin (das becke) and with
the other hand the can (die kannten) of water, also the towel on his
shoulder, so that after the circumcision Raabod shall be able to wash
his hands. Raabod circumcises the Child, Josaphat lifts his clothes
or the shift (hembdlin) on one side and Amalech on the other side,
then Zacharias speaks ´[*four lines*]. Raabod has a sponge
(schümlin) full of blood hidden in his hand, has a sharp
stone, so that he can act as though he were cutting it off, then
Urias offers him a small box (büchsslin) in which there should
be powder so that he can sprinkle it on. . . . Once the Child
is circumcised, Joseph takes it, carries it home again, and this
time the angels in Heaven sing: Dies est loetitiae etc.

Thereupon give the Three Kings the final signal and have them ride
in.
Let the star down.

John the Baptist:
John the Baptist beside the Fountain and those who are allocated to
him, they begin to walk steadily. Then John the Baptist speaks in a
loud voice, standing by the Fountain. [*After John's speech:*] Meanwhile the Jews have come to join them and he addresses them. . . .

[*When John has just talked about baptizing:*] Music, during which he
is to baptize several.
. . .
The Savior stands still. Then John undresses him and baptizes him.
The Holy Ghost comes over him, and then God the Father speaks
[*two lines*].
John dresses the Savior again and says. . . .

The 1616 manuscript reveals further details of this episode:
The Savior makes himself ready (stellt sich) for baptism, both angels
stand beside him. John undresses him, the angels hold the robe
(gwandt).

John baptizes him, at the same moment the Holy Ghost comes over
him.
Holy Ghost.
God the Father stands up in Heaven, stretches out his hands and
says [*two lines*]. John puts the clothes (kleider) back on the Savior.

The Resurrection and Harrowing of Hell:
[*The first stage direction relates to the end of the preceding scene.*]
Urias goes away and the four [*guards*] begin to sleep. Then it be-

gins to thunder. Then the Savior pushes (stost) the tomb open and
puts one foot down outside the tomb. Then several of the dead are
to arise, and then the First Angel comes and says to the Savior [six
lines]. Angels sing "Christ is arisen," after which Christ climbs
(stigt) out of the tomb saying [four lines]. Now the Savior with the
angels goes in front of Hell and stands there. Then the angels sing:
"You princes of Hell are vanquished, open the gates at once." Angels
sing. The Savior kicks Hell with one foot, saying: "You princes of
Hell, open up the gates! The King of Honor (Eeren) is outside!"
The devils let out a wild cry, then the Savior takes a chain and
binds Lucifer. [Three more speeches.] Now the angels sing: "Come
you blessed of God the Father." [In margin: advenisti desiderabilis
etc.] Then in margin: Savior to patriarchs. After this speech:
Thereupon the Savior takes Adam by the hand and leads them out
onto the square, for they follow after him. They then all fall to
their knees in front of him. At this point also note in the margin:
Here the people in Purgatory are to speak in biblical order. Pay
attention to the numbering. [This numbering does not go beyond 1
and 2 for Adam and Eve. In the oldest extant MS. of this scene
(1545), the order was not biblical.] Now the Savior goes toward
Heaven with the patriarchs, who enter the bottom of the Haus zur
Sonne. Then the [Second] Angel comes to Mary saying [six lines by
Gabriel]. The angels sing: Regina Celi, letare, alleluya, then the
Savior appears to his mother Mary saying [six lines each]. Savior
departs, puts on gardener's clothes.

The PARIS RESURRECTION also contains a description of the
Harrowing of Hell:
Here all the devils except Satan bring culverins and other weapons
(ferremens) into Hell and close their gates with great bolts (correilz). And the Anima Christi with the above-mentioned four [an-
gels] and the soul of the Penitent Thief go towards Hell, holding
Satan bound. And the Anima Christi strikes the gates of Hell with
his cross. [The Attolite portas dialogue follows.] Here the Anima
Christi breaks the gates of Hell with the cross and goes inside with
the four angels and the soul of the Penitent Thief. Then the souls
in Limbo sing this hymn melodiously: Conditor alma sidera. Then
the Anima Christi should remain near the room of Limbo (chambre
du Limbe) until the devils have fled from there.

The series of stage directions towards the end of the first N.
TOWN PASSION play gives a full picture of the action of Christ's
betrayal:
Here Jesus with his disciples goes into the place, and ten people
shall come in, well-arrayed in white armor and coats of mail, and
some dressed in other garments, with swords, halberds, and other
strange weapons, [and] cressets flaming, and lanterns, and lighted
torches; and Judas in front of them all, leading them to Jesus by

signs (be contenawns). [*Jesus speaks to them.*] Here all the Jews
suddenly fall to the earth when they hear Christ speak, and when he
tells them to rise, they rise again. . . . Here Judas kisses Jesus and
immediately all the Jews gather round him and lay hands on him,
and pull him about as if they were mad, and make a great outcry
against him all at once; and after this Peter says:

> "I draw my sword now at this time;
> Shall I strike, Master, I'd be glad to know?"

And immediately he strikes off Malchus' ear, and he cries: "Help!
My ear, my ear!" And Christ blesses it and it is healed. . . . Here
the Jews lead Christ out of the place with great clamor and noise,
some pulling Christ forwards and some backwards, and leading him
out thus with their weapons raised and lights burning. And in the
meantime Mary Magdalene shall run to Our Lady and tell her about
the taking of Our Lord.

In the second N. TOWN PASSION *play another series of stage directions describes the events following the Crucifixion.*
Here four or five poor men shall stand and watch the Jews, and the
Jews shall come to them and make them hang the thieves. . . .
Here the ordinary men shall set up the two crosses and hang the
thieves up by the arms; and meanwhile the Jews shall throw dice for
his clothes and fight and squabble. And in the meantime Our Lady
with the three Marys shall come, and St. John with them, setting
themselves down in front of the cross, Our Lady swooning and
mourning. . . . Here Our Lady shall rise and run and embrace the
cross. . . . Here they shall take Our Lady from the cross. And here
Pilate shall come down from his scaffold with Caiaphas and Annas
and all their followers, and shall come and look at Christ; and Annas
and Caiaphas shall say scornfully. . . . Here Pilate shall ask for pen
and ink, and a board (tabyl) shall be brought to him with Hic est
Jhesus Nazarenus rex Judeorum already written on it. And he shall
pretend to write, and then go up a ladder and put the board above
Christ's head; and then Caiaphas shall make him read it.

In the BURGOS PASSION (1520) *each of the three short
scenes is preceded by a prose prologue which summarizes the action
to come and gives stage directions:*
In this brief scene (contemplacion), devout madam, four prophets
appear: David, Solomon, Isaiah, and Jeremiah. They are seated like
judges (a manera de juyzio) in a hall into which Our Lady enters.
She appears distraught, searching for her son. She asks the prophets
who they are, and each tells her his name. She asks them why they
are gathered together and they reply: to pronounce judgment on
Jesus Christ. Our Lady utters laments and departs, disconsolate.
Then Christ enters to bid farewell to his mother before going to his
death.

. . .
In this short scene of the Ecce Homo, an honorable man leads Christ
round a room (una sala) with a rope around his neck, the crown of
thorns on his head, and clearly suffering from his torture. When
Our Lady sees this man, so disfigured, she asks St. John who he is,
and St. John tells her it is her son. Then Our Lady laments to the
people (alas gentes).
. . .
Now Our Lady and St. John are at the foot of the cross and Joseph
of Arimathea and Nicodemus approach. Our Lady asks them why
they have come and they answer: to take away the body of Christ.

    The DUTCH *play of the* WISE AND FOOLISH VIRGINS, *which*
survives only in a nineteenth-century transcript, contains indications
of movement at several points in the action:
Then they [*the Foolish Virgins*] go away from there, and the Wise
ones go to meet the bridegroom, and they make the curtain (scuift)
for Heaven open and sing Sanctus. Meanwhile Our Lord sits, and the
bride before Our Lord with the Joy of Contemplation, and two angels on each side swing censers.
. . .
Now he [*the bridegroom*] goes to Heaven and the Wise Virgins bow
to him, and when he is in the Heaven the bridegroom stands still
and the bride and the others all kneel and the angels swing the
censers until the Benedictus is over; then the angels stand up and
the Wise ones remain kneeling and sing Suscipe nos Domine.

Here he crowns Charity and puts a ring on her hand and then all the
rest, one after the other during the music (pause). When they are all
crowned, the bridegroom goes and sits down and the bride beside
him, then Te Deum laudamus and Sanctus are sung; and then they
all kneel but the bridegroom alone remains sitting.

When the Te Deum has been sung, the Wise ones go and sit on the
bench before the bridegroom, and music is played (men speelt pause)
after which Heaven is closed and Hell is opened.

    A *detailed scenario with movement and music is provided for*
the SIENA NATIVITY *play:*
On the feast of the Nativity of Christ, the shepherds shall be first
arranged with sheep and dogs and bagpipes and everything they need.
First an angel shall come during Mass (infra la messa) over the hut
(capannuccia) with a light in his hand at the time of the Gloria, and
he shall announce the Gloria in Excelsis Deo. The choir shall reply
and the angels shall stand behind the canvas of the scaffold (palco);
they shall reply. After Ite Missa Est has been said, an angel shall
appear and announce the feast. When he has announced the feast,
he shall go among the shepherds and remain in a hidden place until

Jesus is born. After the birth of Jesus, he shall come out and announce to the shepherds that which he has to announce. And immediately there shall be amidst the shepherds thunder (?uno scoppietto) and lightning, at the proper time. After the annunciation of the angel, the Virgin Mary with Joseph and a handmaid shall go to be registered (si vada a fare scrivere). And she shall come back and go onto the scaffold (palchetto). When she has reached the scaffold and everything is ready, two angels shall come and lift the canvas, and Jesus shall be born; and the angel shall appear to the shepherds. And immediately the angels shall be at the hut. They shall come out and sing in chorus; with great reverence they shall adore the Lord and, while the shepherds approach, they shall dance, and the angel who has announced to the shepherds shall depart from them and go to the hut with the others; and four stanzas of the Verbum Caro shall be sung while the child is swaddled. And when the child is swaddled the shepherds shall come to pray.

A succession of movements is specified for the Ascension in the FRANKFURT *Director's Roll:*
After this the Lord (dominica persona) is to go ahead of his disciples and coming to Paradise, having taken the banner, he is to take up the souls and make his way towards the place where he is to be ready (velit) to ascend. The souls, dressed in white clothing, are to follow the Lord (dominum) singing:

Summi triumphi re

until they come to the steps where they are to ascend. The throne, where the Majesty (Maiestas) is to sit, is to be there, very fine and high and sufficiently broad to be able easily to receive the souls, having steps by which they may easily climb to the top.

Here, as he ascends, the Lord shall sing:

Pacem meam do vobis

Then the Lord and all the souls with him:

Ascendo ad patrum meum

After which the choir (?persone) shall sing this verse:

Concedit iubilans

until they have ascended the throne. Now Jesus is to be crowned by angels, and he shall sing:

Pater manifestavi

The apostles on the ground (in terra) are to watch the Lord's ascension, and the angels are to say [?sing] to them:

> Viri Galilei, quid admiramini etc.
> You men of Galilee there. . . .

After this the Church is to begin to dispute with the Synagogue.

Many stage directions refer to walking. All too often they are as unspecific and uninformative as the following example from MONS:
Here the ten apostles in their working clothes (habits mecaniques) walk with Jesus.

Occasionally walking serves to fill in time before a character rejoins the main action, as in this example from MONS *which precedes Mary Magdalene's entrance into the house of Simon the Leper:*
At this time, Mary Magdalene should stroll (ghambier) about the playing area (parcq) until she has been given her cue (adverty).

More obviously walking is used to indicate a change of location, as in LUCERNE *at the end of the scene with the Samaritan woman where the Savior's words: "Stand up, you disciples, let us go to Jerusalem; there we shall have things to do" are followed by the stage direction:* They walk round in a circle (Sy gand im ring umb).

The above two purposes may be combined as in the following direction to the Virgin and Mary Salome from MONS:
Then they set out to go to their lodging (logis) and should walk about on the stage (pietier le hourt) until they are told.

Slightly differing purposes are apparent in the following examples also from MONS:
Here Jesus should be warned to leave his mother's house and walk about the playing area (parcq) so that Abias may meet him.
. . .
Note that Human Lineage should speak this couplet quite close to Paradise. And if by chance he is far off (loing) when he begins it, he must approach while speaking.

In the ANGLO-NORMAN ADAM, *the devil walks among the audience before he goes to tempt Eve:*
Then he shall go away from Adam, sad and downcast, and go to the

gates of Hell and talk with the other demons. After that he shall
move around among the people (discursum faciet per populum), then
he shall come to Paradise on Eve's side and speak to Eve with a
bland and smiling face, saying. . . .

A special kind of walking-about seems to be called for in the
CORNISH ORDINALIA *from a number of different characters by the
Latin word* pompare, *perhaps to 'strut' or 'parade':*
And King David shall perform (ludet), and he shall parade about
(pompabit).
. . .
Lucifer shall parade about if he pleases (pompabit . . . si placet).

Several plays make use of silent movement for the dead. At
MONS *and in the* ADMONT *Passion Play it occurs at the moment of
Christ's death on the cross.*
ADMONT:
The Lord dies and bows his head; as a sign of the earthquake the
shots are fired; the dead come out, just allow themselves to be seen
and go away again; the angels sing the Tenebre. [*Latin text fol-
lows.*]

MONS:
Then [*Jesus*] bows his head to the right. Note that there should be
great earthquakes and the veil of the Temple should break, the
stones split, and the dead rise and go hither and thither without
speaking.

In LUCERNE *at the Last Judgment:*
They arise at the bottom of the square on the stand out of the
grave into which the dead bodies have been put when they were
carried away, and they walk, divided between the two sides (zert-
heilt an beiden orten), up the square towards the Temple and the
stalls, allow people to see them as if they were appearing, do not
speak, and then go immediately back down through the grave out of
which they came.

*The difficulties inherent in organizing the movement of large
numbers of people is evident in the amount of information from*
LUCERNE, *recorded in both texts and elsewhere, which even the
experienced Cysat found it necessary to write down. This can be
illustrated from the David and Goliath episode. After Augustine's
introductory speech the text begins:*
This is the army that King Saul has:
Abner, the general (feldhouptman), Salmon, Eliab, all in armor
(harnast).
Herod's ensign (fendrich) and eight more men in armor.

Musicians (spillüt) and four footsoldiers (trabanten), two from King Saul's and two from Herod's stall.

Followed immediately but separately by:

The order for the procession (ußzug): musicians, trumpeters, drummers, pipers (pfyffer).

Abner, the captain, alone, in armor, and before him a shield-bearer.

Salmon, Eliab, both in armor ⎤   these four with round shields,
Josaphat and Naason, both in ⎬—— quivers (kochern) and cross-
    in armor ⎦   bows (flitschbögen)

Two footsoldiers of King Saul.

The ensign, alone, in armor.

Two footsoldiers of Herod.

Josue, Johel, Sampson, Samuel, all in armor with their shields and clubs (kolben).

Now the Jews, King Saul's people, in armor as an army make a circuit (thund ein umbzug) until they are once more in front of Saul's stall.

Then Goliath with his guards steps forward on the stand.

Even fuller details are given in Cysat's preliminary notes:

GOLIATH

1. Two trumpeters together. ⎤
2. One drummer ⎬— --together
   One piper (pfyffer) ⎦
3. Two archers with bows: Hiram and Hanan, Jamuel the runner between them.
4. Banner-bearer, is to be the standard-bearer of King Melchior.
5. Shield-bearer.
6. Two of Nebuchadnezzar's footsoldiers.
7. Goliath alone.
8. Two personal servants: Vago, Nebo.
9. Two archers with bows: Annas, Zophar.
10. Two of Nebuchadnezzar's footsoldiers.

THE ARMY OF THE JEWISH KING SAUL

1. Two trumpeters.
2. One piper and one drummer.
3. Three archers with bows.
4. Shield-bearer.
5. Sisera the chief commander alone.
6. Abner, Captain. ⎤
   Eliah, lieutenant ⎬— together
   Salmon, sergeant ⎦
7. Achab, Haman.
8. Two footsoldiers.
9. Banner-bearer alone.
10. Two footsoldiers
11. Barber-surgeon (Feldschärer) with a boy.
12. Two with partisans: Zambri, Lucillus.
13. Three archers with bows.

Small-part actors like the footsoldiers above were used to fill up the retinues of the major figures. The complexity of the movements required is evident from the following stage direction included by Cysat in the manuscript of the 1597 text 150 lines before the scene to which it refers:
Note on Herod's banquet. Have two footsoldiers go from the herald's stall (Proclamatoris höff) to Herod's, also the trumpeters and musicians. The Steward (trucksäß) and the four knights now leave Herod's stall and take up positions where previously Putiphar and Sother were—that is, at the very bottom of the square below the Synagogue—and they are joined by the following Jews: Raabod, Urias, Sedechias, Salathiel. The Marshall (Marschalk) stays in his stall. *The 1616 version after the list of four names adds:* the remainder are the guests at Herod's feast.

Whenever a crowd scene is required the same group of people is used:
FIRST DAY
When Mardochaeum is being honored, then all that are Jewish are to be there and step forward, young and old, in so far as not otherwise occupied. Likewise, when John the Baptist preaches, the crowd of Jews, young and old, shall approach and listen, in so far as not otherwise occupied.

SECOND DAY
When the Savior is brought before Pilate, likewise.
Again, when he is brought to Herod, likewise, on the departure again likewise.
Again, before the Condemnation again at Pilate's: his blood upon us, etc.
Again, in the leading out [*to Calvary*] to approach.
Again, in Whitsun to approach.

Processions within the action also call for careful planning. The crowd of Jews mentioned above brings up the rear of the organized procession to Calvary.
John goes with Mary towards the Savior, then comes first Barrabas in front with the murderers.
And Annas and Caiaphas.
Urias and Jechonias.
Pilate and Herod.
Then the Savior with the cross.
After him Mary with John and the women Magdalene, Martha, Veronica, M. Jacobi, M. Cleophas, M. Salome, etc.
After that the Jews with their procession (züg).

The following extract from the minutes of the first general meeting preceding the 1597 performance shows that Cysat appre-

ciated also the need to avoid unnecessary, distracting movement:
People are also to be warned that throughout the performance of the
play any participant, whether it be at a time he has anything to do
or not, in all his actions, apart from what his role, his lines, and the
play contain and require, in what he does as much as in what he
refrains from doing, is to behave and show himself seemly, quiet,
and decent, without any horseplay, foolish behavior, chattering, and
laughter, also without running around.

While most characters at LUCERNE *appeared in the opening
procession, a very small number were kept in reserve for special
entrances later:*
This is the order of the Three Kings' mounted entry (ynrytens).
Each has a specially constructed (besonder zuogerüstes) animal:

        A camel   -   Balthasar
        An elephant - Caspar
        A dromedary - Melchior

and on each animal a boy sitting, who carries in his hand the container in which is the offering and each container different, none
like another. King Balthasar, the Moorish king, and all his retinue
are to be black-skinned and dressed in white. The others accoutered
(zuogerüst) differently according to their taste.

The Entry
A trumpeter in front, on horseback.
Next a knight (rütter) bearing the banner, on horseback.
The beast, together with the boy on it.
A lackey (Lackey) on foot.
The king on horseback.
Two footsoldiers (Trabanten).

On Adam and Eve at LUCERNE, *see above, p. 130.*

Compare the BOURGES PARADE (monstre) *in Section D.*

*Occasionally the manuscripts find it necessary to note ex-
plicitly some individual movement of particular significance.*
PARIS RESURRECTION:
Here Mary Magdalene, searching thus through the garden where the
tomb was, saw the two angels who bowed down before Jesus, who
was coming from behind the Magdalene in the dress (en guise de) of
a gardener. As a result of which bowing, she looked behind to see
whom they were bowing to. Jesus, as the gardener, speaks to the
Magdalene.

LUCERNE: *Mount of Olives:*
The Savior goes right up to (zvollen zruor) the Mount of Olives,
prostrates himself in the shape of the cross, lies still for some time,
gets up onto his knees, and with upraised hands looks up into Heav-
en, saying. . . .

MONS: *Joseph's doubts about Mary:*
Here remind Mary to raise her belly (eslever son ventre) to show
that she is pregnant.

MONS: *Raising of Lazarus:*
A reminder here to hold their noses when they move the stone away
[*from Lazarus' tomb*].
. . .
Here they lay down the stone and each one holds his nose.

MONS: *Judgment of Christ:*
Then Pilate summons Jesus. Note here that Pilate enters his pre-
torium (pretoire) which is a square court (?parquet), and there is a
raised, much adorned chair (cayere) there and another, second chair
in which Pilate seats himself for the trials (les prochez) and inter-
rogations of Jesus, and he shall not seat himself on the raised chair
until he pronounces sentence of crucifixion on Jesus. Note here that
no one but Pilate shall enter the said court (parquet), and he shall
sit down in the second chair with Jesus alone in front of him whom
he has taken by the hand to place him there. And all the other
Jews remain outside.

The play of St. Martin at SEURRE *had specific instructions
for presenting the Mass on the stage:*
Here there should be an altar well dressed with everything necessary, at which St. Martin will come to sing Mass. Then he shall be
vested and it shall be neither more nor less than would be used for
an archbishop. He can say the whole Mass, but he will not conse-
crate. Then when it reaches the Elevation of the Body of God, to
chest height only, there must appear above his head a whirlwind of
fire cunningly made without touching his head and it shall stay there
a short time bright and shining, then go away and disappear by a
cunning device (par subtil moyen). And St. Martin who appears not
to have seen it will finish the rest of his Mass.

*Movement out of the playing area altogether is sometimes
indicated.*
MONS:
Then Noah's wife enters the ark first, then all the others follow--
that is to say, the men first, and then their wives and Noah last--
and those who have no more to say that day should go out through
the trap doors (secrez) in the ground.

LUCERNE:
They sit down together for a little time outside Paradise until
Jerome has finished speaking. They then both depart and are not to
be seen again.

. . .

Moses departs. Has nothing to do. Likewise all the grumblers, men
and women, young and old, together with the goldsmith, are not to
be seen again, and there remain only the people in the Temple.

11. DANCE

In biblical plays dances mostly occur in two broadly different contexts--those of spiritual joy and of worldly pleasure. At the Nativity they appear as a naive, innocent expression of joy.

In the HESSE NATIVITY *play Joseph invites his servant to rejoice with him:*
"Sellenfro [= *happy at heart*], my servant, sing with me and let us be glad, because the Savior is sent to earth to us."
. . .
And then the servant and Joseph dance round the cradle singing (corisant per currabulum cantando): In dulci jubilo.
Later in the play this dance is repeated with the Child Jesus (cum puero).

In the REVELLO *Passion the shepherds dance after hearing the news of Christ's birth:*
Having said this, Abiron [*a shepherd*] plays on his pipes. And the other shepherds dance in pairs. And Anania and his partner act as if (finga) they do not know how to dance like the others. [*Abiron rebukes them, seven lines.*] Then Abiron places himself at their head, dancing and playing and the other shepherds dancing.

From Spain come several examples of longer sequences of dancing which sometimes in themselves advance the action. At SEVILLE *in 1540, a contract was made between the Tanners' Guild and a certain Gonzalo Guerra, leader of a group of dancers:*
I undertake to provide at Corpus Christi this year a dance (una danza) composed of seven dancers: the Magi, a lady, and three pages. The seven dancers will come out of a tent (un pabellón), and the Magi will go up to Mary and the Child Jesus, who will be figures (que han de ir de bulto) at a crib (un portalico) together with St. Joseph, a mule and an ox and a drummer (un tamborino), and will offer gifts and worship. I shall present myself, with the dancers, at the time when the procession and banner of the said guild comes out of the Cathedral, and we shall accompany the procession, dancing (andaremos danzando) for as long as it lasts, for a fee of 8 golden ducats. Further, I undertake to give you a preview (el ensayo) of the dance at Whitsun.

There are detailed directions for movements, gestures, and the dance of the shepherds in the SUAREZ DE ROBLES NATIVITY *play which dates from the sixteenth century:*

173

The shepherds are to appear in two lines (en dos hileras repartidos) preceded by the person playing the psaltery (Psalterio) or little drum (Tamborino). To the sound of this instrument they are to advance dancing (yran dançando) to the middle of the church, and there they will dance a few figures (haran algunos laços). The shepherds are to be followed by the angels with candles and, if possible, by eight angels carrying the canopy of the Holy Sacrament under which are to walk Our Lady and St. Joseph, and they shall walk up to the steps of the high altar, where there is to be a cradle shaped like a manger (una cuna al modo de pesebre), and in it they shall place the Child Jesus. Then Our Lady and St. Joseph shall kneel, their hands in a pose of contemplation (puestas las manos como contemplando), and the angels shall take up their positions on each side, their faces turned towards each other and looking at the Child (los rostros bueltos unos a otros, y mirando hazia el Nino). Meanwhile, the shepherds shall finish their dance, and then an angel shall go into the pulpit and speak as follows. As the shepherds listen, they are to seem afraid as they look upwards and all around (mostraran espan- tarse mirando para arriba a una y otra parte).

ANGEL   "Do not be afraid,
                   Shepherds . . .
                   and because I hear
                   Angelic music,
                   I must delay no longer."

At this point the angel disappears. The angels grouped around the Nativity (Nacimiento) sing this song (villancico):

                   "Glory to God on high
                   We offer, as to the King of Heaven,
                   And on earth let there be peace
                   To man and all creatures,
                   A thousand hymns of praise we sing
                   To you, celestial King,
                   And we adore you. . . ."

At this point, the angels stop singing and, without moving from their positions (sin mudarse donde estan), the shepherds speak, beginning with Anton, the first:

ANTON   "I can hear music and sounds
                   Over there by the town . . . ."

Here they dance a figure (hazen un laço de dança) and dance to- wards the Nativity group, and before they stop they dance the same figure before it, after which the angels sing this song (villancico), and the shepherds reply:

ANGELS   "Sweet shepherds,

Where are you going, tell us?"

SHEPHERDS   "We come full of joy
              To seek God here. . . ."

After the song is over, keeping the same order as hitherto, the first
shepherd, Anton, says:

ANTON   "Illustrious company,
              Tell us what has caused you
              So to rejoice. . . ."

Now Anton is to dance forward and, after improvizing a dance
(desque ha hecho alguna mudança), is to kneel and say:

ANTON   "I adore you, my creator,
              Chief of all shepherds . . .
              Receive my gift. . . ."

Here he can offer a rattle (un sonagero) or some other thing. Then
the instrument is to be played, at which Anton will stand up and
dance, and at the same time Rebanado will come forward, and both
will dance to the music, Anton dancing back to his original position,
and Rebanado moving forward to the place where Anton was kneeling, and they shall stop at the same time. The others are to do the
same.

[*Shepherds adore Child and offer gifts. Joseph thanks them. Mary
offers to be advocate.*]

ANTON   "Let us sing in praise
              Of this boy
              And since he has
              Taken away our sins
              Let us dance a little
              Around this shelter (portal)."

REBANADO   "You begin, Anton,
              And we shall follow you;
              After we have finished
              We shall return to our flocks."

Now the shepherds sing the following song (villancico). Anton and
Rebanado begin, and then the others join in. After the verse has
been sung, the angels answer, singing "There in Bethlehem" (Aca en
Belen). Then the shepherds dance a figure (hazen un laço) and,
after they have done this, they sing a verse, the angels answer, and
they dance again, and so on until all the verses have been sung.
They are to sing to the tune of "At the gates of the King/ A flower
has been born" (A puertas del Rey nacio/ una flor).

Such lengthy or repeated dances are not usually found in the context of worldly pleasure.   In these dances there are often strong overtones of evil or cruelty.   Such is true of the dance of Human Kind and the Sins in the Noah part of the MONS play.

At LUCERNE *the dance performed by Herodias' daughter which leads up to the beheading of John the Baptist is indicated only briefly in text and stage directions:*

> Rea, the daughter:
> "My lord and father, if it is your will . . .
> I will perform a dance which I can do well."

> Herod to his daughter:
> "My daughter, you have my permission!
> If you can do something exotic (<u>frömbds</u>), then
> begin it. . . ."

Rea dances, and the musicians accompany her (<u>machend iro die spillüt zetantz</u>).

The fact that the 1616 manuscript here adds a scene with five devils makes the nature of the dance evident.

At the corresponding point in the MONS *text the information is almost as brief:*
Then she shall dance a morisco (<u>une mourisque</u>) accompanied by a drum (<u>tamburin</u>), then the drum shall be silent for a while and the girl continues to dance.

The dancing of the Jews round the crucified Christ in the second N. TOWN PASSION *is of a related kind.   It acts as a grim antithesis to the dance of joy round the cradle:*
Here they shall stop and dance briefly around the cross.

Dance can also be used as a complicated form of movement from place to place, as in the VIENNA EASTER PLAY:
The Jews dance to Caiaphas and sing.
. . .
The Jews dance to Pilate and sing in Hebrew (<u>Jodisch</u>).

12. MIME AND GESTURE

Pretended action is frequently called for in the plays. The following examples are selected to illustrate the variety of such action in a wide range of plays. Many of these, though calling for mime, do not specify how the mime is to be performed.

There are several examples in the CATALAN SAINTS' PLAYS:
Then the two [*St. Eudalt and St. Prancaci*] are to pretend to climb the mountain (fingesquen de muntar a la montanya). . . .
. . .
Then St. Christopher shall put the Child on his shoulders, take his staff, and pretend that (farà spares qui) the weight is too great. . . .
. . .
They shall take a hoe and pretend (feran spares de) to dig. . . .

Various scenes in the CHESTER *cycle also require mimed action. The Latin directions use the phrase* facere signum:
Then Moses shall make a sign (faciet signum) as though he were cutting the tablets [*of the Law*] from the mountain, and, writing on them, let him say to the people. . . .
. . .
Then he [*Herod*] shall make a sign as if he were dying. . . .
. . .
Then he [*Simeon*] shall rub the book as if deleting the word virgo, and afterwards he places the book on the altar. And the angel shall come and take the book, making a sign as if he were writing; and he shall shut the book and vanish.

A similar phrase is found in the English stage directions:
Then Noah, with all his family, shall make a sign as though they worked on the ship with various tools.
. . .
Here let Abraham take and bind his son Isaac on the altar, and let him make a sign as though he were going to cut off his head with the sword. Then let the angel come and take the sword by the point and prevent it from moving.

The LUCERNE *scene which combines the Presentation in the Temple with the Flight into Egypt calls also for simulated emotion:*
Then Simeon takes the Child on his arm and speaks towards Heaven, upwards to God. When Simeon says the Nunc dimittis, Joseph and Mary look at him as if they were amazed by his speech. . . . As Mary and Joseph go out of the Temple to their position, then the Synagogue sings. By the end of its song, Joseph is lying as if asleep

177

for Raphael to instruct him to flee to Egypt.

    In the MERCADÉ VENGEANCE *a complete battle is mimed:*
The soldiers of both sides come together and fight and strike down
some of the extras (ceulx qui pas ne doivent parler) on both sides.
Trumpets sound cheerfully within and without [*the city*] as long as
the battle lasts at the discretion of the leaders [*of the battle or of
the play*]. And the men must fight without wounding each other;
and they must let themselves be killed in pretence.

    *Many references to gesture are brief, and some are included
in passages which have been quoted to illustrate other staging matters. A single text which contains much information about the use of
gestures in a Church music drama context is the* CIVIDALE *planctus.
It is important for the frequency of its stage directions and also
for its detailed association of gesture and speech.*
Here begins the lament (planctus) of Mary and others on Good Friday.

Magdalene   Here let her turn to the men with arms out-
             stretched

             "O brothers,"

             Here to the women

             "and sisters,
             where is my hope?"

             Here let her strike her breast

             "Where is my consolation?"

             Here let her raise her hands

             "Where all salvation"

             Here, with head bowed, let her place herself
             (sternat) at Christ's feet

             "O my master?"

Mary the Virgin
             Here let her strike her hands [*together*]
(Maria maior)

             "O misery!
             Alas, misery!

So wherefore,"

Here let her indicate Christ with open hands

"dear son,
do you hang thus,
when you had life"

Here let her strike her breast

"before time was?"

John   Here with hands outstretched let him indicate
              Christ

"Celestial king
on account of evil men"

Here throwing himself forward (<u>projiciendo</u>)
let him indicate the people

"you absolve penalties
foreign to you,
lamb without sin."

Mary Jacobi   Let her indicate the cross with open hands

"Pure flesh, precious to the world,
why do you wither on the altar of the
                cross,"

Here let her strike her breast

"a sacrifice for sins?"

. . . [38 *lines of text omitted.*]

Magdalene   Here on bended knees before the cross

"O benign Father,
O glorious master,"

Here let her indicate herself

"do not abandon me:"

Here let her strike herself

"behold a sinner,
you who have saved me!"

Mary the Virgin   "O Mary"

    Here let her indicate Magdalene

      "Magdalene,"

    Here let her indicate Christ

      "sweet disciple of my son,"

    Here let her embrace Magdalene around the neck
with her two arms

      "complain with me, my sister,"

    Here embracing Magdalene let her turn in
another direction

      "complain passionately with me"

    Here let her indicate Christ

      "the death of my sweet son,"

    Here let her indicate Magdalene

      "and the death of your master,"

    Here let her indicate Christ

      "his death who"

    Here let her indicate Magdalene

      "so loved you,"

    Here let her indicate Magdalene

      "who all your sins"

    Here let her stretch out her hands downwards
(relaxat . . . deorsum)

      "has released (relaxavit) from you,"

    Here, embracing Magdalene as she did at first,
let her finish the verse:

      "most sweet Magdalene."

. . . [*14 lines of text omitted.*]

Mary Jacobi   Here indicating [*those*] all around, and with her
hands to her eyes afterwards, let her say:

> "Who is here who will not weep
> if he sees the mother of Christ"

Here let her strike herself

> "in so much sorrow?"

Mary the Virgin
    Here let her turn to the people with open hands

> "O all you who pass by the way"

Here let her put her hands to her eyes

> "weep with me,"

Here let her indicate Christ

> "and my sweet son
> equally bewail, and see"

Here let her strike herself

> "if there is like sorrow"

Here let her strike herself

> "to my sorrow"

Here let her strike herself

> "Alas, alas, wretched Mary!"

Mary Salome   Here turned to Mary the Virgin

> "Be consoled, lady,
> mother and queen.
> Why do you lose yourself (<u>deficis</u>) in grief,"

Here let her indicate Mary the Virgin

> "morning star?
> Your son raises"

Here let her stretch wide her hands

"the world from ruin."

Mary the Virgin
                    Here let her indicate Christ

                    "My most dear son,"

                    Here let her indicate herself

                        "my sweet love,
                        why do I now see you"

                    Here let her indicate the cross

                        "hanging on a cross;"

                    Here let her indicate the thieves

                        "placed between two thieves;"

                    Here the crown of thorns

                        "crowned with thorns;"

                    Here let her indicate his side

                        "your side, my Son,
                        pierced with a spear?"

                    Here let her strike herself

                        "Alas, alas, wretched Mary!"

John   Here let him indicate Christ

                        "Why do you offer upon the altar of the
                            cross
                        flesh which is devoid of sin,"

                    Here let him strike himself

                        "flesh knowing no guilt?"

Mary the Virgin
                    Here let her turn to the people and stay [thus]
                    until the words "Take the reward" and then. . . .

                        "O treacherous minds
                        and perfidious tongues!

> O suborned witnesses
> and false judges. . . .!"
> [*The very end of the text and directions is missing.*]

The opening rubric of the ANGLO-NORMAN ADAM *contains general instructions about manner of speaking as well as about gestures:*
. . . and let Adam be well instructed when to reply, lest in replying he is too quick or too slow. Not only he but all the characters (persone) should be instructed so that they speak appropriately and make gestures (gestum) fitting what they are saying. And in the verse let them neither add nor omit a syllable, but speak everything clearly and say what they have to say in the proper order. Whoever has named Paradise, let him look at it and indicate it with his hand.

Later directions in ADAM *also refer to gesture:*
Meanwhile let demons run about in the place (per plateas), making suitable gestures (gestum . . . competentem). And let them come near to Paradise, pointing out the forbidden fruit to Eve, as if persuading her that she should eat it.
. . .
When Adam and Eve shall come to the land they have cultivated (ad culturam suam) and have seen the thorns and thistles, struck with violent grief, they shall throw themselves on the ground, and remaining there shall beat their breasts and their thighs, showing their grief by gesture (gestu).

C. AFTERMATH

AFTER THE PLAY

Documentation of clearing-up after the performance is spo-
radic and diverse: the only exception to this is in the area of
finance. The majority of the non-financial references are to
dismantling or to storage.

Dismantling of the scaffolds for the SARAGOSSA *Nativity*
in 1487 took place almost at once:
I also made a payment on the second day of Christmas for dismantling the platform (tablado) on which their Majesties sat on
Christmas Night, for the Queen's people wanted to take it saying
that they were royal insignia (que eran insignias reales) to
dismantle and store the wood safely, 2s.
On the third day of Christmas to dismantle the scaffold (los
cadahalsos) of the shepherds' play (entremes) to make way for
the Feast of the Innocents, 5s.

At MONS *there was some discussion about whether to*
retain the stage because the Prince had expressed an interest in
seeing the play in a few weeks' time:
Therefore there was a discussion of what should be done in this
matter and also what should be done about the enclosure of the
auditorium (parcq). Agreed that all the enclosure should be
taken down while retaining the stage (hourt) complete and having it guarded by one man during the day and two at night and
covering over Hell, and that they should send to the Prince to
know his pleasure at his convenience (sans soy trop haster).

At TOLEDO, *Alonso del Campo, a chaplain of the Cathe-*
dral, was in charge of organizing the Corpus Christi plays from
1481 until 1499. The inventory of the contents of his house
made after his death in that year includes some of the props
kept there between performances:
Items of wood
    --a wooden mold (molde) for an angel.
Items of earthenware
    --a plaster mold for a woman's mask (cara de
       muger);
    belongs to the sacrarium (sagrario)
Masks (Rostros)
    --seven women's masks
    --four men's masks
    --four angels' masks
    --some wooden hands with their arms
    --an old lance.

Props stored in VALENCIA *for the* CORPUS CHRISTI *cele-brations were requested in 1413 by the King of Aragon for his coronation festivities:*

Then the honored Micer Johan Mercader, Governor of the King-dom of Valencia, came before the council and showed a letter of credence from the King [*Ferdinand I of Aragon*] and informed the council that the King begged and asked the said council to lend for his coronation festivities the masks, wings, and albs (testes, ales e camjs) of the angels, which the said city had for the feast of Corpus Christi.   And he said that he would offer to give all necessary assurances that he would have them re-turned to the city as soon as the above-mentioned celebrations were over.   Concerning this request, the council, after a vote, decided that the said masks, wings, albs, and other ornaments of the angels of the Corpus Christi procession should be lent to the King, and to the said Governor on his behalf.   It was agreed, however, that the said Governor should give assurances and should appoint a person of Valencia who would be able to guarantee the return to the city of the said items immediately after the coronation in the condition they were in when lent, without damage or hurt.   And on the same subject the said council asked the honored representatives chosen to attend the said celebrations that while they were in Saragossa they should immediately afterwards recover the said items and have them sent back quickly and securely.

The sets and stage properties for the play of Tobias at LINCOLN *in the 1560's were stored in various places around the town:*

First, Hell mouth with a lower jaw ⎤ stored at (lying at) Mr.
Item, a prison with a covering ⎬ Norton's house in the pos-
Item, Sarah's room ⎦ session of William Smart

Item, a great idol with a club ⎤
Item, a tomb with a covering
Item, the city of Jerusalem
    with towers and pinnacles ⎬ stored at (remanyng in)
Item, the city of Rages St. Swithun's Church
    with towers and pinnacles
Item, the city of Nineveh
Item, the King of Nineveh's palace
Item, old Tobias' house
Item, the Israelite's house and the
    neighbor's house ⎦

Item, the king's palace at Laches
Item, a firmament with a fiery cloud
    and a double cloud--
                in the custody of Thomas Fulbeck, alderman.

From England there are also numerous references to the
storage of pageant wagons used regularly in civic processions
and performances of biblical plays. While many were stored in
pageant houses specially built for the purpose, there are occasional references to storage elsewhere.
LINCOLN, 1539:
Also it is agreed in this Common Council that a large door shall
be made at the former school house so that the pageants may be
put inside; and every pageant to pay annually 4d, and Noah's
ship 12d.

CANTERBURY, 1523:
Item, paid to the Prioress of St. Sepulchre's for the standing of
the said pageant in her barn, 20d.

1530:
Item, paid for a pair of shoes given to Thomas Johnson of the
palace for the standing of St. Thomas' pageant there, 10d.

CHESTER, Coopers', 1572:
More paid to John Joanson for putting the carriage in his cellar,
18d.

YORK, 1377:
For a tenement in which three Corpus Christi pageants are
kept, by the year, 2s.

The text of a play also had to be stored as is implied in
this reference to the Coliseum Passion at ROME:
Item: a parchment book in which shall be recorded the Passion
of our Lord Jesus Christ and every other play performed by
our company, which book shall not be lent to any person nor
taken from our premises.

Both dismantling and storage may involve expenditure as
is shown by this entry from MONTFERRAND:
7 November 1477. Jehan Percheron, our treasurer (collecteur),
paid to Jehan Giollet and Jehan Coraill, carpenters . . . the
sum of 13s 4d T which we owe them for having dismantled the
scaffolds they had made.

Sometimes damaged items had to be made good; also at
MONTFERRAND:
Item: for having repaired (?adubé) a bench belonging to
Pierre Ailher which had been broken during the said Passion,
2s 6d.

Account entries have provided evidence in almost all the preceding sections of this book. They cover the most diverse aspects of a production.

SARAGOSSA *Nativity, 1487:*
The chapter ordered that Master Just be given as a gift for the supervision (?el magesterio de facer) of the whole Christmas play (toda la representacion de la natividat) 5 gold florins or 80s.

PARIS ENTRY, *1502:*
To Jean Marchand and Pierre Gringoire, composer (compositeur) and carpenter who have prepared (fait) and composed the play (mystère) given (fait) at the Châtelet of Paris for the Entry of the noble Legate, organized the characters (personnages), dressed and garbed them, as was appropriate for the play and also for having made the scaffolds (eschaffaults) necessary for it and provided the wood to do so, £100.

ABBÉVILLE, *1466:*
Waitier de Visme, bathhouse-keeper (estuveur) for those who played the devils in the Judgment on the stage (hourd) in the market, who went to clean and bathe themselves in the baths of the said Waitier.

From ROMANS *we have a series of entries recording the whole process of putting up and taking down the awning:*
Paid 27 April for eighteen pots (pos) of wine, total 6s, and for 3s given for bread and meat (chert) to those who erected three large wooden poles (piesses de boes) at the Cordeliers to support the awnings (tantes) and ropes. Paid the same day for having several ropes and millstones (?mofles) carried from Paradise as far as the Cordeliers to help erect the three wooden poles aforementioned, total 3d T.

18 May paid to the said Gregoire for a large, square piece of iron (gros fer carré) to set into the wall of the Church of St. Francis [*the church of the Cordeliers*] to fix the awning, weighing 3½ lbs., total 3s 6d.

Item, I have paid for taking down the awnings and ropes . . . 3 florins.
Plus the money paid to repair the walls of the Franciscans [*i.e. the Cordeliers*] both on the side of the meadow of the said Franciscans as on the side of Monsieur de Rocha and to replace the tiles of the said church . . . 30 florins 8s T.

Plus, I have paid to Guillaume Fores for the awnings for the play (tentes du jeu) which he supplied . . . 61 florins 8s T.

After the MONTFERRAND *production of 1477 proceedings were instituted to recover money due:*
14 February 1478.   To all those who will see or hear this present declaration. Jehan Loste, bachelor of civil and common law . . . councillor of our Lord the King and his governor of Montferrand . . . makes it known that . . . the consuls, having admitted owing to Jehan Talande 8s 4d for . . . a certain quantity of ironware (aiz) which they had from the said claimant to use on the scaffolds to play the Passion. *The consuls must pay the sum due, otherwise they may suffer* seizure, sale, and expropriation of their goods, *or* all other reasonable and proper ways and means *which may be used.*

In another judgment on 2 March 1478, the consuls admitted owing to Colas Riolet the sum of 8s 4d T in respect of a certain quantity of laths (late) *used for the scaffolds to play the Passion recently played at the Abbey* (Mostier).

After this same production danger money was asked for by those working in Hell:
Further, the said Mercier asks of the said consuls, both for himself and his servant, for having worked for the said Passion in Hell as long as the said Passion and Mystery lasted, and having put himself thereby in great danger to his person and of being killed by the culverins, in which he has given and worked much time and thought to have damaged his face and worked as much as the carpenters, the sum of £4T (paid 31s).

The risk of legal proceedings combined with the dangers of working in Hell resulted in the following ROYAL EXONERATION *by Charles V after a fatal accident in the Paris Passion of 1380:*
We, Charles . . . make it known to all present and future, that we have been notified on behalf of Guillaume Langlois that as, on the Tuesday after Easter last, at the plays (jeux) which were ordained and performed in the honor and remembrance of the Passion of our Lord Jesus Christ in our good city of Paris by some of the burghers (bourgeois) and other good people of the same, the said appellant (exposant) had been requested, begged, and ordained by those who in the said plays were performing the parts of the characters (faisoient les personnages des figures) of the adversaries and devils to be at the said plays to fire the cannons at the proper time so that their parts might be better performed, as it is the custom to do at the said plays each year in Paris . . . [*one Jehan Hemon joins Guillaume as assistant*] and they prepared and set in order these cannons

to fire and make a noise at the moment of ordering of the Crucifixion (sur l'appointement et arroy de cruxifiement) as it is
customary to do in the said plays in remembrance of the death
and Passion of our Lord Jesus Christ; and because in the place
where the said appellant and Jehan Hemon were standing, a hot
ramrod (broche) was put and thrust into a cannon that was in
that place, the wad (cheville) of this cannon flew out from the
explosion (par force de feu s'en issy et sailli) sooner and in a
different direction than the said appellant and Hemon had
thought or expected in such a way that the said Hemon was
accidentally struck by the said wad on one of his legs and injured and the said Guillaume also was burnt and scorched by
the explosion of fire and was at great risk and mischance of
being killed or seriously harmed. . . . [Jehan died of his injuries but had previously signed a declaration before witnesses
totally exonerating Guillaume, who, however, preferred also to
obtain the royal confirmation of this. The King exonerated him
from any charge of criminal negligence though leaving it open to
anyone to pursue him in a civil action.] Given in Paris in
April of the year of Grace 1380, and the 17th of our reign.

   A similar exoneration was granted by Charles VI following
a fatal accident during a rehearsal of "Theophilus" at AUNAY-
LES-BORDY on 19 June 1384:
We, Charles . . . make known to all those present and to come
that we have been notified by the kinsmen (amis charnelz) of
Fremin Severin, resident at Aunay near Livry, that as the
inhabitants of the said town of Aunay and the neighboring area
had undertaken on the Sunday after the Nativity of St. John
Baptist [24 June] to present a play (uns jeux) or commemoration
of the Miracle which Our Lady performed at the request of
Theophilus, in which play there was a role of someone who had
to fire a cannon; and it befell that on the Sunday before the
said Feast of St. John just past, the said inhabitants were in
the church of the said town of Aunay to rehearse their parts,
the said Fremin who had to take care of the said cannon had
filled the barrel (bouete) of the said cannon with paper only,
without any fire or wood being there, and at the moment when
he should let off the said cannon, this Fremin had said to the
people who were there "stand back, you run a great risk in
being so near." Nevertheless, the late Perrier le Roux by
chance stood in front of the said cannon when it was let off so
that in the letting off of the said cannon the paper which was in
the barrel (boite) of the said cannon struck him in the eye;
which late Perrier le Roux died the following Friday. . . .

   Occasionally the full final accounts survive, as the fol-

lowing extract from MONS *shows:*
Presented by these accountants with the account by the said
Bricquenaix from the Treasury for this year, to the honorable
eschevins and the Council. 4 April 1502, since Easter [*i.e.,
new style date*]. This is the account of all moneys whatsoever
involved in the Mystery of the Creation of the World, the Flood
and Nativity, the Passion and Resurrection of our Lord God,
performed in the said town in the month of July 1501 . . . as
follows. Firstly the amounts received from the moneys taken by
those empowered to take the money for the enclosure (parcque)
and galleries of the stage (galleries du hourt) of the said mystery. [*They are given separately for each of the eight days.
There were eight men involved working in pairs. The amounts
vary from £126 11s on the Thursday, 4th day, to £306 11s 6d
on the Sunday, 7th day. There are listed items of income from
sale of properties, wood, etc. Then the final total.*] Sum total
of income of this account: £1338 4s 4d. [*Then follow all the
expenses, with running totals every week or so from 1 February
1501 to 16 August 1501 ending with an indemnity to the account.*] For the care and trouble taken and had by the treasurer both for taking care of the stages (hourts), enclosure
(parque), and other accessories and things needful for the said
mystery of the Passion, and for having kept the accounts of the
income and expenditure of the moneys employed herein by the
said town and also for having been ready on each day [*of the
play*] both late and early and for a long period of time, is here
added, including his salary for the drawing up of these accounts in this matter and doing them out in duplicate, in which
he has had great toil, trouble, and diligence, together, the sum
of £28. . . . Total of expenditure £2281 18s 6d.

   Similar accounts survive from ROMANS *where a profit of
58 florins 5s 7d was made.*

   The complete accounts of the wache *and play of* WYMOND-
HAM *in Norfolk, which have survived for one year, 1538, give
an idea of one dramatic activity in a small town and its financing, though there are one or two items that may not refer to
the play:*
First, the amount of 6s 10d received as the arrears of the last
account, of Robert Kett and his fellows, as it appears in the
foot of the same account;
Also, the amount of 22s ½d received in money collected before
the play;
Also, of 8s 4d received from William Reynold for wheat and
manure (?midden) collected;
Also, of 9s received for 4 measures (combe) of malt collected;
Also, of 8s received for cheeses collected;

Also, of 9s received in money after the play;
Total sum of all receipts: £3 3s 2½d.
From which was paid:
Imprimis, paid 2s 6d for 8 pounds of serpentine powder [*fine gunpowder*];
Item, paid 21d for 3 pounds of <u>pyle</u> powder [*?another sort of gunpowder*];
Item, paid 7d for 500 saddlers' nails;
Item, paid 16d for half a ream of white paper;
Item, paid 2½d for 1 pound of glue;
Item, paid 3d for foil;
Item, paid 2d for bowstrings;
Item, paid 5d for packthread;
Item, paid 6d in expenses for a man and horse buying the said ware;
Item, paid 3d for bread and ale at the rehearsal of the play (?<u>recordyng the play</u>);
Item, paid 1d to John Mannyng for a piece of ash for laths (<u>splentur</u>);
Item, paid 2d to a man for splitting the same laths for the giant;
Item, paid 19d to Mr. Cusyng for canvas for the same giant;
Item, paid 2d to John Usher for cutting the clothing of the same giant;
Item, paid 2s 4d to Thomas Wennok for making the same giant;
Item, paid 3d for packthread and bowstring for the same;
Item, paid 4s for blue and red buckram for two vices' coats;
Item, paid 4s to the trumpeters for serving the watch and play;
Item, paid 4s 8d to the minstrels, entertainments (<u>revels</u>), and dancers;
Item, paid 10d for canvas for a coat-armor for John Amyas;
Item, paid 3s to William Kett for wood and sticks;
Item, paid 16d to William Kett for 16 pounds of tallow for the cresset light;
Item, paid 8d to the same William for pitch and resin for the same light;
Item, paid 6d to William Kedell for making the same light;
Item, paid 4d for half a bundle of gray paper;
Item, paid 8d for a pair of shoes given to William Garrard;
Item, paid 4d to Thomas Chylderhowse for a pair of devil's shoes;
Item, paid 1d for wire;
Item, paid 8d to William Garrard for digging turves and working in the . . . .
Item, paid 4d to Robert Ludborugh for working in the same place by. . . .
Item, paid 10d to John Newman for making the hearths in the same place;
Item, paid 2s 8d for the carriage of timber, clay, turves and for old pieces of timber;

Item, paid 16d to William Kett for old timber to lay over the
vault; Item, paid 9d to Thomas Bell for working in the same
place for two days;
Item, paid 6d to Mother Kett for baking two bushels of wheat
and brewing a measure of malt;
Item, paid 12s to Thomas Paker for supervising the properties
of the play;
Item, paid 16d to William Cowper for meat for the players;
Item, paid 18d to the same William for meat;
Item, paid 4d to Richard Howse for a horse for three days;
Item, paid 1d to a man for treading clay for molds;
Item, paid 2d to a man for gathering moss to clothe a wodewose;
Item, paid 5d for lath and nail for a window in the Town House;
Item, paid 3s 4d to John Skarndell in part payment of 7s 6½d.
Total sum of all expenses: 59s 2½d.
And so remains in the hands of Thomas Wyndam and William
Rowse: 4s 1d.

      The extant material from LUCERNE *includes summaries*
of expenditure in 1571, most extravagant of all the Lucerne
productions, and in 1583.   These and all the Lucerne accounts
are given in Gulden, Schilling, *and* Heller.   *12 h = 1 s;*
40 s = 1 g.   Batzen (b), = 3 s, occurs occasionally.
Points to note concerning the Easter Play.
From the earliest times until the most recent Easter Play the
City Council have taken it on themselves to bear the general
expenses and also to provide the evening meal (daß Nachtmal) on
both playing days for the performers (den gmeinen Spil ge-
sellen) and for those on duty on the square and at the entrances.
    But abuses and irregularities have occurred in more re-
cent times; this has since been improved and brought to an
end.
    In 1571 was spent:
First, the City Fathers, as is customary and usual, have had
the main spectator stands (die gemeinen Brüginen) and other
equipment (Rüstung) set up and the square got ready by their
work-people.

Then the specific items and pieces of of equipment:	g	s	h
Crosses, biers, Hell, golden calf, pillar, tomb for the Resurrection (urstende grab), brazen serpent, tablets of the Law, sun and moon, manna, well, water rock, Mount of Olives, stars, Judas' clothing	61	17	-

Item: the City Council had

bought 5 barrels of Alsatian wine for use during the play for the local people and visitors	222	32	-
Furthermore, for extra wine was spent a further	027	02	-
Item: expenses incurred entertaining visitors and for those who accompanied them as well as for the workpeople and the Councillors' servants	284	05	-
Item: for the food consumed in all the stalls on the square in addition to the wine mentioned already as being provided by the City Council, for the performers and for the visitors on both days	196	33	-
Item: the watch, who guarded the city on both days, were given their food and drink besides their pay-- this was	028	32	-
Item: for the performers (spil gsellschafft) both evening meals on both days as is usual; made	082	14	-
Item: there were 156 musicians (spillüt), local and visiting. They were recompensed with cloth and money	327	24	-

TOTAL	g1233	s4	h-

In 1583 was spent:	g	s	h
First, the stands and equipment as previously.			
Item: costs to the city (der gmein umbkosten) for specific pieces of equipment and other items were greater than previously; reason, that several items had to be made afresh, including 600 brass tokens for the evening entertainment, and for preparing the horns. All added up to	128	-	-
Item: the watch, for food and pay	039	30	-
Item: the expenses incurred entertaining visitors in the inns as well as in the rooms, at the Courthouse, and on the square, together with those accompanying them, and for wine. Added up to	404	-	-

The cost of entertaining was
   higher than previously, and this
   was for food and wine, for no
   wine had been bought as previously.
Item: the four leaders of the choir
   (praesidenten der Cantory) were
   paid an honorarium (vereert)   9   -   -
Item: the singers in the choir, plus
   the musicians, as well as the
   servants of the Councillors and the
   stage staff on the two days consumed   66   20   -
Item: to the master carpenter for his
   work-people for setting up the
   equipment, for doing whatever
   work needed doing on stage, for
   being on guard and being on call   31   32   -
Item: for the performers for both
   evening meals as customary   126   30   -
Item: the expenses for local and
   visiting musicians added up to   143   36   -

              TOTAL   g969 s36 h-

   The following extracts show the details of some of the
payments made by the LUCERNE *City Council after the 1583*
performance:
Paid for the powder for the smoke in   g   s   h
   the Mount of Olives and the eclipse
   to Master Niclaus Schyterberg,
   without the gunpowder   1   18   -
Paid to Master Peter Mattmann, the
   tiler, for the wires, rings, ropes,
   and equipment to operate the star
   and the Holy Ghost   1   33   -
Paid to Master Jost Biderman, the
   cooper, for cloth for the Mount of
   Olives and Hell's Mouth, also for
   nails and hair [*manuscript reading*
   uncertain] for them. Item: for a
   new thunder barrel in the attic of
   the Courthouse and for renovating
   the barrel of the old thunder barrel
   on the Butchers', also for the
   barrel for the well and the barrel
   for the water rock. Item: for hoops
   (reiffen) for the choir of the Temple and his payment for making all
   these things makes   15   20   -
Paid to Master Jost Biderman, who

played the part of Judas, for hair and purse (seckel) together with the strap (band) in which he hung which does not belong to the Brotherhood, 30 batzen; also for 7 ells of yellow London cloth for his coat (rock) at 20 batzen; cost of cutting and making up 17 s; makes altogether	13	7	-
Paid to Hans Pali the saddler for getting ready the bellows for the manna	1	2	-
Paid to Lienhart Etter the girdler for covering (bschlahen) the synagogue books, 16s, and to the cabinet maker (dismacher) for making them 1 g 20 s, without the parchment; makes	1	36	-
Paid to the said girdler for 600 brass tokens for the evening hospitality (gsellschafft leisten) for visitors and performers, for brass and for the making	3	14	-
Paid to the serving man (stuben knecht) at the Tailors' for what was consumed at the Savior's meal in the stall of Zacheus. Was done as a favor to master Jörg Schyterberg, in view of his age, it is not to be repeated in the future.	2	-	-
For the scepter of the Director's page in the play	-	27	-
Item: paid for four silver medallions (schowpfennig) presented by the City Council and the Brotherhood to the four gentlemen who got ready and organized the music and singing for and in the play: namely master organist and master schoolmaster from Baden and our own schoolmaster and organist, makes	9	-	-
Item: paid for expenses (zeerung) on the several occasions before the performance when the members of the Committee appointed by the City Council met to make arrangements	2	35	-
Item: wages and expenses for the messenger to go to Solothurn to fetch the four drums (Tromen)	3	36	-

Paid to master Anthoni Falenter,
   the cabinetmaker, for making the
   boxes for the manna   3   12   -
Paid to Caspar Thürmgen [*MS. un-*
   certain] the powder-maker, for
   12 lbs. of powder for the guns
   and the thunder, makes in total,
   as I have paid him on 27 April '83   3   -   -
Paid to Hansen Heckli, schoolboy
   (schuoler), who assisted the
   play by delivering messages
   (mit dem umbsagen) and the Jews'
   songs, for a coat, as alms   7   32   -
Item, paid to master Niclaus Gyssler,
   potter beside the Parish Church
   (im Hoff), for two candlesticks
   and the calf in the Easter Play.   1   10   -
Item: paid to Peter Knecht, merchant
   (kremer), for a barrel for the
   Pool of Siloam in the Easter Play.   -   27   -
Item: paid to master Hanss Heinrich
   Wegman for working as painter in
   the chapel [*from where the per-*
   formers set out in procession for
   each day's performance] on the
   actors' clothing and beards, also for
   a heaven with blue clouds for the
   manna, for everything   3   3   -
Item: paid to master Uoli Hardmeyer,
   the master carpenter, for the
   carpenters who worked during the
   Easter holidays from the feast day
   until the end of the play,
   erecting the equipment on the square
   and being present throughout the
   two days of the play, ready to
   carry out whatever work became
   necessary, and for guarding the
   square during the same period;
   made in total   31   32   -
Item: paid to master Ignatius
   Hürliman, the cabinet-maker, for
   various work he did in connection
   with the play. Namely: a hollow
   cross, like the Savior's cross,
   for use in the scene where he is
   led out to execution, and a small
   thin cross for use at rehearsal
   (im probieren zbruchen). Also
   a case for on top of the cross in

which the dove is to be at the Death.
Item: two horns for on Moses' hair,
and the tablets for the Ten
Commandments.
Item: two biers, one for John the Baptist,
the other for the remaining dead.
Item: a pulpit (Cantzel) was got ready
for use by the Doctors of the church
but not used, but was subsequently
sent to the Spitalkirche.
Item: a lid for Lazarus' grave, lifts
up (?erhept).
Item: the title on the cross.
Item: the pillar for the scourging.
Item: the equipment for the well
winding-gear.
Item: a wooden arch for above Herod's
chair.

Make altogether   g16   s37   h-

The final accounts at VALENCIENNES *show a profit of
more than £1000 T which was shared among those who had
financed the play as allowed for in the contract (see Section
A.1, above):*
Item: as all those who wanted to come and hear and see the said
Passion had to pay, great and small, the sum of 6 deniers for
each session, and those who wanted to be up on the scaffold
(hordement) made specially in this place (lieu) paid 12 deniers,
and the receipts for the whole 25 days were £4,680 14s 6d.
Item: when all was over there was a public sale of all the costumes and properties (utensilles) which had been used to perform the said Passion, which realized the sum of £728 12s 6d.
Item: the expense to be set against the above receipts amounted
for the scaffold (hourdement), costuming of the actors, and all
other properties used for the secrets and related matters (af-
faires pertinent) to the sum of £4,179 4s 9d   [MS. wrongly:
£4,079].
Item: the rest of the money, which amounted to the sum of
£1,230 2s 3d, was divided and shared out by the supervisors
among the originators and players, to one more and another less
according to whether they had major or minor roles.

*Sometimes towns made retrospective payments to groups of
actors for their performances. Where the performance had been
on a cart, the town paid an amount for each "carting" as at* ST.
OMER *in 1454:*
To Jehan Descamps, called Wastelet, and his companions, and to
the son of the lady (demiselle) Leurant d'Antoing and his com-

panions for the plays that they have done in the past (par le
temps passé) they have acted both before the scelle [House of
the Seal] and before the dwellings (hostels) of my lord Bailiff
and others in the town: to each of them 16s, making 32s and
henceforward for each "carting" (carée), 4s.

*The accounts for 1456 from the same town record that since the
beginning of 1455 there had been a series of these performances
by Descamps and his friends:*
For having made many entertainments and delights through
plays (jeux de personnages) on carts and wagons (cars et
carios) . . . for each carting which in this period has amounted
to 36 cartings (carées) . . . 4s. Making £7 4s.

*Town councils sometimes rewarded actors who had brought
credit to the town by winning prizes in local drama festivals.*
ST. OMER, *1462:*
To Jehan Descamps, called Wastellet, Jacques de le Steghele,
Bertelemieu Lartisien, Pierquin le Cordier, and others to the
number of 24, who, for the honor of this town, have traveled to
the town of Aire and maintained themselves there for five whole
days, ending on the 28th day of this present month, in order to
act there several plays (jeux de personnages), both moralities
and farces (soties), to win certain prizes which were being
given by those of the said town of Aire to the best actors, in
which those mentioned above have borne and acquitted themselves so well that they obtained the principal prize and two
others, over one of which there was some discussion (ilz sont
demourés en debat). For this and to help with their expenses
in this matter, is [given] by order of the Council (messeigneurs) on this last day of June 1462, £12.

LILLE, *1418:*
To Grard One-Eye was given by courtesy to him and some
companions, performers of entertainments with characters (es-
batements de personnaiges), in honor of their having performed
in an entertainment which was held at Douai where they gained
a silver lion for the second prize and to help towards their
expenses in taking part therein: £12. [*The exact nature of
this performance is not clear, but in 1432 a group went to
Béthune explicitly to perform a play (jeux de personnaiges).*]

*Those who took part in the LUCERNE performances were
rewarded both materially and spiritually. They were provided
with an evening meal at the City Council's expense on both
evenings after the performance, for which they were issued
tokens. A council minute of 1583 states:*
Tokens (Wortzeichen) are to be given to the people in the play.

These the city councillors at municipal expense will entertain to
the evening meal on both days on the proviso that they will pay
for nobody who does not have a token. [see also pp. 196, 198.]

*It seems that the performers were also granted Indulgence by
the Church, although the only relevant extant document is
Cysat's request for the Indulgence for the 1597 performance:*
This is a copy of the request made to the Reverend Father the
Prince Bishop of Veglia, Johann de la Turre, Papal Legate in
the [Swiss] Confederation, concerning the Indulgence for the
performers in the Easter Play and also the spectators, submitted
at the beginning of Lent, 1597. Some time ago Your Reverend
Grace was informed by the [Joint] Committee of the Brotherhood
of the Crown of Thorns of Our Lord and of the priests and
Council of this City of Lucerne that these gentlemen have the
custom of presenting at various intervals around Eastertime to
the people, who attend in great numbers not only from the city
itself but also from the countryside, also from other places
(Orten) and territories (Herrschaften) within and outside the
[Swiss] Confederation several days' journey distant, for the
whole of two successive days, in the form of a play (In spils
wys), with great devotion, at great expense and very decor-
ously, the outstanding mysteries and stories (Misteria und His-
torien) of the Old and New Testaments, including the scenes of
the Passion of Our Lord, and in order the Nativity, his Life,
Miracles, and his whole Passion, Resurrection, Ascension, and
Whitsuntide [these last two were additions in Cysat's 1597 re-
vision], all of which brings great consolation and edification not
only to Catholics but also to non-Catholics who attend in considerable numbers and esteem and value it very highly; the said
gentlemen humbly petition you that in order to arouse increased
fervor and devotion you will favor them with spiritual gifts and
Indulgence both for the performers and the spectators, it being
their opinion that in this matter the performers should be re-
garded rather more favorably than the spectators. However,
this and everything they wish to entrust to Your Reverend
Grace, having hereby reminded you of this matter and having
requested you to further it (die sach zefürdern). They wish
Your Grace every blessing from God, with a long life, etc.
Signed in the names of those indicated above (wie obstat).
Translated into Italian by Renward Cysat, Knight, Town Clerk
of Lucerne.

*The organizers of the Coliseum Passion in ROME provided
not only a meal for those involved in the play but also spiritual
nourishment for the audience afterwards:*
The officials and members of the company shall be obliged to
meet in S. Lucia at the time of the service (allo offitio): and
there shall devoutly dress themselves in their tabards (sac-

chi) . . . : and then they shall proceed with the Crucifix in procession to the Coliseum and go to the places appointed by the said producers: and they shall observe silence throughout the said Passion: at the end of which they shall return in procession to *S. Lucia.*

Item: the said Lord Guardians and the Chamberlain (Camerlengo) shall order a meal to be prepared in a convenient manner for all the musicians and the officials themselves and other persons who have helped during the play in any work necessary on the platform . . . observing the same [*procedure*] for the other plays. In the same Coliseum, when the said Passion is ended, two men wearing the tabards of our [*company*] and carrying torches shall guard a Crucifix at the place appointed and adorned with a pallium: so that the people (brigate) can go to the said Crucifix to pray and offer alms.

It was customary in France to sell off timber and properties after the performance. Among the items sold at MONS were cloths which had been used for the Creation:
From Guis le Josne for a sky (ciel) of painted cloth on which were some gold stars, sold on the Market Place (le Marchié) with other pieces from the said Mystery (Mistere) 1 April, 1502, 15s 7d.
From the same for other pieces of cloth looking like windows (à manière de verrières), 4s.
From the same for another piece of cloth painted to look like damask (damas), 9s.
From the same for another piece of cloth painted red, 8s.
From the same again for another piece of cloth having the sun and moon represented on it (deduit), 22s 2d.

There was a variety of clearing up to do after the MONS play:
To Pierart de Lattre, for four days he spent in putting the wood and other things belonging to the town in the barn of the Town Hall (Maison de la Paix) and also for having dismantled the feet of the benches (deffait les piés des bans) made for the said stage and playing area (Hourt et parcque), at 5s per day: 20s. [*Three other men are paid 4s a day to do the same (ottel)*].
To Billet and his nephew for half a day spent by them in unsewing (desquedre) some of the same cloths (toilles) returned to Collart Camus, paid 2s 6d.
To Collart Camus, cloth merchant, who had supplied the stage (Hourt) with 379½ ells of coarse cloth (toille de canevas), of which 108½ ells were returned to him, leaving 271 ells bought from him at the price of 3s 4d per ell, total £48 9d . . . and

for the reduced value (?<u>admenrissement</u>) of the said 108½ ells of
cloth returned to him, at the price of 6d per ell: 54s.

To Jehan Escarpeau, beadle (?<u>sergent</u>) in the town of Mons, for
his journey made on the orders of the honorable councillors
(<u>Messrs. Eschevins</u>) to the town of Amiens to take back and
return to the administration (<u>ceulx de la Loy</u>) of the said town
the paper books (<u>les quayers en papier</u>) of the said mystery of
the Passion which they had lent to this town of Mons, with the
special effects for the purpose (<u>les secres a ceste cause</u>), on
which journey he spent five full days, ending on the 24th day
of August, 1501, at a cost of 25s per day: £6 5s; and for a
bag (<u>pannetiere</u>) which he bought to put the papers in, 10s.
Total: £6 15s. [*The same man with two others also undertook
the guarding of the playing area* (<u>la garde dudit parcque</u>) *during the performance.*]

To Collart Doureau, cook in the same town . . . for his salary
for preparing the supper for the actors in the Passion, given
afterwards on the 13 July 1501 on the said stage (<u>Hourt</u>), was
paid, in addition to the £24 17s then given to the actors to
celebrate together (<u>pour eulx recreer ensemble</u>), herewith, 50s.

D. EYE-WITNESS ACCOUNTS AND EXTENDED DESCRIPTIONS

1. PHILIPPE DE MEZIERES,
PRESENTATION OF MARY IN THE TEMPLE (1372)

Philippe de Mézières' Office for the feast of the Pre-
sentation of Mary in the Temple was first celebrated in Avignon
on 21 November 1372. The surviving text of the drama asso-
ciated with that office was probably composed soon after;
whether an earlier version was performed in 1372 is not known.
The text as it survives is almost certainly not a description of
the performance in 1372 but an ideal version, composed for later
performance by de Mézières himself. The only account of a
later performance of the drama is a brief one contained in a
description of the celebration of the feast, again at Avignon, in
1385. For comparison, the relevant section of that description
is translated here at the end of the full version.
The primary manuscript containing the Presentation drama
also contains a letter recommending the celebration of the feast,
the Office and the Mass, and other liturgical material related to
the feast, as well as the 1385 account, and belonged to Philippe
de Mézières himself.

Certain people devoted to the mother of him who "giveth
wisdom to the wise and knowledge to them that have understanding," who "revealeth deep and hidden things and knoweth
what is in darkness," with whom the light is "revealing mysteries
which shall come to pass," from whom every best and perfect
gift comes down, are pleased to make known that on the twenty-
first day of November (in commemoration of that day on which
the mother of his eternal Word without sin, through earthly
parents according to their vow, was presented in the Temple of
the Lord so that she might for ever be near him whom to serve
is to rule) they have ordained a celebration with certain dramatic representations (representationibus) containing most devout speeches, new actions, and devices (signis); through
which they might make known to all those believing in Christ
that through this Presentation of a most humble virgin in the
Temple the whole universal foundation was laid; by which also
the mind stirred by the flesh as if through visible signs and
actions, according to the teaching of the apostle, shall be
enabled to come to a knowledge of the invisible and visible mysteries of God--as is clearly set forth in what follows:

And first, about the twenty-two people who shall put on the
performance (pro representatione fienda) and their names;

Secondly, about their costumes and various accessories (in-
dumentis ipsarum et ornamentis diversis);

207

Thirdly, how the place (locus) is to be laid out for the whole
performance (pro representationibus omnibus);

Fourthly, about making the procession and its order;

Fifthly, about putting on the performance (de representatione
fienda) and the Praises of Mary;

Sixthly, about the celebration of the Presentation of Mary, with
solemn Mass, and a short sermon.

First, there shall be a young and most beautiful girl (virgo),
about three or four years old, who shall represent Mary, and
with her, two other most beautiful girls of the same age.   Then
there shall be Joachim and Anna, and also two angels, Gabriel
and Raphael.   Then there shall be nine angels representing the
nine orders of angels. After that there shall be a most beautiful
woman, aged about twenty, who shall be called Ecclesia and who
shall represent the Church. Then there shall be a woman of
advanced age who shall be called Synagoga, and who shall represent the law of Moses and the Old Testament.   Also there
shall be two young men playing instruments. Then there shall
be the archangel Michael and Lucifer.   Finally there shall be a
bishop with a deacon and a subdeacon.

    Having given the names of the people who shall put on
the performance, it is necessary to speak of their costumes and
accessories. Mary shall wear a pure white tunic of sendal without any unnecessary decoration, with a narrow hem encircling
the lower edge of the tunic, visible on the outside of the tunic.
And the tunic shall be loose-fitting everywhere except the
sleeves which shall be tight; nor shall she wear a girdle over
the tunic.   Over that she shall have a cloak, also pure white,
of sendal or silk open in front the whole length of the body,
with a cord of gold embroidery for fastening the cloak over the
breast, in the manner of a bridal cloak. And around the neck
of the tunic and all along the opening of the cloak there shall
be put a narrow strip of gold embroidery; and encircling the
lower edge of the cloak there shall be a hem, visible on the
outside of the cloak.   Mary's head shall be bare and her hair
hanging loose behind over the shoulders.   She shall have,
however, on her head a golden circlet of silver gilt, the width
of the middle finger, with a halo of fine silver gilt, of a moder-
ate width, fixed to the circlet at the back of her head.   This
shall be the ornament for Mary's head.   She shall have no
rings, nor a girdle, nor anything else on her but of white or
gold, showing the innocence and virginity of Mary and the puri-
ty of her love.
    The two girls accompanying Mary: one shall be dressed
in green silk or sendal representing the humility of Mary, and

the other in the color blue or azure (celestino) representing
Mary's faith and hope, for according to the apostle, "Our
dwelling-place" (but even more so that of Mary) "is in heaven."
These two girls shall not wear cloaks as Mary does, but shall
have loose-fitting tunics with hems at the lower edge as is said
above. Nor shall they have girdles over their tunics. But on
their bare heads, they shall wear circlets of silver without the
halo, of the width previously mentioned, and hair let down loose
behind, as above for Mary.

Joachim, Mary's father, shall be dressed in the alb of a
priest, girt above like a priest with a stole around his neck and
coming down over the breast in the form of a cross, as a
priest, and over that an ancient but not torn cope. And he
shall have on his head a covering of fine material, fairly long
and, if it may be managed, decorated in some way, with which
he shall cover his head and neck. And the two ends of the
covering shall hang down the length of two hands-breadths and
a bit more over the shoulders on top of the cope to the right
and to the left. He shall have a long, full, and white beard
coming down over his breast, and shall hold in his hand, outside the cope, a smallish glass vessel full of red wine.

Anna shall be dressed in white linen, both body and
head, in the manner of an old honorable matron, and shall carry
in her hand a round loaf, pure white and reasonably large.

The two angels Gabriel and Raphael are to be dressed in
white amices, girt above with stoles around their necks and
crossing over the breast. On their heads they shall wear hats
close-fitting to the head above the ears, and around the head
at the top they shall have a triangular or rectangular shape,
not too broad, with two lappets behind as on the mitre of a
bishop. And these hats shall be of white sendal or silk or
paper or parchment with a border (frizello) around the hat,
painted in some way and covered with flowers painted on top of
the hats. And whoever wants to may put around the hats narrow fringes of silk of various colors. The two angels shall have
two wings of some kind, and shall carry in their right hands a
red rod of some sort.

The nine angels shall be dressed like Gabriel and Raphael
except that the three who shall represent the higher order of
angels (namely cherubim, etc.) shall have their hats, as described, painted red; the three of the second order of angels
shall have blue hats, or of azure color, and the three of the
third order of angels white hats. All nine shall have a lily on a
slender rod of a green color; and the lily of the first order
shall be gilded, and the lily of the second order of an azure
color, and the third of a silvery color.

Ecclesia shall be a very handsome young man about twenty
years old, without a beard and dressed completely in gold in
the costume of a deacon, with the most beautiful hair of a
woman extending over his shoulders. And on his head he shall

wear a gold crown with lilies and precious stones. Against his
breast shall be fixed with a cord a silver gilt chalice without
paten, which chalice shall signify the New Testament. And in
his left hand he shall carry a long cross, along the upright and
cross-piece of which shall be a red rod the width of the thumb,
and the cross shall be gilt throughout without any decoration.
In his right hand he shall carry a round apple, all gilt, signifying the universal rule of the Church.

Synagoga shall be dressed in the manner of an aged
woman in an ankle-length ancient tunic made of some cloth of a
plain color and a cloak black and torn. Her head shall be
dressed as an old woman's with some covering of a dark color,
and in front of her eyes and face a black veil through which,
however, she can see. In her left hand she shall carry a red
banner the black pole of which shall appear broken, the banner
leaning on her shoulder. On this red banner shall be written in
letters of gold S.P.Q.R., which are the arms of the Romans.
And in her right hand she shall carry two tablets of stone tilted
towards the earth, on which stone tablets shall be written letters like Hebrew letters signifying the law of Moses and the Old
Testament.

The two young men who play soft instruments shall be dressed
as angels except that they shall not wear stoles or wings, but good
hats of a green color.

Then there shall be the archangel Michael, who shall be
dressed in the finest armor from foot to head, and on his helmet or bascinet or barbute he shall have a gilded crown, sign
of a victorious soldier and sign of Christ triumphant. In his
right hand Michael shall carry a naked sword, shining and
raised towards heaven; and in his left hand he shall carry an
iron chain with which Lucifer, following behind Michael, is
bound around the neck.

Lucifer shall be costumed (ornetur) in such a way as
befits the same, most vile and abominable [personage], with
horns, teeth, and a hideous face. And with his right hand
Lucifer shall hold a crook or hook of iron carried over his
shoulder, and with his left hand he shall hold the chain, as if
he wished to rebel against Michael.

How the place (locus) is laid out for putting on the performance. In the church between the great west door and the
door of the canons' or brothers' choir, in the middle of the
church but somewhat nearer to the door of the choir than to the
west door so that it can the more clearly be seen from all parts
of the church, a construction of wood or a stage (stacio) is to
be erected, six feet in height. On top it shall be boarded in
the manner of a platform (solarii), and this platform shall reach
across the church--namely, from north to south, ten feet in
length, and from east to west the platform shall be eight feet in
length. And against the middle of the platform towards the

west door there shall be as many steps as are possible from the
paved floor of the church to the platform; and likewise there
shall be similar steps opposite the door of the choir for descending from the platform, so that any step is about three feet
in length and hence it takes up as little of the platform as can
be managed. And these steps are to be enclosed on both sides
with boards or planks so that no one can go up except in the
proper way for the performance.

On the platform in the space between the two flights of
steps, the way shall be level. But on the north side there
shall be a bench for sitting on, extending across the platform
from west to east. And this bench shall be long enough for
Joachim and Anna to be able to sit down at either end and Mary
in the middle, but so that Mary's seat is raised just enough   *why?*
that, with the three sitting down, the head of Mary sitting in
the middle shall be on a level with her father and mother. And
between the bench and the edge of the platform towards the
north a space is left for Gabriel and Raphael who shall stand
there behind Mary on their feet. On the south of the platform
beyond the way between the steps, there shall be two seats as
high as the aforesaid bench upon which Joachim and Anna shall
sit. One of these seats shall be placed to the east of the platform and the other to the west, on which Ecclesia and Synagoga
shall sit looking at Mary, so that anyone mounting the platform
by going up the steps can pass freely between Ecclesia and
Synagoga to the edge of the platform towards the south. At
the four corners of the platform there shall stand, at the
northern corners Gabriel and Raphael, and at the southern the
two young men playing instruments. The platform is protected
all round by a narrow board at a height above the platform of
two feet, in the manner of a railing, so that the said platform
may appear more fitting for a performance and so that those
who are on the platform may not easily fall off it. This platform, the bench, and the seats shall be covered with carpets.
Therefore let the structure or platform (edificium seu solarium)
be made of very strong planks and well joined together, lest
because of the pressure of people standing around it it should
somehow be able to collapse.

Furthermore, between the seats of the canons or brothers
and the high altar, to the north against a wall or pillar in a
prominent position shall be constructed another platform of large
timbers, but a small one, namely, in height seven or eight feet.
The platform shall be six feet square at the top, and all around
this square it shall be protected with a narrow board, one foot
above the platform. And the platform shall be covered with
carpets; and on the carpet almost in the middle of the platform
shall be placed a small stool covered with some fine silk cloth,
with a small silk cushion for Mary to rest upon (ad apodiandam)
while hearing Mass. And directly in the middle of the platform
shall be placed on the carpet a large silk cushion for Mary to

sit on; and the aforesaid stool immediately in front of Mary.

It shall be arranged for some place near the church, as
for instance the ground-floor room of some house adequate for
the purpose near the church, sufficient to hold all the people
getting ready or dressing for the performance--which place
could perhaps be the chapter-house of the brothers, but shut
off in front with curtains--in which our sweet Mary with her
company shall get ready and, prepared and arrayed as is de-
clared above, shall await the procession.

About making the procession and the ordering of it. The
bishop or archbishop who is to celebrate Mass, dressed in his
episcopal vestments and carrying his pastoral staff, a deacon
and sub-deacon with all the clergy preceding him, the priests
dressed in copes or other vestments from the high altar, shall
start the procession by singing in a loud voice Salve Regina and
the procession shall go by a direct way towards the place where
Mary is, singing all the time. And when the whole procession
shall have crossed the place or chapter house, immediately after
the bishop has passed, the curtains or door shall be opened.
And first one of the orders of angels with a white rod in his
right hand shall come out as if showing and clearing the way.
And this angel shall immediately follow the bishop at about two
paces from him, in such a way, however, that no person shall
interpose himself between the bishop and the angel. The angel,
following the bishop and keeping the same distance, shall clear
the way on the right hand and the left with his rod.
And the eight other angels shall follow the angel, walking
one behind the other according to his order and hierarchy,
the cherubim and seraphim coming last, each carrying in
his left hand the lily described above. Immediately after the
nine angels, Synagoga shall follow, head cast down and carrying
her banner and tablets of stone, as was stated above. And
after Synagoga, Ecclesia shall follow, beautiful, with her cross,
the chalice at her breast, and the golden apple in her right
hand. Immediately after Ecclesia, the two young musicians shall
follow, walking together and playing their instruments. After
the musicians shall follow the two young girls walking together.
And the one dressed in green shall carry in her right hand a
green candle, three-quarters of a pound [in weight], and the
other young girl a similar candle of an azure color.

Immediately after the two young girls, our sweet Mary
shall follow carrying in her right hand a candle similar in
weight but pure white, and in her left hand she shall carry a
pure white dove at her breast. And on the right side of Mary,
Gabriel shall walk with his red rod raised, and on the left side
of Mary in the same way Raphael walking reverently step by
step with Mary, not coming too near the person of Mary but
always looking at her. After Mary, Gabriel and Raphael,
Joachim and Anna shall walk together, looking continually at

Mary, and carrying the bread and wine, as is stated above.
And after them, Michael the Archangel shall come, in armor,
with his sword gleaming upright in his right hand and with his
left, with the chain a yard long, he shall drag Lucifer, roaring
and at times howling and as if going along unwillingly. As Mary
goes out from the chapter house or the place where she awaited
the procession, immediately one of the angels places himself
between the two musicians, and, going with the procession, he
shall begin in a loud voice a song in the style of a rondeau
about the blessed Virgin with the instruments accompanying,
and this in the vernacular to excite the people to devotion. And
all the angels with Ecclesia, Gabriel and Raphael, and the musicians shall reply. The clergy, who before were singing Salve
Regina, when they hear the angel singing, shall be quiet, and
all shall be quiet except the angels who shall sing the said
rondeau continually, one beginning and the others replying,
going processionally up to the platform constructed in the middle of the church.

And after Michael and Lucifer, the nobility and local dignitaries (persone autentice vulgares) shall walk, and afterwards
the people of both sexes. The procession shall go through the
cloister to the door which leads to the open space (plateam)
which is in front of the great west doors of the church. In
which place (platea) the procession shall form a circle going
round the place and returning to the great door of the church,
walking and singing as above as far as the aforesaid platform.
And it is to be observed that every member of the clergy going
in the procession shall carry a lighted candle in his hand. And
if the noblemen, local dignitaries, and the people wish to carry
candles in procession in honor of the new Light come from the
womb, afterwards illuminating the whole world, they shall without doubt be rewarded by that same Light. When Mary goes
out from the chapter house with her company, certain strong
young men shall be appointed who shall hold in their hands the
shafts of spears bound one to another with rope crosswise all
along the procession from the bishop to Lucifer inclusive, and
walking processionally in this double row so that Mary with her
costumed company going between the spears shall not be an-
noyed by the press of people and shall have a clear path in so
far as the men holding the spears in their hands shall walk
opposite each other outside the spears on the side of the people, holding back the people with the spears. Nor shall anyone
be allowed to go between the two rows of spears except Mary
and her company, apart from two, three, or four sergeants or
keepers of the peace (servientibus aut clientibus justicie) who
may be within the spears to ease the press of people, lest Mary
and her company become oppressed by the crowd.

When the procession enters the church, the bishop with
his clergy shall cross near the platform and go to the high altar, and there in his throne he shall wait with the clergy for

the performance on the platform, and afterwards for the making
of the Presentation of Mary to the bishop himself. And Mary
shall stand still with her company between the spears in front
of the platform which has been erected, between the platform
and the great west door of the church, with the angels singing
continually until the bishop can reach his throne and all the
people have entered the church. And note that the procession
must begin very early in the morning, about sunrise, because
the ceremony of the performance (misterium representationis) is
long and very devout, and at that time the days are short.

Of the performance and the Praises of Mary. The performance is thus: Gabriel and Raphael with Mary, Joachim, and
Anna, and with the two musicians playing and leading, shall go
quickly to the foot of the steps of the platform, with the other
angels, Ecclesia, Synagoga, Michael, and Lucifer standing fast
in their places and waiting. The ascent of the steps of the
platform is to be guarded carefully by the sergeants-at-arms
and retainers (servientes . . . armorum seu clientes) so that no
one may presume to go up except those so ordered for taking
part in the performance (ad representationem fiendam ordinati).
Then Gabriel first shall go up onto the platform, and with his
rod, turning himself to all sides (with a gesture not with a
word), he shall impose silence upon all with his rod. And
straightaway, Mary, alone without any help, shall go up onto
the platform by the steps, with a joyous expression. And if
she shall not be able to carry her candle in going up, Raphael
shall carry the candle. And Mary shall in going up carry her
dove in front of her breast, with the instruments playing. And
when Mary is on the platform, with her face raised to the high
altar, immediately Raphael shall go up, and together with Gabriel they shall place Mary in her seat, referred to above, towards
the northern end.
And then Gabriel and Raphael shall bow to Mary with
great reverence and shall go behind her, Gabriel standing at
the corner of the platform towards the east, always looking
towards Mary and with his rod held upright, and Raphael likewise in the other corner of the platform behind Mary, with rod
held upright. Mary shall hold the dove in her lap with both
hands, sometimes kissing it and placing it against her breast.
And Mary's candle shall be placed by Raphael on a candlestick
in front of Mary, and the two candles of the two young girls
shall be placed thus when they have come up on the platform,
on two candlesticks exactly like Mary's candlestick. Then the
two girls shall ascend together holding their candles, and shall
seat themselves at Mary's feet. And then the two musicians
shall go up and place themselves in the corners of the platform
toward the south side, one in each corner of the platform,
facing Mary and playing. Immediately after the musicians have
gone up, Joachim and Anna shall go up, and, with heads slight-

ly bowed as though reverencing Mary, they shall sit upon the
bench described above: Mary in the middle facing towards the
south, Joachim sitting on Mary's left towards the east, and Anna
on Mary's right towards the west.   And at once Synagoga first
and after her Ecclesia shall go up, and they shall sit upon the
stools previously indicated; namely Synagoga on the east side,
and Ecclesia on the west side, looking towards Mary and holding
in their hands, Synagoga banner and tablets, and Ecclesia cross
and apple, as is stated above.   And so the way shall remain
clear on the platform between the two flights of steps--the
ascent to the platform on the west, and the descent from it on
the east, between Mary, Joachim, and Anna all alike seated,
with Gabriel and Raphael standing behind at the corners of the
platform to the north, and Synagoga and Ecclesia, with the musicians standing behind in the corners of the platform on the
south side and playing.
      Now we come to the Praises of Mary.   At first, when si-
lence has been imposed by Gabriel and Raphael with their rods,
the first angel, who shall hold a white rod in his right hand
and his lily in his left hand, shall go up onto the platform with
rod held upright.   And when he comes before Mary, he shall lay
his rod on the carpet and bow deeply to Mary, and immediately
place himself between Synagoga and Ecclesia and the musicians
with his face raised up to Mary. With the instruments and all in
church falling silent, holding the lily upright in his left hand
and, with his right, indicating Mary, he shall begin in a loud
voice, as it were singing, to say:

> 'Who is she who rises up in the desert as a column
> of smoke from spices of myrrh and frankincense?   Is
> this the rod that shall arise from the root of Jesse?
> And the flower rises up from his root and the spirit
> of the Lord rests upon it; the spirit of wisdom and
> understanding, the spirit of knowledge and counsel,
> the spirit of piety and strength, and the spirit of
> the fear of the Lord.'

When this is said, the instruments shall play and the said angel
shall come before Mary and, bowing himself before her, shall
take up his rod and shall go down from the platform by the
steps on the eastern side.   And he shall stop between the steps
and the entry to the choir, where the strong young men shall
be holding the spears across in two rows, as is previously
stated, for receiving both the angels and Mary when they come
down from the platform and go through the choir to the high
altar to present Mary to the bishop.
      As the first angel comes down from the platform with the
instruments playing, the second angel shall go up onto the platform
by the western steps, and with his lily in his left hand he shall bow
deeply to Mary and position himself in the place where the angel

had been between Ecclesia and Synagoga and the musicians. And in
the same way, holding the lily upright in his left hand and extending
the right towards Mary, he shall say in a loud voice:

>'Behold our joy approaches!'

Then moving his hand from right to left and bringing it back to
Mary, he shall say:

>'Consider and behold a beautiful virgin, pleasing to
>God, shining in purity, delighting the angels, per-
>severing in honor, and adorning the world! Day of
>unbounded joy and great exultation for all crea-
>tures! For behold the ark of the Lord, vessel of
>divine wisdom, and preservation of shipwrecked
>human nature, who today is presented in the tem-
>ple, is dedicated to God, and is for ever bound to
>the honoring of almighty God.'

When this has been said, the instruments shall play and the
angel shall bow before Mary and go down with the first angel
and stand waiting in his place. The third angel shall say in
the place as above:

>'The virgin goes up into the temple and angels
>descend to her. She is called 'handmaid' and shall
>be 'lady.' She is said to be humble, and she shall
>humble God. She shall vow virginity, and shall
>conceive God. You are a virgin, the model of vir-
>gins; a woman, the grace of women; a lady, the
>pattern of ladies. You are blessed because through
>you virgins shall be honored, women shall be
>blessed, and all saints through you shall be re-
>warded.'

The fourth angel shall say:

>'Behold virginity, behold humility, behold gracious-
>ness, behold purity, behold innocence, behold per-
>fect love in whom unbounded goodness shall dwell,
>and behold her who shall become wife, mother, and
>temple of God!'

And it is to be noted that all the angels shall speak and sing
their verses or songs in the same place; and in going up onto
the platform, in standing, in singing, in bowing before Mary, in
going down from the platform, and in waiting between the eastern steps of the platform and the entrance to the choir, they
shall follow the procedure which is set out above regarding the
first two angels. The fifth angel shall sing these words (can-

tabit dicens):

> 'O great foundation upon which human frailty shall
> be borne up, upon which universal faith shall be
> built, from which perfect virginity begins, and in
> which unbounded goodness shall be brought to per-
> fection! From you, through you, and in you, the
> supreme godhead shall be praised.'

The sixth angel shall sing and say:

> 'O lady, wonderful in the sight of men, in the
> sight of angels, and in the presence of God! Who
> shall praise you worthily, who shall call upon you
> worthily, since in the world you are without parallel
> and in nature without blemish and in heaven you
> will be with unbounded honor?'

The seventh angel shall sing and say:

> 'Hail, our lady; hail, restoration of human nature;
> hail, mediator of divine justice and one in whom the
> mercy of God is shown; because you will be mother
> and virgin, God and man, faith and a human heart.
> Truly wonderful the ascent of a girl ascending; but
> more wonderful the wisdom of a girl working; but
> most wonderful the bending down of God de-
> scending, she will be joy to the holy Fathers and to
> all who love God because with her we shall always
> rejoice with God for ever and ever.'

The eighth angel shall say or sing:

> 'Hail, Mary, full of grace, the Lord is with you,
> and more with you than in heaven. In you he shall
> dwell, taking on flesh from you; with you he shall
> be and with all who are with you, who love you,
> who honor you. The Creator will be with you, O
> creature; the master, O handmaid; the husband, O
> wonderful wife! We bless you, we praise you, we
> worship you for ever and ever!'

The ninth angel from the cherubim shall sing these words:

> 'O inestimable affection! O vast tenderness! O
> infinite love!'

With his hand indicating himself, then with his hand indicating
Mary, he shall say:

>'Behold her to whom shall be given the price of
>human redemption, the gift of endless honor, and
>the reward of supreme perfection. This is the
>virgin, humble mother of the Son of God, who shall
>be overshadowed by the Holy Spirit. She shall be
>called handmaid chosen above all others and shall be
>rewarded forever with God the Father.'

Then, with the instruments playing and the nine angels waiting
on the ground between the platform and the entrance to the
choir in the order according to which they walked in the procession, Anna, the mother of Mary, shall rise and, standing on
her feet in her place, with the instruments silent, she shall
raise both her hands to heaven with the bread in her left; and
with the husky voice (voce grossa) of a woman, a widow and
advanced in age, she shall say:

>'Listen, sons of Israel, rejoicing with me, because I
>shall tell the wonders of God. One barren is made
>a mother'

--indicating herself with her hand--

>'and has brought forth rejoicing in Israel. Behold,
>I shall be able to offer gifts to the Lord, and my
>enemies shall not be able to prevent me. The Lord
>God of hosts has remembered his Word and has
>visited his people with his holy visitation.'

When she has said this and kissed Mary, she shall sit in her
place as before, and for a short while the instruments shall be
played. Then Joachim shall rise to his feet, standing in his
place, and likewise he shall raise his hands to heaven with the
wine in his left. And turning himself to right and to left,
beckoning with his hands, he shall say in a husky voice:

>'Rejoice, all women, because your reproach shall be
>wiped away; and you, all men, because God is born
>man from her!'

--indicating Mary with his hand, then turning to the angels--

>'and you, all angels, because your places shall be
>restored!'

Then he shall turn himself in every direction and shall say:

>'And you, all creatures, because you shall be
>honored through her.'

And with hands raised to heaven, kneeling with his face to the south as when he was seated, he shall end, saying:

> 'Let us all therefore rejoice and be glad and praise the Father and the Son and the Spirit.'

And then he shall rise and, having kissed Mary, shall sit in his place as before. And the instruments shall be played for a short while.

Then Ecclesia shall rise from her stool, and, standing on her feet looking at Mary, she shall sing in a loud voice these words (dicens):

> 'Let the heavens rejoice and the earth be glad! Behold our redemption approaches; behold the gathering of the sons of God approaches.'

And indicating herself with her right hand, in which she holds the golden apple, she shall say:

> 'Behold the new mother, full of the fruitfulness not of the Law, but of Grace; not of fear, but of love; not of bondage, but of freedom. For behold this virgin,'

--pointing at Mary--

> 'who shall conceive and bear a son, who shall save his people from their sins. Glory be to the Father and to the Son and to the Holy Spirit; as it was in the beginning, is now and always, and forever and ever.'

And all the angels shall reply: Amen. And Ecclesia shall remain in her place sitting on her stool, as before. And after some music, Synagoga shall rise to her feet, standing in her place with her face inclined to the left. As if sorrowful, she shall turn to all sides and shall sing, as if weeping, these words:

> 'Who shall give a spring of tears to my eyes so that I may bewail my wretched desolation? Behold her'

--indicating Mary--

> 'through whom this truth shall be brought to pass: When the holy of holies comes, your anointing shall cease.'

And then immediately Gabriel and Raphael shall come and, as if
in anger, drive off Synagoga from the platform by the western
steps. And then Synagoga going down shall throw away banner
and tablets to right and to left in the temple off the platform;
and thus she shall flee out of the church, upright, weeping and
complaining; and she shall not appear again. And Gabriel and
Raphael shall not go down from the platform but shall return to
their places. And the instruments shall play for a short while
and until the people have quietened their laughter at the expulsion of Synagoga.

To the sound of the instruments, Michael shall go up onto
the platform and shall lead Lucifer with him, as if advancing
unwillingly and howling. And after Michael's bow to Mary, he
shall place himself where the angels sing their songs. And
Lucifer shall be near Michael, but when he shall cross in front
of Mary he shall pretend to be (finget se) fearful and trembling
and shall let himself fall on his face. And Michael shall drag
him as if by force to the place aforesaid, namely where the
angels have spoken their verses. Then Michael, with his face
towards Mary, holding his shining sword aloft and holding in
his left hand the chain of the kneeling Lucifer, shall say in a
loud voice:

> 'Hail, lady most high, whom the heavens, earth,
> sea, the abyss, and all creatures obey! Command
> and I shall obey you!'

And with the point of his sword indicating Lucifer, he shall
say:

> 'Behold the rebel against God, the scandal of an-
> gels, the enemy of human nature! You, indeed,
> have received from God the power of treading
> underfoot, of overcoming and tormenting him on
> behalf of God Almighty. He is placed under your
> sentence, is given over to your will, and is bound
> under your feet.'

And then Michael shall place Lucifer bound thus and howling
under Mary's feet, and she shall beat with her feet upon him
and drive him away from her. And at once he shall be pushed
from the platform by Michael, Gabriel, and Raphael down the
western steps to the ground; and he shall not appear again in
the celebration (in festo). And the instruments shall play and
Michael shall place himself where Synagoga was, looking always
at Mary.

After a short time, Ecclesia shall rise from her place and
shall bow before Mary and shall go down from the platform,
standing in her place with the angels. And after Ecclesia, the
two musicians shall go down playing their instruments; and

immediately after them, the two young girls shall go down carrying their candles in their hands. And Mary with her candle
in her hand, immediately after them, between but a little in
front of Gabriel and Raphael, without a gap, shall go down from
the platform in the company of the angels, in their order as
previously stated. And immediately after, Joachim and Anna
shall go down. And lastly Michael, as if directing the procession, going through the choir to the high altar where the bishop
is waiting dressed in a chasuble for celebrating Mass with his
deacon and sub-deacon, one on the right the other on the left,
standing upright against the altar facing Mary as she approaches. When Michael has come down from the platform with Mary
and her company between the two rows of spears, she will be
ready to walk towards the altar. At once two of the angels
shall begin with a loud voice: Veni Creator spiritus, and all
the angels shall reply: Mentes tuorum visita, the whole verse.
And when the verse is finished, the two angels shall begin
again: Qui paraclitus etc., and the others shall reply as before. And going at a slow pace to the altar, the whole hymn
shall be completed. When Mary finds herself before the altar,
the angels shall divide in front of the altar to the right and to
the left of Mary, Mary remaining on the step of the altar in
front of the bishop between Joachim and Anna, with Gabriel and
Raphael remaining in the middle behind Mary with their rods, as
if guarding Mary, and the two young girls to right and left.
Joachim and Anna shall stand upright; Ecclesia shall place herself at the right corner of the altar facing Mary or the people,
and Michael shall do the same at the left corner of the altar.
When the hymn is finished, the two singing angels shall begin:
Emitte Spiritum tuum et creabuntur, and the others shall reply:
Et renovabis faciem terre. Then the bishop shall say in a loud
voice: Deus qui corda. And after Veni Creator is begun, the
instruments shall play no more. One thing is to be observed:
that when Mary with her company has come before the altar and
the angels divide, as has been said, those strong young men
who shall carry the spears in a double line shall make one large
rectangle with their spears in front of the altar, in which rectangle Mary and her company shall be safe from being crushed.
Nor shall the sergeants-at-arms permit any persons to enter
unless they are of the company of Mary, in order, that is, that
the ceremony (misterium) of the Presentation of Mary can be
seen by all without obstruction.

Now to the Presentation of the blessed Mary in the Temple. It should be observed that all the things shown above in
gestures, words, actions, and representations (signis, dictis,
factis, et representationibus) clearly enough describe Mary's
ascent of the steps and her Presentation. And how important
this is appears in her Praises and the often repeated songs--and
the universal and joyous foundation of our redemption and

restoration. Now to the Presentation of Mary: this Presentation
is celebrated this day in the Church of God not undeservedly
by the faithful in angelic rejoicing and the jubilation of those
devoted to the mother of God.   Anna standing upright, with the
bread raised in her left hand and with her right holding Mary's
left arm, shall say in a loud voice:

> 'Receive, O Lord, our fruit ordained by you from
> eternity; blessed by you, made known by your
> angel, wondrously conceived, gloriously born,
> guided by you, and by you chosen as your
> dwelling-place.'

Then Joachim, standing upright, his right hand with the wine
raised and with his left holding Mary's right arm raised with the
candle, shall also say in a loud voice:

> 'Blessed be the Lord God of Israel because he has
> given us offspring (visitavit nos in prole) and has
> prepared redemption for his people.   Receive, O
> Lord, our vow, the fruit of our barrenness, be-
> cause you have comforted our old age, you who
> command the safety of Jacob.   Come quickly and
> descend on her, that your prophets may be found
> faithful and the human race be released through her
> from its Babylonian bondage.'

When this is said, Joachim and Anna shall pray for a short time
with their heads bowed to the ground, Mary remaining on her
feet.   And quickly they shall rise and lead Mary holding her
candle and her dove in front of the bishop and, kneeling, they
shall present her to him.   Then the bishop shall say in a loud
voice, in the person of God the Father:

> 'Come, my friend, come, my dove, because there is
> no blemish on you.   Come from Libanus, chosen from
> eternity, so that I may receive you as the chosen
> bride of my beloved Son.'

And then the bishop shall receive her in his arms, turning to
right and left, and shall make her kiss the altar, and shall put
her down on the ground.   Joachim and Anna shall offer on the
altar the bread and wine, kissing the altar, leaving Mary in
front of the altar with the two young girls, who shall also kiss
the altar, and shall go down to the angels.
      Then Gabriel and Raphael shall lead Mary between them
onto the platform set up between the altar and the seats of the
choir on the north side, as stated above.   And the two young
girls shall go up also onto the platform with Mary; on which
little platform no one shall stay except Mary and the two young

girls, with Gabriel and Raphael behind Mary, remaining standing, with their rods upright as if guarding Mary. In front of
Mary's little stool, on which she shall rest herself while hearing
Mass, there shall be three candlesticks in which the candles of
Mary and the young girls shall be placed. And on the stool
shall be a beautiful little book, the pages of which Mary shall
turn as if saying her hours, and at the time when she shall be
sitting on the large cushion and the young girls near her on
the carpet. At the Gospel, Mary and the young girls shall rise
and hold their candles in their hands; and Mary shall bear
herself in a grown-up way and devoutly at the Mass, Gabriel
and Raphael instructing her. When the Mass has begun Mary
shall let her dove fly away. And let it be noted that when
Mary is on this small platform, Joachim, Anna, Ecclesia,
Michael, the nine angels, with the musicians playing, each in
his position: the angels first, with Ecclesia, the musicians,
Joachim and Anna, and Michael walking behind, bowing their
heads in front of the bishop and the altar, and afterwards
deeply before Mary, shall process out with the instruments
playing, and they shall go to the place where they got ready
and shall leave their costumes and accessories (vestimenta sua
et ornamenta), all which accessories shall be carefully looked
after for performance in a future year.
    When the aforesaid have retired from in front of the bish-
op and Mary, the bishop shall begin: Confiteor, and the cantors of the choir shall begin: Gaudeamus, the Office of the
Presentation, Mary remaining on the platform until the end of
the Mass, facing south, and the young girls and the two angels
shall look almost continually at Mary. And if it shall seem that
a short sermon about the feast day (de solempnitate) can be
given during the Mass, and that time allows, let it be done.
But because the ceremonies (misteria) were long and devout, it
shall be left to the judgment of those in charge, on condition,
however, that either during the Mass or after the meal so solemn a ceremony of the Queen of Heaven shall not be lacking
entirely in a sermon or homily. When the Mass is finished,
Mary with her angels and young girls shall go down from the
platform, and, kissing the altar, she shall offer her candle, and
the young girls also. And immediately the musicians who withdrew shall approach, and with them preceding and playing,
Mary, between Gabriel and Raphael, the young girls falling
back, accompanied by a great crowd of noble ladies, especially
of girls and boys of every kind, shall be carried to the house
where she will eat by some man of high stature; or else riding
on a horse, and the angels also upon two horses with Mary
between, making a short progress through the city if the
weather is fine. At the meal Mary shall be placed in her costume in a higher place on a royal throne, accompanied by as
many young girls as possible at the table, Gabriel and Raphael
serving attentively, punctiliously, and with profound reverence

until the end of the meal.

And may he who is able to serve the sweetest Virgin Mary
more fervently and ardently, and is able to repeat and make
known through performance (recensendo) her most worthy
praises, [may he] reach out to me, I pray, a helping hand
because truly he shall not be deprived of his reward. And let
it be noted that the songs above-written for the Praises of the
Virgin, which shall be sung or spoken in a loud voice by the
angels and the other people above mentioned, are most religious
and are, chiefly for the faithful who understand Latin, sure to
move them to tears because of their devotion. But because the
common people do not understand Latin, if it shall seem expedi-
ent, and our most sweet Mary inspires the hearts of her faithful through grace, these often-mentioned songs may be translated into the vernacular, and they may be delivered in the
same way in the vernacular. Doing or not doing this, I leave
to the faithful piously reading the present play (representationem) of the spotless Virgin.

This ceremony of the Presentation of the Blessed Virgin
Mary in the Temple, newly shining from East to West, the Blessed Virgin has wished to have so celebrated in the said parts as
it has been celebrated in Italy and afterwards in the Roman
Curia. Through whom and of how much power and devotion is
this ceremony shall appear more clearly to the reader in the
letter about the Presentation of Mary in the Temple and its
novelty in Western parts, which letter must be placed at the
beginning of the Office of the Presentation. Wherefore I humbly
pray the faithful follower of Mary reading this letter, office,
and present play (representationem) that in such a new devotion
of the Virgin he may see fit to intercede for my wretched soul
with the Empress of the Empyrean Heaven and anchor of my
hope. Amen.

An account of the performance in 1385:

. . .At the solemn Mass in praise of the Virgin and through the
devotion of her faithful followers, a certain play (representacio)
was performed by fifteen young girls of three or four years of
age, the best-looking of whom represented Mary accompanied by
the said young girls. And thus diversely costumed in a devout
procession in which Joachim and Anna were represented (figu-
ratis), and with angels preceding and following the Virgin, she
was led with instruments of music to the altar. And there she
quickly climbed the fifteen wooden steps leading to the altar and
was presented in figure (figuraliter) by her parents and devoutly received by the high priest of the law of the Old Testament, dressed in the costume of the high priests of the Jews.

When she had been presented at the altar with praises and
psalms, delivered in a loud voice by the angels, Joachim and

Anna and Mary herself, she was led into the midst of the choir
and cardinals onto a higher place (loco eminenciori), as has
been mentioned, with her company, and there she waited until
the end of the celebration of the Mass. . . .

There are clearly marked differences between the 1385 and
the earlier versions and, while it is true that the later account
is very much briefer and that it is not intended as a script,
these differences do seem to indicate changes made in the performance. The main differences are in the costume of the officiating priest and in the existence of the fifteen steps in 1385.
It is worth remembering that considerable stress is laid on the
fifteen steps in de Mézières' letter which is prefixed to the
text of the Office, yet there is no mention of them in his full
text of the "Presentation" drama.

2. BARKING ABBEY:
EASTER CELEBRATION (LATE FOURTEENTH CENTURY)

*The Easter celebrations from Barking Abbey in Essex are
translated here as an example of a late and elaborate development
of the earliest of Church dramas. The first section describes the
Good Friday ceremony, the Burial of Christ, and the second the
Easter ceremony of the Harrowing of Hell and the Resurrection.*

*Barking Abbey was the largest and wealthiest of the English
nunneries. The ceremonies described here are attributed to the influence of Lady Katherine de Sutton who was abbess between 1363
and 1376, though the manuscript in which they appear is fifteenth-
century.*

*The parish church at Barking was closely connected with the
nunnery and there is no reason to suppose that the phrase populorum
concursus (translated here as "congregation of the people") refers
only to the nuns. The church of the nunnery was totally destroyed
in the sixteenth century, and it is unfortunately therefore no longer
possible to map out precisely the movements of the ceremonies.*

When, however, the holy cross has been adored, the priests,
raising the cross from the aforesaid place, shall begin the antiphon
Super omnia ligna, and with the choir following they shall all sing it
together (concinant), the cantrix beginning. They shall carry the
cross to the high altar and there, as though they were (in specie)
Joseph and Nicodemus taking down the image from the cross (de
ligno), they shall wash the wounds of the Crucified (crucifixi) with
wine and water. While they are doing this, the convent shall join in
the responsory Ecce quomodo moritur justus, the priest beginning, the
cantrix replying, and the convent joining them. After washing the
wounds, they shall bear it [the image] with candles and censer to
the sepulcher, singing these antiphons: In pace in idipsum; . . .
Habitabit; . . . Caro mea. And when they have placed it reverently
in the aforesaid place, fittingly decorated with a covering of carpets, by a pillow also (tapetum palleo auriculari quoque), and with
most beautiful cloths, the priest shall close the sepulcher and begin
the responsory Sepulto Domino. And then the abbess shall offer a
candle (cereum) which shall burn continually in front of the sepulcher, nor shall it be extinguished until the image, taken from the
sepulcher after Matins on the night of Easter with candles, incense,
and procession, shall be put back in its place. And so, these things
being done, the convent shall return to the choir and the priest to
the vestry.
. . .

Note that according to an ancient ecclesiastical custom the
Resurrection of the Lord was celebrated before Matins and before
the ringing of any bell on Easter Day. And since the congregation
of the people in those times seemed to freeze in devotion, and

human torpor greatly increasing, the worthy lady, Lady Katherine of
Sutton, then being responsible for their pastoral care, desiring to get
rid of the said torpor completely and the more to excite the devotion of the faithful to such a renowned celebration, ordered with the
unanimous consent of the sisters that immediately after the third
responsory of Matins on Easter Day the celebration of the Lord's
Resurrection should take place; and the matter was arranged in this
way.

First the lady abbess shall go with all the convent and with
certain priests and clerks dressed in copes, and with each priest and
clerk carrying in his hand a palm and an unlit candle. They shall
enter the chapel of St. Mary Magdalene, signifying (figurantes) the
souls of the holy Fathers descending into Hell before the coming of
Christ; and they shall shut the door of the aforesaid chapel on
themselves. Then the officiating priest (sacerdos ebdomodarius),
dressed in an alb and cope, coming to the said chapel with two
deacons, one carrying a cross with the Lord's banner hanging from
the top, the other carrying a censer in his hand, and with other
priests and clerks with two boys carrying candles approaching the
door of the said chapel, shall begin three times this antiphon: Tol-
lite portas. This priest indeed shall represent (representabit) the
person of Christ about to descend to Hell and break down the gates
of Hell. And the aforesaid antiphon shall be begun at each repeti-
tion in a louder voice (altiori voce), which the clerks repeat the
same number of times, and at the beginning each time he shall beat
with the cross at the aforesaid door, signifying (figurans) the breaking down of the gates of Hell. And at the third knock, the door
shall open. Then he shall go in with his ministers.

Meanwhile a certain priest being inside the chapel shall begin
the antiphon A porta inferi, which the cantrix shall take up, with
the whole convent: Erue Domino etc. Then the officiating priest
shall lead out all those who were inside the aforesaid chapel, and in
the meantime the priest shall begin the antiphon Domine abstraxisti,
and the cantrix shall follow: Ab inferis. Then all shall go out from
the chapel, that is, from the Limbo of the Fathers, and the priests
and clerks shall sing the antiphon Cum Rex glorie in a procession
through the middle of the choir to the sepulcher, each one carrying
a palm and a candle, signifying (designantes) victory recovered from
the enemy, with the lady abbess, the prioress, and all the convent
following, as if they are the early Fathers (sicut sunt priores).

And when they have reached the sepulcher, the officiating
priest shall cense and enter the sepulcher, beginning the verse Con-
surgit. Then the cantrix shall follow with: Christus tumulo; the
verse: Quesumus auctor; the verse: Gloria tibi Domine. And
meanwhile he shall carry out the body of the Lord (corpus domini-
cum) from the sepulcher, beginning the antiphon Christus resurgens in
front of the altar with his face turned to the people, holding the
body of the Lord enclosed in crystal in his hands. Then the cantrix
shall join in with: Ex mortuis. And with the said antiphon they

shall make a procession to the altar of the Holy Trinity in solemn
state, namely with censers and candles. The convent shall follow
singing the aforesaid antiphon with the verse Dicant nunc, and the
versicle: Dicite in nacionibus. Prayer: Deus qui pro nobis filium
tuum. And this procession shall signify (figuratur) in what way
Christ proceeded after the Resurrection into Galilee with his disciples following.

These things having been performed, three sisters selected by
the lady abbess shall come forward, and, having taken off their black
vestments in the chapel of the Blessed Mary Magdalene, they shall
put on most beautiful surplices (superpelliciis), snow-white coverings
being placed on their heads by the lady abbess. Thus prepared,
therefore, and bearing silver jars in their hands, they shall say Confiteor to the abbess, and, absolved by her, they shall take their
stand in the appointed place with candles. Then she who represents
the person (speciem pretendit) of Mary Magdalene shall sing this
verse: Quodam Dei. And when that is finished, the second who
signifies (prefigurat) Mary Jacobi shall reply with the second verse:
Appropinquans ergo sola. The third Mary, having the part of Salome
(vicem optinens), shall sing the third verse: Licet mihi vobiscum
ire. After proceeding to the choir, they shall sing these verses
together, with weeping and humble voice: Heu nobis internas mentes. These verses ended, Magdalene alone shall say (dicat) this
verse: Heu misere. Jacobi shall reply: Heu consolacio nostra;
Salome: Heu redempcio Israel. In the fourth verse they shall all
join together, thus: Iam iam ecce. Then the Marys going out from
the choir together shall say (dicant): Eya quis revolvet.

When, however, they have come to the sepulcher, a clerk
dressed in a white stole shall be seated before the sepulcher, representing (gerens figuram) the angel who rolled the stone from the
mouth of the monument and sat upon it, who shall say this: Quem
queritis in sepulchro o Christicole? The women shall reply: Jhesum
Nazarenum querimus. The angel shall answer (subinferat): Non est
hic surrexit. And when he has said, Venite et videte, they shall go
into the sepulcher and kiss the place where the Crucified (crucifixus)
was laid. Mary Magdalene meanwhile shall take the sudary which
was over his head, and shall carry it with her. Then another clerk
in the person (in specie) of the other angel sitting in the sepulcher
shall say to Magdalene: Mulier quid ploras. She shall answer (sub-
iungat): Quia tulerunt Dominus meum. Then the two angels joining
together shall say to the women: Quid queritis viventem cum mortuis, etc.

Then they still doubting the Resurrection of the Lord shall say
mourning to each other: Heu dolor etc. Then Mary Magdalene sigh-
ing shall join in with: Te suspiro etc. Then on the left-hand side
of the altar the Persona shall appear, saying to her: Mulier quid
ploras quem queris. She, thinking him to be a gardener, shall reply:
Domine si tu sustulisti eum etc. The Persona shall answer: Maria.
Then she, recognizing him, shall prostrate herself at his feet saying:
Raboni. The Persona, however, drawing back shall say: Noli me

tangere etc. When the Persona has disappeared, Mary shall com-
municate her joy to her companions with joyful voice singing these
verses: Gratulari et letari, etc. When these are ended the Persona
shall appear at once to the three women on the right of the altar
saying: Avete nolite timere etc. Then prostrate on the ground they
shall hold his feet and kiss them. Which done, one after another
they shall sing these verses, Mary Magdalene beginning: Jhesu ille
Nazarenus etc. These verses being finished, the Marys standing on
the step before the altar turning to the people shall sing this response: Alleluia surrexit Dominus de sepulchro, with the choir replying to them.

When these are ended, priests and clerks representing (in figuram) the disciples of Christ shall come forward saying: O gens
dira. Then one of them shall approach and say to Mary Magdalene:
Dic nobis Maria etc. She shall reply: Sepulcrum Christi. Angelicos
testes. With her finger she shall point out the place where the
angel was sitting, and shall hold out the sudary for them to kiss,
adding this verse: Surrexit Christus spes nostra. Then these final
verses shall be added by the disciples and choir: Credendum est.
Scimus Christum.

Then Magdalene shall begin Christus resurgens, with the clergy
and choir joining at the same time. These ended, the hymn Te Deum
laudamus shall be solemnly chanted, the priest beginning. And meanwhile the aforementioned priests putting their proper clothes on
again in the chapel, crossing through the choir with candles, shall
approach the sepulcher to give thanks and make a short prayer
there. Then they shall return to their station (stacionem) until the
abbess shall order them to go out to rest.

3. VALENCIA ASSUMPTION PLAY
(EARLY FIFTEENTH CENTURY)

The surviving text probably dates from the early fifteenth century. The play was performed over two days, in the Cathedral, as part of the liturgy for the Feast. The text contains Mary's part and cues and also unusually detailed directions for movements, gestures, and facial expressions for Mary and others. The ordering of processions is given; the use of raising and lowering machines is indicated, but the machines themselves are not described. The play was apparently almost entirely sung, and directions for the music are given.

When Mary has gone up onto the scaffold (quadafal) she shall go to her chamber (cambra), which is to be prepared and enclosed with curtains (tàcada ab los vels entorn), and she shall enter by the door with her two handmaidens, who are to follow her. And when she has reached the seat (setial), she shall sit down in a modest manner and shall have in her hands a small book of hours (hunes horetes) which she shall read. And the handmaidens shall pull back (pleguen) all the curtains so that Mary can be seen by the people (lo poble). And the said handmaidens shall sit down in front of Mary some distance from her, with their faces turned towards her. And when the time has come to begin the play (lo misteri), Mary, seated, shall sing (diga) the following words, addressed to the maidens, to the melody of Ab cant daucells, and the maidens are to stand up:

[*Mary expresses her wish to join Christ.*]

Immediately, the maidens, kneeling, shall reply with the following words (cobla), sung to the melody of Si cascun iorn me daz de vos:

[*Maidens' reply.*]

After their song (cobla), Mary is to get up from her seat, walk modestly around her room up to the door, go out, and then go to visit the holy places (los santuaris). The maidens shall follow her after closing the curtains, and they shall shut the door. And when Mary is in front of the Garden of Gethsemane (lort de Cherico) she is to kneel and, with hands folded and held high towards heaven, is to sing the following words to the melody of Aixi com dos infants petits. And the maidens are to kneel with Mary.

[*Mary reflects on Christ's arrest in the Garden and on her own loneliness.*]

And after this speech, she is to stand up, devoutly make a

230

bow with her head, and go to the Hill of Calvary (<u>Monticalvari</u>). And when she is in front of the Cross, she is to kneel some distance from it, then stand up, go up to it, and kiss the place where the feet were nailed. Then she shall stand back a little, kneel, and sing the following words to the same melody:

[*Mary addresses the Cross, where her Son hung to save Mankind. She begs that she may be taken from this world.*]

After this speech, she is to do as before, the maidens are to adore the Cross, and then Mary is to go to the Sepulcher (<u>sepulcre</u>), kneel, and sing the following words to the same melody:

[*Mary addresses the Sepulcher, where Christ was laid. Begs her Son to take pity on her.*]

And after this speech she shall go and kiss the Sepulcher, and shall then go to the Mount of Olives (<u>Mŏt Olivet</u>) and shall sing to the same melody:

[*Mary addresses the Mount of Olives. Begs Christ to guide her at the hour of her death.*]

When she has finished her speech she shall stand up, and if she is able to reach the representation (<u>forma</u>) of Christ's feet she is to touch them with her lips or hands. And then she is to return devoutly to her house (<u>casa</u>), and when she reaches the door she is to turn towards the altar, then go into the house and sit down on her seat. And very shortly afterwards, as there is not [*much*] time, she is to stand up, then kneel and, looking up towards heaven with folded hands, is to sing the following words to the melody of <u>Ab cant dauzells</u>:

[*Mary prays to Christ that she may join him.*]

And immediately she is to sit down again on her seat, and claps of thunder (<u>trons</u>) are to be made, the angel is to descend (<u>devall</u>), and when the angel is before Mary, she is to look at him very humbly, and the angel is to sing his words to the melody of <u>Cercats duymay</u>:

[*Angel addresses Mary.*]

When the angel gives Mary the palm, she is to take it humbly and with great reverence. Kneeling, she is to hold it reverently and kiss it. Then she shall stand up, and when the angel has finished, Mary is to reply, singing to the melody associated with her (<u>en son so</u>):

[*Mary makes three requests: that the angel tell her his*]

name; that the apostles be brought to her; that she should
not see Satan at the hour of her death.]

And when she has finished, she is to sit down again, and the
angel is to reply to her three requests using his melody:

[*Angel's reply.*]

When the angel has gone in again (<u>sen serà entrat</u>), and the
thunder has been made, Mary is to get up from her seat and, kneeling, thank God for the angel's embassy, and then she shall sing the
following words in her accustomed melody:

[*Mary gives thanks to God that her requests are to be grant-*
ed.]

Then immediately Mary shall sit down again on her seat and
turn towards her handmaidens, singing in her accustomed melody:

[*Mary asks them to fetch the people so that she can bless*
them before her death, and so that they can witness her
Assumption.]

Immediately the handmaidens are to reply to the melody of
<u>Quant vey la lauseta mover</u>. Then the handmaidens are to go to the
people and address them:

[*They address them as the people of God.*]

And the people are to reply:

[*The people's words.*]

Then the women and maidens are to say [*or* sing] their
words.
And then the people are to go to Mary, enter her door, bow
before her, kissing her hand, and are to say [*or* sing] their words.
Then the women and maidens are to say [*or* sing] their words. Then
Mary shall stand up immediately, telling them why she has summoned
them, blessing them and making the sign of the cross over them,
touching them with the palm.

[*Mary's speech, announcing that she will die within three*
days.]

When she has finished, she shall sit down again, and then,
taking leave of them, shall say:

[*Mary exhorts them.*]

When Mary has finished, the people are to take their leave
saying [or singing] their words, and the women are to do the same.
And they are to kiss her hand and make their way straight to
Gamaliel, leaving by the door. And when they are with Gamaliel
they are to greet each other, kissing and embracing each other and
giving their hands to the ladies. And they shall say [or sing] their
words:

[People's speech.]

And Gamaliel is to reply:

[Gamaliel's speech.]

And they are to stay there together.
At once John shall come to Mary's door, knock on it with the
door knocker, and say:

[John addresses the handmaidens.]

And the handmaidens are to answer, telling him to enter. And
when John is before Mary, he is to address her:

[John's words to Mary.]

Mary shall reply to him, still seated. Then she shall stand up
and, putting her hands on his shoulders, she shall embrace him, and
after saying [or singing] her words shall sit down again.

[Mary's speech, welcoming John.]

Immediately, the other apostles come and knock at the door
and say [or sing] their words in turn.

[Apostles ask that the door be opened to them.]

St. John replies:

[St. John greets them.]

And when they are in front of Mary, they say [or sing]:

[Apostles greet Mary.]

When they have finished, Mary shall stand up and, saying [or
singing] her words, go among them, putting her hands on the shoulders of each one as if embracing him gently, returning to her seat
before she has finished her speech.

[Mary greets them and tells them why they have been brought

to her.]

And the apostles are to sit down in turn (?per cors) some
distance away. And Mary, still seated, is to address them:

[*Mary begs for news of their success in the world.*]

And the apostles are to reply, saying [*or* singing] their words:

[*Apostles answer Mary.*]

And when they have finished, Mary, seated, is to console
them:

[*Mary exhorts them to be diligent in preaching their
faith, and tells them not to fear persecution, for they will
have their reward.*]

And then the Christian people are to approach with Gamaliel
and all the other people, and, by way of the message that they have
brought, the people are to say [*or* sing] the following words:

[*They greet Mary.*]

Then Gamaliel with the others shall approach Mary and shall
kiss her hand, saying [*or* singing]:

[*They greet Mary.*]

Then the three Marys shall say [*or* sing]:

[*They greet Mary.*]

Then the women and maidens shall say [*or* sing]:

[*They greet Mary.*]

And at once Mary shall reply to them all:

[*Mary tells them that Christ will lead her to Paradise.*]

Then there is to be thunder, and the three princes are to
approach, saying [*or* singing]:

[*They greet Mary.*]

And when they have finished, Mary is to stand up with great
humility, kneel, and say [*or* sing]:

[*Mary tells them she has longed to join her Son, and he,*

obedient to her, will grant her wish.]

And after Mary has spoken [*or* sung] these words, there is to be thunder, the heaven is to open (<u>obras lo cel</u>), and meanwhile the apostles, princes, and others are to help Mary onto her bed. And Mary is to remain kneeling, watching the descent (<u>lo devallament</u>) of Christ. When Christ is before her, Mary is to rush to kiss his feet, and shall say [*or* sing]:

[*Mary greets Christ.*]

Christ is to reply, addressing his sweet mother. Also another song to his mother, to its own melody.
Then the prophets are to address Mary:

[*Prophets' words.*]

Then Mary, turning towards Christ, is to say [*or* sing]:

[*Mary thanks Christ.*]

And when she has finished, she is to take St. James by the hand and lead him to Mary Salome, saying [*or* singing]:

[*Mary tells St. James how delighted his mother will be to see him.*]

Afterwards St. James shall say [*or* sing] to his mother:

[*He greets her.*]

And then his mother is to answer:

[*She greets him joyfully.*]

And when Mary Salome has finished, St. James and the Virgin Mary are to turn to Christ and kneel. And then with Moses and Abraham they are to sing to the melody of <u>pus amor nol quen sia pacients</u>:

[*They pray for the people of Israel.*]

Christ replies. When Christ has finished, Mary is to stand up, take Christ's hands, kiss them, and show them to the people on all sides, saying [*or* singing]:

[*Mary shows the hands which created the whole world.*]

After she has spoken [*or* sung] these words, Mary is to tell the handmaidens to bring a large candle (<u>ciri</u>) from the box, and give

it to St. Peter, and St. Peter is to hold it, lit, until it is asked
for.

Christ replies:

'Come, then, my spouse.'

The same speaker:

'I shall set you on my right hand.'

Then Mary is to take the candle in her hands and say [or
sing]:

[*Says she is ready, and commends her spirit to Christ.*]

And when she has finished, Christ, taking the soul from her
body (trahent la anima del cors), shall say [or sing]:

[*Commands Mary's soul to come forth.*]

When Christ has spoken, Mary shall fall into the arms of the
handmaidens as if dead (faent com es morta). Meantime there is to
be loud thunder, and they are to place Mary beneath the stage (devall lo cadafal). And they are to carry up the image (la ymage) and
say all the rest of the office.

On the second day of the play (en la segona iornada), after
St. Michael has returned the soul to the body, those who are beneath
the stage (devall lo cadafal) are to receive the image quickly and
make thunder and smoke, and the living person (la viva) is to emerge
suddenly.

And when she is on the tomb (lo sepulcre), Mary is to appear
amazed as if she had never been in this world before and to look
around her in astonishment. And the angels are to kneel reverently.
And while Mary is on the tomb (lo moniment), the angels, kneeling,
are to say [or sing]:

[*Angel's song:* 'Mother of God, full of Grace.']

After the song, they are to stand up and with great reverence
lead Mary from the tomb. And then Michael and Gabriel are to
stand before her, one on each side of her and some distance away,
in such a way that everybody can see her. The prince is to stand
behind her. And they are to sing and bow to her. And Mary is to
turn towards them and they to her. And thus they are to proceed
to the entrance to the choir (ala porta del cor), and here Mary is to
stand facing the altar (girada vers laltar). And the angels are to
stop singing. Christ is to address the apostles:

[*Christ's words.*]

And the apostles are to reply:

[*Apostles' words.*]

And after the apostles have spoken, they are to make their way towards Mary, and when they are in front of her they are to kneel and say [*or* sing]:

[*Words in praise of Mary.*]

And when they have finished, they are to get up very reverently and move forward in procession.

And then Gamaliel and Lazarus are to come with the others and say [*or* sing] their words, and then to do the same as the apostles:

[*Words of praise to Mary.*]

Similarly, the people are to say [*or* sing] their words:

[*Words of praise.*]

Similarly, the Marys are to say [*or* sing] their words:

[*Words of praise.*]

Similarly, the handmaidens of the Virgin are to say [*or* sing] their words:

[*Words of praise.*]

Similarly, the women and maidens are to say [*or* sing]:

[*Words of praise.*]

And when all have finished they are to join the procession which moves from Mary towards Christ.

And Mary is to begin to walk through the procession, and the angels are to sing as before. And when Mary passes by each one he is to bow his head low towards the earth, and when she is in front of the apostles, they are to say [*or* sing]:

[*They greet Mary.*]

Similarly, Gamaliel, etc:

[*Words to Mary.*]

Similarly, the Christian people:

[*Words to Mary.*]

Similarly, the three Marys:

[*Words to Mary.*]

Similarly, the handmaidens of the Virgin:

[*Words to Mary.*]

Similarly, the women and maidens:

[*Words to Mary.*]

Then Mary is to walk through the procession touching each on the shoulders as if taking her leave, saying [*or* singing]:

[*Mary's farewell.*]

When this is over, Mary is to walk towards Christ, and when she is in front of him she is to kneel humbly. And she is to make as if to take off the chaplet, and the angels are to take it from her reverently and to give it to the handmaidens, and Mary is to say [*or* sing]:

[*Mary begs to leave the world.*]

Christ replies:

'Come then, my spouse.'

The same speaker:

'I shall set you on my right hand.'

The same speaker:

[*He asks the archangels to bring her to him.*]

And after Christ has said these words, the angels are to lead Mary humbly and raise her up with Christ. Then the angels, apostles, and everybody else are to crowd round Christ and Mary, and thunder and smoke are to be made, and Christ and Mary are to exit. And at once the lifting machinery (la ara celi) is to rise. As it begins to rise the apostles are to say [*or* sing]:

[*Words of praise to Mary.*]

And the angels in the dome (<u>cembori</u>) are to sing:

[*Praise Mary.*]

They sing another song:

[*Praise Mary.*]

And when the heaven has been closed, the apostles are to form a procession and everybody else is to follow. They are to begin to sing <u>Te deum laudamus</u>. And singing this, they are to proceed in order to the chapter house (<u>capitol</u>) to disrobe, and there they are to have their lunch if they have food with them.

4. FLORENCE: FEAST OF JOHN THE BAPTIST (1439)

Every year the people of Florence celebrated the feast of their patron saint, John the Baptist, with several days of festivities.
In 1439, a Greek writer, attending the Ecumenical Council in the city, described the celebrations. We have translated from the Italian version since the Greek original no longer survives.

On 23 June there is a big procession and a celebration in which the whole population takes part and during which they perform prodigies and almost miracles, or representations of miracles. For they resuscitate the dead; and the leader (caporione) routs the devils; they crucify a man, like Christ; and they perform the Resurrection of Christ; they dress up some men as Magi, and by means of men they represent the Nativity of Christ with the shepherds, the star, the animals, and the crib. Moreover they have a procession with statues and relics of saints and effigies (imagini) and precious crosses, preceded always by trumpets and other musical instruments. How shall I describe how they represented St. Augustine by means of one dressed as a friar, and they put him 25 ells (braccia) high, and he walked about and preached. But they also imitated hermits with beards, and they walked high on wooden stilts, and it was a most awesome (orrendo) sight. And we also saw some sacred images being carried around, some enormous, some impressive (sublimi), like sorrowful things (come cosa dolorosa). What shall I say of St. George who performs the miracle of the dragon? Having done all these things on 23 June, on the day of the 24th they showed all their riches and exhibited gold and silver in abundance and plenty of vestments, having on the day of the celebration consecrated in the Church of the Precursor first of all nearly one hundred banners and then thirty castles albeit of wood but splendidly made; and then candles and torches in great numbers and finally men who were kept in prison, carrying wreaths and olive branches. All these things were done with much pomp, with flutes and trumpets, and every other kind of ceremony (onoranza); and one could see the whole of Florence revelling, both men and women, and the spectacle was great and splendid. Even the night was not dark, but bright and ablaze with lights. Not only on the lower part of the church, but also high up they had hung big lamps full of wax, a hundred pounds apiece, which lit up the night. As these things were being celebrated by the Florentines, we were made welcome by them to watch this festivity.

In 1454 the traditional procession included floats on which were performed a series of plays from the Creation to the Last Judgment.
For St. John the order of events was changed. It was customary to

have the parade (mostra) on the 22nd, the procession with companies
(compagnie), friars, priests, and floats (edifizj) on the morning of the
23rd, and the offerings (offerte) in the evening, and on the 24th the
horse race (palio), and they were rearranged in this way: that is to
say the parade should be on the 21st, and on the morning of the
22nd the procession with all the floats (edifizj); what these were in
the said year and how they processed I shall now proceed to tell. On
the 22nd the cross from Santa Maria del Fiore led the way with all
the choir boys and after them six cantors; next came the companies
of Jacopo the tailor's cutter and Nofri the cobbler with about thirty
boys dressed in white, and little angels; third, the float (edifizio) of
the Angel St. Michael, above which was God the Father in a cloud,
and in the square before the Signoria (al dirimpetto a' Signori) they
performed (fecero Rappresentazione) the battle of the angels when
Lucifer was cast out of Heaven with his fallen angels (maladetti);
fourth, the company of ser Antonio and Piero di Mariano with about
thirty boys dressed in white and little angels; fifth, the float of
Adam which in the square performed the play (fe' Rappresentazione)
of God creating Adam and Eve, and giving his commandment to
them, and of their disobedience so that they were cast out of Paradise, with first the temptation by the serpent and other relevant
events (appartenenze); sixth, a Moses on horseback with a large
group of mounted elders (principali) of the people of Israel and
others; seventh, the float of Moses, which in the square performed
the play (fe' le Rappresentazione) in which God gave him the law;
eighth, several prophets and sibyls with Hermes Trismegistus and
others who foretold the incarnation of Christ; ninth, the float of the
Annunciation which performed its play (fe' la sua Rappresentazione);
tenth, the Emperor Octavian with many horsemen and the sibyl, to
perform the play in which the sibyl foretold that Christ was to be
born, and showed him the Virgin up in the sky (in aria) with Christ
in her arms. And it happened that when the float was before the
Signoria, and Octavian had dismounted and stepped onto the lower
level of the float (in sull'edifizio sotto)--that is, into the temple--to
start his performance, a German came upon them wearing only a
loose shirt, and at the foot of the float he asked, 'Where is the
king of Rome?' And there were some who answered, 'Look, he is
there'; and showed him Octavian. He climbed onto the float: many
believed that he was one of those who had to take part in the festival (festa) and therefore he was not hindered. First of all he
seized the idol which was in the said temple and threw it into the
square; then, turning to Octavian, who was dressed in purple velvet
worked (broccato) in costly (ricchissimo) gold, he seized him, threw
him headlong onto the people in the square, and then seized a pillar
to climb up to some children who were standing above the said
temple as little angels; and as he did this, some bystanders inter-
vened having clubs (mazze) in their hands, and beating him fiercely
they pulled him with difficulty to the ground. Having got up from
the ground he again tried to climb up, but he was hit with clubs
from below and from above and overpowered. Eleventh, the Temple

of Peace (Templum Pacis) with the float of the Nativity to perform
its play (per fare la sua Rappresentazione); twelfth, a float in the
shape of a magnificent and triumphal Temple, which octagonal temple was adorned all round with the seven Virtues and the Virgin
Mary on the east side with the Christ Child, and around the temple
Herod performed his play; thirteenth, the three Magi, with a troop
of more than 200 horses most magnificently adorned, came to bring
their offerings to the Christ Child; the Passion and Entombment
were left out, as they were not felt to be appropriate to a festival
(non parve si convenisse a festa); fourteenth, a mounted troop of
Pilate's soldiers, detailed as guards to the sepulcher; fifteenth, the
float of the Entombment, from which Christ arose; sixteenth, the
float of Limbo, out of which he brought the Patriarchs; seventeenth,
the float of Paradise, into which he led the said Patriarchs; eigh-
teenth, the Apostles and the Marys, who were present at the Ascension (Assunzione); nineteenth, the float of the Ascension of Christ,
that is, the one from which he went to Heaven; twentieth, the
mounted troop of three kings, queens, damsels, and nymphs with
carts and other matters belonging to the Living (appartenenze al
vivo); twenty-first, the float of the Living and the Dead; twenty-
second, the float of Judgment, with the stretcher for tombs (barella
de' sepolcri), Paradise, and Hell, and its play (Rappresentazione) as in
faith we believe it shall be at the end of time. All the above-
mentioned floats performed their plays in the square before the
Signoria, and these lasted until the sixteenth hour (in fino alle 16
ore) [after sunrise?].

5. FLORENCE: ANNUNCIATION AND ASCENSION (1439)

Abramo, the Russian bishop of Souzdal, visited Florence in
1439 for the Ecumenical Council. In his diary he describes two
performances in churches there which used elaborate machinery.
Exceptionally we have included these two descriptions even
though we were unable to translate from the Russian original. The
following translations are of the German versions by Wesselofsky;
they have been compared with d'Ancona's Italian versions, which
sometimes diverge appreciably, and at appropriate points both Ger-
man and Italian terms have been included, always in this order.

A learned Italian has created in Italy a magnificent work.   In
a monastery in Florence there is a big church dedicated to the name
of the Virgin [*SS. Annunziata*] and over its entrance a scaffold
(Gerüst/tribuna) ten and a half feet square was set up, with a
small, skillfully constructed ladder (Leiter/scala) leading to it.   Both
scaffold and ladder were draped with curtains (Vorhängen/tende).
The scaffold was meant to represent the heavenly spheres from
where the Angel Gabriel is sent down to the Holy Virgin by God the
Father; on top of the scaffold there is a throne on which a man of
majestic appearance is seated, dressed in priestly robes with a crown
on his head and the Gospel in his left hand, as God the Father is
represented.   He is surrounded by many children artfully arranged
around him and at his feet an image of the heavenly powers.   Seven
circles surrounded the throne and the children; the smallest of the
circles had a diameter of about two ells (Ellen/braccia), then there
was another which was two spans larger, and so on, and there were
a thousand lighted oil lamps on them.   Four small children crowned
and dressed as angels, holding cymbals, a cittern, or a tambourine in
one hand, stood facing one another on the largest circle, amid the
lamps.   All this represented the seven heavens, the heavenly powers,
and the inextinguishable angelic light, and everything was surrounded
by the said curtain (Vorhänge/cortine).   In the middle of the church
at a distance of 175 feet from the entrance there was, stretching
from one wall to the other, a stone structure/bridge (Gerüst/ponte)
or partition (tramezzo), built on stone columns 21 feet high and 17½
deep, draped with red materials (Stoffen/stoffe); on it, on the left,
there was a wooden bed, also adorned with magnificent materials,
and, beside it, close to the pillow, there was a richly covered seat.
Seated on it there was a beautiful youth richly dressed in maiden's
clothes with a crown on his head and holding a book which he was
reading in silence, very much like the Virgin Mary to look at.   On
the same scaffold/platform (Gerüst/palco) there were four costumed
men with long beards, long flowing hair, and narrow gold circlets on
their heads.   They were simply dressed in long, ample white surplices with girdles; a narrow scarlet band went from the right
shoulder to the left side: their appearance and clothing were those

of Prophets. All this, as well as that which was on the aforesaid
higher scaffold (Gerüst/tribuna), was covered with precious Italian
and French cloths (Tüchern/panni) and red curtains (Umhängen/cor-
tine). Five thin but strong ropes (Stricke/canapi) were stretched from
the stone platform (Estrade/palco) in the middle of the church to the
high scaffold facing it. Two of them were fastened not far from
the young man dressed as the Virgin, and on them by means of a
third, very thin rope (Stricke/canapo) the angel sent forth by God
descends and then jubilantly returns up above after the Annunciation.
The other three ropes lead precisely to the center of the platform.

When the time comes to begin the great and marvelous spectacle, many people gather silently in the church, their eyes fixed on
the scaffold in the middle of the church. After a short while the
curtains and hangings are drawn back and one can see, seated on the
magnificent seat by the small bed, the man who represented the
Virgin. All this was full of beauty, wonder, and grace. Then on the
same platform appear the four Prophets, each of whom has a scroll
(Schrift/scritto) in his hand, containing the ancient prophecies of the
birth and incarnation of Christ. They move about on the platform,
each looking at his own scroll, stretching out their right hands towards the upper scaffold (tribuna), which is still veiled, saying:
'Thence the salvation comes to mankind'; or one says to another,
looking at his scroll: 'The Lord shall come from the South.' Then
they dispute among themselves, after which each one tears up his
scroll and throws it away as erroneous: then they take other scrolls
and walk to the front of the scaffold and bow to each other, and
each one examines his own scroll, striking it with his hand and ar-
guing with his companions. One of them says: 'Thence shall God
come to seek the lost sheep'; and another says other things. So
they continue their dispute for about half an hour. Then the curtains of the upper scaffold open and from there comes a volley of
shots imitating Heaven's thunder, and the Prophets with their scrolls
are not seen again. Up on the scaffold is God the Father surrounded by more than five hundred burning lamps which revolve continually, going up and down. Children dressed in white, representing the
angels, surround him, one striking the cymbals, others playing flutes
or citterns in a scene of joyful and inexpressible beauty. After
some time, the angel sent by God descends on the two ropes already
mentioned to announce the conception of the Son. The angel is a
beautiful, curly-headed youth, dressed in a robe as white as snow,
adorned with gold, exactly as celestial angels are to be seen in
paintings. While he descends he sings in a low voice, holding a
branch (Zweig/ramoscello) in his hand. The descent is effected in
this way: behind him there are two small wheels secured, invisible
from below because of the distance, into which the two ropes fit,
while some people who cannot be seen stand up above and by means
of the third very thin rope lower and lift up the angel. The angel,
therefore, having descended and arrived before the Virgin Mary, who
is resting, courteously addresses her, holding the aforementioned rod

(Ruthe) in his hand. Then follows the Annunciation which is an
abbreviation of the Ave Maria; to which the Virgin quickly stands up
and answers in a sweet and modest voice: 'O young man, how dare
you come to my threshold and enter my house? What foolish speech
is this about God being with me and being incarnated in my womb?
I do not trust your words, for I have no experience of marriage and
I know no man. Go away, young man, lest Joseph should see you
and cut off your head with an axe while you linger to address me in
my house. I beg you, go away, or he will drive me out of the house
too.' But, seeing her fear, the angel answers, 'Fear not, Mary; I am
the archangel Gabriel, whom God has sent to you to announce the
conception of his Son. Believe in what I say: you will conceive
without seed; the Holy Spirit shall come upon you and the power of
the Highest shall overshadow you.' Having listened to these words,
Mary lifts up her eyes and sees God in all his power and magnificence blessing her. She folds her hands in her lap and humbly says,
'Lo, I am God's handmaid: let what you have said befall me.' The
angel hands over to her the beautiful branch (Ruthe/verghetta) and
ascends. Mary remains standing, watching his ascent. In the meantime a fire comes from God and with a noise of uninterrupted thunder passes down the three ropes towards the middle of the scaffold,
where the Prophets were, rising up again in flames and rebounding
down once more, so that the whole church was filled with sparks.
The angel sang jubilantly as he ascended, and moved his hands about
and beat his wings as if he were really flying. The fire poured forth
and spread with increasing intensity and noise from the high scaffold, lighting the lamps in the church but without burning the
clothes of the spectators or causing any harm. When the angel arrives back at his point of departure the flames subside and the curtains close again.
        I saw this marvelous and most skillfully contrived spectacle in
the city of Florence, and I have described it to the best of my
ability: but some of it is impossible to describe, for it was so in-
expressibly beautiful.

Florence Ascension, 1439:
        In the famous city of Florence I saw something even more
marvelous. According to an old custom, the Latin Church (die La-
teiner/i latini) celebrates the memorial of the Ascension of Our
Lord, who ascended to heaven to the Father on the fortieth day
after the Resurrection. This celebration takes place on the Thursday
of the sixth week after Easter in the Church of the Ascension of
Our Lord [*Santa Maria del Carmine*]. This is what I saw. The
church is 560 feet long from the front wall to the altar and is 140
feet wide. Like that of the church of SS. Annunziata, of which I
have already spoken, it has a stone platform (Estrade/tramezzo) 140
feet long standing on 28 foot-high columns. On this platform on the
left hand side can be seen a stone castle, magnificently adorned,
with towers and bastions, representing the holy city of Jerusalem;

opposite, against the wall, there is a hill, ten and a half feet high, to which leads a staircase, two spans from the floor. The hill is surrounded by red materials. Above it, at a height of about 56 feet, there is a wooden scaffold 28 feet wide and 28 deep with planking (Brettverschlag/tavolato) on all sides and beautifully painted beneath and all around. On the top of this scaffold there is a round opening of 14 feet in diameter, covered by a blue hanging, on which the sun, moon, and surrounding stars are painted, representing the first heavenly sphere. When the time comes this hanging is lifted, which signifies that the gates of Heaven are opened; and inside a man can be seen with a crown on his head, representing God the Father: he stands in a miraculous way above the gates of Heaven, looking down on the Mount of Olives, where his divine Son, the holy Virgin, and the Apostles are standing together. He blesses them, apparently suspended in mid-air. Around him there are small children in great numbers with flutes, citterns, and chime bells. Among these children, who represent the angels, and around God the Father there is a vast number of burning lamps. At the top of the opening which represents Heaven is fixed a paper disc, the bottom rim of which touches the upper rim of the opening and the top rim of which points upwards; on this, life-size angels are painted. Seven thin and strong ropes with skillfully constructed iron gear wheels go from the opening of Heaven to the Mount of Olives. A young man representing Jesus Christ in the act of ascending to the Father is beneath these ropes. Above the church altar, high up in the wall, there is a little stone room about 21 feet square; on the side of the church it is covered with a red curtain on which can be seen a crown in a circle, which ceaselessly revolves to the right and to the left. Everything is marvelously ordered and nothing similar has ever been seen.

Towards the ninth hour many people come to this church to watch the marvelous spectacle. When there is perfect silence in the crowded church, people turn their eyes to the platform and everything that has been prepared there. Then four young children dressed and attired as angels appear, each carrying a flowering rod (Ruthe/ramo), then another comes forth in the appearance of the Son of God and goes towards the city representing Jerusalem, and the angels precede him. He enters Jerusalem, and after a few minutes he comes out again accompanied by two young men dressed as women, who represent the holy Virgin and Mary Magdalene. Then he returns to Jerusalem and fetches Peter, prince of the Apostles, and after him all the other Apostles; and together with the holy Mother, the Apostles, and the four angels he proceeds towards the Mount of Olives. The Apostles walk barefoot and are dressed as they can be seen in holy paintings: some with beards and some without, just as they really were. When Jesus approaches the Mount of Olives he stops, turning his face towards Jerusalem, with the Mother and Magdalene standing on his right. The Apostle Peter, having knelt down before him and received his blessing, goes to his place. The others do the same, taking up their places, some to the right and

some to the left of Our Lord. When they have done that, Jesus
distributes gifts among them. He gives a net to the Apostle Andrew, saying: 'You will be a fisher of men.' Another receives a
book, a third a sword, with the words, 'You will not suffer any harm
from this, if you use it in my name.' Then Jesus proceeds to the
Mount and climbs its ladder (Stiege/scala); the Mother and Magdalene
stand on his right, the Apostles in their places at the foot of the
mount. Then Jesus says, 'Since everything concerning me is ful-
filled, I return to my Father, who is also your Father, and to my
God, who is also yours'; and he moves away to reach the summit of
the Mount, where the machine with the ropes is prepared. The
Apostles bow to one another, weep, and say sorrowfully, 'O Lord, do
not forsake us, for we are orphans.' But Jesus answers, 'Do not
weep, I will not leave you as orphans, I am going to my Father and
I shall ask him to send you the Spirit of Consolation and Truth, who
will teach you all things: for if I do not go, the Paraclete will not
come to you.' After these and other words there is a clap of thunder, Christ appears on top of the mountain, the heavens open, and
God the Father can be seen miraculously suspended in the air, enve-
loped in a great light which pours forth from the innumerable lamps;
the small children representing the angels move around him while
harmonious music and sweet singing are heard. The taller angels
which are painted on the disc also revolve around so that they seem
to be alive. From the Heaven where God the Father is, a very
beautiful and ingeniously devised cloud descends on the seven ropes:
it is round and surrounded by revolving discs which move quickly; to
right and left two children can be seen dressed as angels with golden
wings. While the cloud is still on its way, Jesus takes two golden
keys and says to Peter, 'You are Peter and upon this rock I will
build my church, etc.', and blessing him, he gives him the keys.
Then, with the help of the seven ropes he ascends towards Heaven,
keeping himself upright, blessing Mary and the Apostles with his
hand. It is a most marvelous and incomparable sight. The ropes are
activated by invisible and most ingenious gear-wheels so that the
person representing Jesus Christ seems indeed to be ascending by
himself; and he reaches a great height without swaying. The holy
Virgin and the Apostles, on seeing that the Lord is going away, shed
tears. When he has reached the cloud, this envelops him from head
to foot and the two angels who stand one on each side of him kneel
down before him. At this moment many lamps which are also within
the cloud are lit shedding splendid light. But Jesus continues to
ascend, accompanied by the two angels, and as soon as he reaches
the Father, the music stops and it grows dark. Then the Virgin and
the Apostles turn their eyes towards the room above the altar: the
curtain is pulled from the place which represents the upper heaven
and the light comes back.

6. PERUGIA: SERMON AND DRAMATIC SPECTACLE (1448)

Sermons were often included in the plays, and sometimes a dramatic spectacle or procession might be used by a preacher to enhance his sermon, as in this account for 1448 from the chronicles of the city of Perugia:

On 29 March, which was Good Friday, the said Friar Ruberto started again his daily preaching in the square. On Holy Thursday he preached on Communion and invited the whole population to come on Good Friday; and at the end of the said sermon on the Passion he performed this play (rappresentazione): that is, he preached at the top of the square outside the door of San Lorenzo where a platform was prepared (?era ordinato un terrato) from the door to the corner towards the house of Cherubino degli Armanne. And there, when it was time to show the Crucifix, out of San Lorenzo came Eliseo de Cristofano, barber at the Gate of Sant'Agnolo, representing (a guisa de) the naked Christ with the cross on his shoulder and the crown of thorns on his head; and his flesh seemed beaten and scourged, as when Christ was scourged. And there several armed men (armate) took him to be crucified. And they went down towards the fountain, around the crowd, as far as the entrance to the Scudellare, and they turned (argiero) at the Exchange (audienza del Cambio) and returned (argiero) to the door of San Lorenzo and went onto the said platform (terrato); and there, in the middle of the platform, someone (una) went towards him in the garb of the Virgin Mary dressed all in black, weeping and speaking sorrowfully, as was done in the similar play (misterio) of the Passion of Jesus Christ; and when they arrived at the scaffold (?pergolo) of Friar Ruberto, he stood there for a long time with the cross on his shoulder, and all the while the people wept and cried for mercy. Then they put down the said cross and took up a crucifix which was already there, and they erected the said cross; and then the wailing of the people grew louder. At the foot of the said cross, Our Lady started her lament together with St. John and Mary Magdalene and Mary Salome, and they said some stanzas from the lament of the Passion. Then came Nicodemus and Joseph of Arimathea, and they freed the body of Jesus Christ from the nails (scavigliarono), put it in the lap of Our Lady, and then laid it in the sepulcher; and throughout the people continued to weep loudly. And many said that there had never been performed in Perugia a more beautiful and pious play (devozione) than this one. And on that morning six friars were professed (?se fecero): one was the said Eliseo, who was a foolish youth, Tomasso de Marchegino, Bino who used to live with the Priors, the son of Bocco del Borgo de Santo Antonio, and Meser Riciere de Francescone de Tanolo, and many others had taken the habit before, because of the sermons of the said Friar Ruberto. And after three or four months the said Friar Eliseo de Cristofano de Porta Sant'Agnolo left the friary and

returned to the barber's trade, and they call him Lord God
(<u>Domendio</u>); and then he married and was a greater scoundrel than
before.

7. IRANZO MAGI CEREMONY (1462-63)

Extracts from a chronicle which describes day-to-day events in a noble Castilian household, that of Miguel Lucas de Iranzo, Constable of Castile, in the second half of the fifteenth century. This private ceremony was repeated, with variations, over a number of years. The author of the chronicle is not known, but, judging by the detail given, he was somebody very familiar with the events described.

In 1462:
And after they had dined and the tables had been cleared away, there entered the hall (la sala) a lady (una dueña) mounted on a little donkey (un asnito sardesco) with a child in her arms. She was acting the part of (representaba ser) Our Lady the Virgin Mary with her blessed and glorious Son, and Joseph accompanied her. And with great devotion, the said Constable received her and led her up to his seat (asiento), placing her between the said Countess [his wife], doña Juana his sister, doña Guiomar Carrillo her [his wife's] mother, and the other ladies and maidens present, and the Constable withdrew to a room (una camara) at the other end of the hall. And a short time later, he came out of the said room with his pages, very well dressed, with masks (visajes) and with crowns on their heads in the manner of the three Wise Men and each with a goblet (copa) in his hands with their presents. And thus he advanced through the hall very slowly (mui mucho paso) in a most dignified manner (con mui jentil contenencia), looking at the star which guided them and which was attached to a cord (un cordel) which was there in the said hall. And thus he reached the far end where the Virgin was seated with her Son and offered his presents amidst a tremendous din of trumpets (trompetas), drums (atavales), and other instruments. And after this had been done, he withdrew to the said room, from which he emerged dressed differently, and then the shawms (chirimias) began to sound, and he began to dance with the said Countess. . . . The said Constable kept and solemnized this feast (esta fiesta) every year, it is said, out of devoutness, and also because it was the birthday of our Lord the King [Henry IV] to whose service he was devoted.

In 1463:
And after they had dined, the three Kings rode up on horseback, following a star attached to a cord which stretched along the street to the door of a hall where the said Constable was, and they dismounted and entered. In the hall there was set up (puesta) another star to guide them, and there they offered their gifts to the good Child Jesus. They carried out all the ceremonies [?plays] (ficieron todos sus actos) with King Herod with great dignity, and after it was all over the said Constable, the Countess, their brothers and

sisters, and the rest, danced for a while. . . .

8. TOLEDO:
CORPUS CHRISTI PROCESSION AND PLAYS (1493)

These accounts from Toledo Cathedral refer to expenditure on the Corpus Christi procession and plays in the year 1493. On a first reading they may appear disjointed and fragmentary, but, although there are a number of obscure items, a fairly clear picture emerges of the preparations during the weeks leading up to Corpus Christi. Floats were cleaned, and carpentry work was started. An artificial donkey and its harness were made from scratch. Costumes, masks, wigs were made or renovated. Painters worked daily. On the day before Corpus Christi, food was prepared, the floats were taken to the Cathedral, and their railings fitted.
On Corpus Christi itself, payments were made to actors and to the many others who had taken part, including ninety-five laborers who had carried the floats through the streets. There then follow details of payments for dismantling and storage. The salary of the organizer, Alonso del Campo, is included as one of the last items. These records give a fascinating glimpse of all that was involved in putting on plays in the Middle Ages.

An account of the expenses for the floats and plays (<u>entremeses e juegos</u>) for the feast of Corpus Christi in the year one thousand, four hundred and ninety-three:
Firstly, to a man who cleaned the floats (<u>carros</u>) and shook out all the other things, one <u>rreal</u>.
For brooms, four <u>maravedis</u>.
Fifteen hanks of rope (<u>sogas yscales</u>) at five <u>blancas</u> the hank.
Three ropes (<u>sogas rrollizas</u>), seven and a half <u>mrs</u>.
One and a half loads of quarter-sawn timber (<u>quartones</u>), ten pieces to the load (<u>cargo</u>), cost nine <u>rreales</u>.
I bought a small cart (<u>carreta</u>) costing eight <u>rreales</u>.
Eight dozen pieces of wood from Avila (<u>avilesa</u>) at twenty-five <u>mrs</u>. the dozen, that is, two hundred <u>mrs</u>.
Two loads of clay (<u>dos cargas de barro</u>) to make the mold for the donkey, eight <u>maravedis</u>.
One yard (<u>vara</u>) of Brittany cloth (<u>bretaña</u>) on which to paint the Veronica, one <u>rreal</u>.

Saturday before Whitsun
Two journeymen carpenters and four assistants (<u>peones</u>) came, their wages were eight <u>reales</u>.
For food and wine, eighteen <u>mrs</u>.
A hundred ship's <u>caravies</u>, two <u>rreales</u>.
Two hundred large <u>caravies</u>, twenty <u>mrs</u>.
Five pounds of six-inch nails (<u>xemales</u>) and nine-inch nails (<u>vellotes</u>), fifty <u>mrs</u>.
Three hundred short nails with large heads (<u>tachuelas</u>), twenty-four

252

mrs.
Two hundred <u>caravies d'entrechilla</u>, one <u>rreal</u>.
Two journeymen painters came to mold the donkey and paint those
things which were necessary, and their wages were four <u>rreales</u>.
To two lads who ground colors, two <u>rreales</u>.
Eight quires of coarse paper, at five and a half <u>mrs</u>. the quire,
makes forty-four <u>mrs</u>.
Four pounds of glue at ten <u>mrs</u>. the pound.
Two pots to boil glue, nine <u>mrs</u>.
Half a measure (<u>hanega</u>) of stive (<u>harija</u>) to make the pastes,
twenty-four <u>mrs</u>.

Wednesday after Whitsun, 28 May
One pound of bright yellow (<u>jalde</u>) cost fifty <u>mrs</u>.
Half a pound of red lead (<u>azarcón</u>), sixteen <u>mrs</u>.
One pound of green (<u>cardenillo</u>), forty-eight <u>mrs</u>.
One pound of white (<u>blanque</u>), twenty <u>mrs</u>.
One pound of vermilion (<u>bermellón</u>), eighty <u>mrs</u>.
Half a <u>rreal</u>'s worth of ocher (<u>ocre</u>), and six <u>mrs</u>. of dark crimson
(<u>alvin</u>), that is, twenty-one and a half.
Five quires (<u>manos</u>) of fine paper for the giants' collars and for four
caps which were made, also for writing out parts (<u>para coplas</u>) and
for other necessary items, at twelve <u>mrs</u>. the quire, makes sixty.
Two journeymen carpenters came, and two assistants; their wages
were six <u>rreales</u>.
Two journeymen painters came, their wages were four <u>rreales</u>.
To a man who ground colors, one <u>rreal</u>.
For bread, wine, and afternoon snack, eighteen mrs.

Thursday, 29 May
Seven planks (<u>tablones</u>), three and a half <u>rreales</u>.
The rough woolen cloth (<u>sayal</u>) for making the hermit's cape and
scapular cost three <u>rreales</u>.
For some sandals, twelve <u>mrs</u>.
The two strings of beads for the hermit cost twelve <u>mrs</u>.
I bought three and a half measures (<u>hanegas</u>) of wheat at seventy-
three <u>mrs</u>. the measure, that is, two hundred and fifty-five and a
half <u>mrs</u>.
For winnowing, seven <u>mrs</u>.
For milling, twenty-four and a half <u>mrs</u>.
Three and a half yards of Brittany cloth for the shift of Our Lady's
soul, three and a half <u>rreales</u>.
For making it up, and for silk, half a <u>rreal</u>.
Four yards of rough white woolen cloth for the gown of the man
who exploded (<u>el rrebentado</u>) at half a <u>rreal</u> the yard.
Three yards of ribbons (<u>çintas</u>) for a girdle for the soul of Our
Lady, six <u>mrs</u>.
Two journeymen carpenters came with an assistant, their wages were
five <u>rreales</u>.
Two master painters came, their wages were four <u>rreales</u>.

To a man who ground colors, one rreal.
Food and wine, half a rreal.

Friday, 30 May
Two consignments (caminos) of water, five mrs.
Three hundred caravies de entrechilla, one and a half rreales.
Twenty-five ship's nails (clavos de barco), half a rreal.
Five hundred short nails with large heads at eight mrs. the hundred.
Six pounds of nine-inch nails at ten mrs. the pound.
One pound of tinplate (lata) for collars, one hundred and seventy-five mrs.
Twine (bramante) and string (cordel), forty-two mrs.
Black and white thread, and saddler's and tailor's needles, sixteen mrs.
Two master carpenters came with an assistant, their wages were five rreales.
Two master painters came, their wages were four rreales.
To a man who ground colors, one rreal.
For his food and wine, half a rreal.

Saturday [sic], 1 June
The red cloth (paño colorado) for the tunic of the man who exploded, one rreal.
Making up this said garment, one rreal.
For hoops (aros) for the giants and for the donkey, twenty mrs.
Twelve ounces of metal foil (?fuella) for the crowns, the monstrance, and for other necessary items, at five mrs. the ounce, comes to sixty.
For indigo (anir danfaz), half a rreal.
For carmine (carmin) ten mrs.
Two ounces of thread, eight mrs.
A strap (correón) for the donkey and for the tomb (sepulcro), half a rreal.
Eight pounds of hemp (cáñamo) at twelve mrs. the pound, ninety-six mrs.
To dyeing these eight pounds at seven mrs. the pound.
To dyeing one garment black and four red, two and a half rreales.
For resin (rresina) and wax (çera) to make pitch (betún), eight mrs.
For preparing the tunics and hose of the patriarchs (santos padres), three rreales.
To eggs for the tempera (temple) eight mrs., and vinegar to make green (cardenillo) two mrs.: a total of ten.
A piece of fine leather (un valdrés), half a rreal.
Two master carpenters came with one assistant, their wages were five rreales.
Two painters came, their wages were four rreales.
To a man who ground colors, one rreal.
For his afternoon snack and wine, half a rreal.

Monday, 3 June
Five rreales were spent on some old sheets to mold the donkey and
other things.
For cork to swell out the hindquarters of the donkey, twenty mrs.
For soaping eight albs (alvas) at four mrs. each.
For soaping the loose gown and headgear of the female giant (la
giganta) and six little shifts (camisicas) for the small angels, seven-
teen mrs.
Four cow's tails, eight mrs.
Four discs (rroldanas) of ashwood for the feet of the donkey, twelve
mrs.
The rings (?aldabas) and their appurtenances cost one rreal.
Two pinches (adarmes) of saffron for the green (verde), seven
mrs.
For half a pound of white, ten mrs.
Two master carpenters came, their wages were four rreales, and an
assistant at one rreal, totals five rreales.
Two master painters at four rreales.
To a man who ground colors, one rreal.
Two pounds of glue at ten mrs. the pound.
Four ounces of tinplate, forty-four mrs.
For making four Jews' masks (caras) and two devils' masks, the
donkey's head, the giants' collars, four angels' caps, renovating
(adobar) the hermit's mask and other masks (rrostros), and putting
the giants together (armar los gigantes), ten rreales.
Nine pounds of nine-inch and six-inch nails at ten mrs.
For the afternoon snack and wine, half a rreal.
For painting the Veronica and the hermit's mask and five other
masks which were painted with oil paints (que se pintaron a olio),
eight rreales.
Two hundred caravies de entrechilla, one rreal.
Two hundred short nails with large heads, sixteen mrs.

Tuesday, 4 June
A dozen glasses, fifteen mrs.
Four jars, four small jugs, and three containers for water, forty-five
mrs.
The donkey's packsaddle cost three and a half rreales.
The rope headstall, girth, breeching, and the halter and bell cost one
and a half rreales.
Twelve gourds for the giants at three mrs. each.
Four rods for keeping order, twenty mrs.
A basket to hold nails, two and a half mrs.
Eight rreales to have five wigs (copias [should read cofias]) made
for the Christs.
To make seventeen wigs with long hair (melenas) for the apostles
and the patriarchs, five rreales.
Two master carpenters came, their wages were four rreales, and an
assistant whose wage was one, a total of five.
Two master painters, their wages were four rreales.

To a man who ground colors, one rreal.
For his snack and wine, half a rreal.

Wednesday, 5 June
Six dozen rockets (cohetes) at seventy mrs. the dozen, that is, four hundred and twenty mrs.
For baking three and a half measures (tres hanegas e media) of wheat, twenty-eight mrs.
To the baker's assistant for fetching and carrying ten trays, ten mrs.
To two women who kneaded the dough, one rreal.
Two measures (cargas) of licorice (oroçuz), two more of fennel (hinojo), and and two more of rramos, four and a half rreales.
Two measures (cargas) of cherries, twenty-one rreales.
Twenty measures (arrovas) of wine, twenty rreales.
For glue and red ocher (almagra), twelve mrs.
Three pounds of nine-inch nails for the nets (rredes).
Three master carpenters came because there was a lot to be done, and six assistants to move the floats (carros) to the church and erect the railings (verjas); the wages of the master craftsmen were six rreales, those of the assistants another six.
Two master painters came, and their wages were four rreales.
To a man who ground colors, one rreal.
For wine and afternoon snack, half a rreal.
The hermit's black robe including the cost of making it up came to two hundred and thirty mrs.
To a man who carted the bread, wine, fruit and other necessary items, twenty mrs.
A pair of geese for the officials' lunch on the day of Corpus Christi, two rreales.

Thursday, Corpus Christi, 6 June
To each of the sixteen priests who carried the monstrance, two rreales.
To the giants, thirty rreales.
To ten trumpeters, forty-four rreales.

The Temptation (Acto de la Tentaçión)
To the person playing Christ, two rreales, another two to the hermit, a total of four.
To four angels, two rreales.
To a devil, one rreal; to the person who let off the rockets, half a rreal.

The Adulteress (La muger adúltera)
To the person playing Christ, two rreales.
To four Jews, seven rreales.
To the woman, one rreal.
To two apostles, two rreales.

The Veronica (La Verónica)
To the person playing Mary, one rreal, to St. John, another, totaling two.
To the people playing St. Veronica and Mary Magdalene, one rreal.
To the two Marys, one rreal.

The Harrowing of Hell (Los santos padres)
Three rreales to each of the eight patriarchs (santos padres), totaling twenty-four rreales.
Their lunch cost two rreales.
To the person playing Christ, four rreales.
To a man whose job it was to set off the rockets in Hell (en el ynfierno), one rreal.

The Resurrection (La Resurreçión)
To the person playing Christ, four rreales.
To the Magdalene, one rreal.
To two apostles, two rreales.
To four angels, two rreales.
To two Marys, one rreal.
To two drummers, two rreales.

The Man who exploded (El rrebentado)
To the man who exploded, four rreales.
To two devils, four rreales.
To two men who walked with the donkey, two rreales.
To the abbot and to two lads who went with him, three rreales.

The Assumption (La Asunçión)
To the person playing Christ, two rreales, one to the person playing Mary, a total of three rreales.
To four apostles, four rreales.
To four angels, two rreales.
To the man who had the duty of receiving the soul (tomar ell anima), half a rreal.

To the angels who walked in front of the monstrance playing instruments (tañendo), eighteen rreales.
To the clavero who guided them, two rreales.
To the organ player, one rreal.
To four men who carried the torches (hachas), four rreales.
To four men who carried the organ (órganos), four rreales.
To ninety-five men (peones) who carried the floats (carros), half a rreal each.
For the hire of four cloaks and hoods for the Jews, two rreales.
To a man who played a small drum (tanborino), two drummers (atanbores), and a tambourine player (pandero de sonajas) who walked with the giants and played at dawn at Whitsun (el día de Pascua).
One pound of candles to enable me to do things in the house that night, and to prepare necessary things in the cathedral, and to pro-

vide light for Hell, forty mrs.

To six officials (ofiçiales) who supervised the performances of the plays (que rregían los actos), two rreales each.

For the hire of nine leather containers and three sacks for two days, twenty-four mrs.

For taking off the railings and taking the floats back to the place where they are kept (asentar los carros en su lugar), and putting everything else away, four rreales.

The wax which was burned in the four torches which preceded the monstrance, the two carried by the giants, my candle which I provided myself, came to seven hundred mrs. altogether.

For the hire of the dwarf's bells, half a rreal.

Nine mrs. for three consignments of water for the wine on the day of Corpus Christi.

Item, added here: one thousand mrs., the salary given each year to Alonso del Campo for organizing (por que trabaja en hazer) the said plays (actos).

Item, two rreales for the scribe who wrote these accounts.

Thus, the total spent on the feast of Corpus Christi in this year of '93, as itemized fully in this book, is 21,124 mrs. Half of this sum was paid by the Fabric Office (la Obra) and half by the Treasury (el Refitor). The items of wood (las cosas de madera) and other appurtenances (atavíos) which remained and which could be kept, remained in the keeping of the said Alonso del Campo. This account was written down on 20 June 1493.

Johan de Sepúlveda
Canon Treasurer

Alvarus Petrus
Canon of Toledo

Johan Ruyz
Apostolic Scribe

Paid jointly by the Fabric Office and the Treasury.

9. SEURRE: MYSTERY OF SAINT MARTIN (1496)

In 1496 the inhabitants of Seurre, near Dijon, staged the "Mystery of Saint Martin" specially written for them by Andrieu de la Vigne. The manuscript of the play contains the following account of the preparations and performance, apparently composed by de la Vigne himself since his signature follows the account.

Praise, glory, honor, and exaltation be unto God, the Virgin Mary, and the most glorious patron of this town of Seurre, my lord St. Martin. In the year 1496, the ninth day of May, the vigil of the Ascension, there assembled in the room of Maistre Andrieu de la Vigne, native of La Rochelle and in the service of the king (facteur du roy), the venerable, discreet messire Oudot Gobillon, incumbent (vicquaire) of the Church of St. Martin in the said Seurre, the honorable Aubert Dupuys, Pierre Loiseleur, Pierre Goillot, George Casote, Pierre Gravelle called Belleville, citizens, and Maistre Pierre Rasoyer, principal (recteur) of the schools for the said Seurre, who commissioned him (marchanderent) to make and compose for them a text which should set out and declare by characters (declairee par parsonnaiges) the life of my lord St. Martin so that on seeing it acted the common people would easily be able to see and understand how the noble patron of the said Seurre lived a holy and devout life. And this text was made and completed as it appears five weeks after that date. And the said life would have been acted on the next feast of St. Martin [*July 4th*] had it not been for the rumor of war and the great number of soldiers (gendarmes) who came to the said town of Seurre, so that the matter was put off for a time. In order to do it, then, the roles were made and set out (faitz et levez) by the said Maistre Andrieu, and the following worthy persons were appointed to distribute and give these out to people proper to perform them: the noble Guyot Berbis, then mayor of Seurre, the noble Guenin Druet, Robin Joliqueur, and Pierre Loiseleur, citizens of the said Seurre who after careful and mature deliberation distributed the said roles to each person as the situation required, receiving from the players the oath required in such case to be prepared to perform as soon as the right moment should come. After which each one individually took care to study his role and to go to the church of the said lord St. Martin or to St. Michael's when it was necessary to see the rites (ceremonies) and ways of doing things (facons de faire) for when they would perform in public, which it was not possible to do as soon as they would have liked because of the aforesaid difficulties. But when they had waited as long as they could, seeing the proper time for the performance passing, the above-named determined and concluded that they would perform the Sunday next after the fair at Sier, for which each made ready. However, again for some bad rumors of war current at the fair it was not possible to play that day, and the fol-

lowing week the grape harvest began in all areas, and they were
forced to wait till it was over, otherwise there would have been
very few people there. After all these things, the good intention of
the said actors to perform the said mystery was not wasted, but the
aforementioned organizers and actors assembled at the said church
and unanimously agreed they would have their parades (monstres) on
Tuesday, 4 October, and would perform the following Sunday, the
feast of St. Denis.

When this decision was reached, the said players carried out
their duty of providing suitable clothes and accessories (accoustre-
ments et habillements). The noble lord the mayor was responsible
for seeing the stages (les eschaffaulx) completed, which he had
started to have erected before the said fair at Sier, and he displayed
much care and great diligence in this. The man in charge of the
special effects (maistre des secretz), Maistre Germain Jacquet, was
sent for from Autun (Ostun). When he arrived, the aforesaid Pierre
Goillot who was treasurer for the said mystery (receveur des
denyers) provided him with everything he needed to make the idols,
trapdoors (secrets), and other things.

When the day came appointed for the parades (les monstres),
it was proclaimed by a trumpeter that all those who had parts in
the said mystery should assemble at midday in Lombardy, each one
dressed in his costume. When the proclamation had been made, the
said players assembled in the said place and were arranged in order
one after the other, mounted, equipped, armed, and adorned so well
that it could not have been improved upon. And it should be explained that they made such a long procession that when God and
his angels left that place riding behind the others, the devils were
already beyond the tower of the prison near the Chantblanc gate,
their route being past the house of Perrenot de Pontoux, along the
horse market as far as the house of my lord the marquis beside the
town walls, and from there along the main street as far as the
aforesaid place. And there was a space of barely two and a half
feet between the horses, and a total of around nine score horses.

When the parade was over, everyone took thought for himself,
and the following Friday the boxes (loges) were handed over to the
actors to furnish them with hangings (tapisseries), including those of
the neighboring towns near Seurre. Wherefore on Saturday, as the
weather was fine, everybody took great pains to adorn the said scaffolds (eschaffaulx). And when the task was completed no one could
remember ever having seen finer scaffolds, better prepared (compas-
sez), decked, hung, nor proportioned than they were. The next
morning, which was Sunday, when they prepared to perform the rain
came down so heavily that it was impossible to do anything, and
continued without ceasing from three o'clock in the morning till
three after dinner without stopping, which was very distressing for
the actors and everyone else. And indeed those who had come from
the towns round about decided to go away when they saw the weather so changed. When the said mayor and others learned of this
they decided when the weather improved that they would perform a

farce in the playing area (sur le parc) to satisfy and please them. So
the trumpeter cried that all the players should at once go, ready
costumed, to the house of M. le Marquis, and all the others should
go on to the mansions. The said cry having been made on one side
and another, everyone did his duty.

Then the actors were put in order and they left the house of
my lord the marquis, following each other so impressively (honnour-
ablement) that when they came to the playing area (le parc) everyone was much astonished. They circled round as was proper, and
then each went to his box (loge), and the only people who were left
in the playing area were the actors in the farce of the Miller copied
previously [i.e., in the manuscript], which was so well acted that
everyone was delighted and nothing more was done that day. When
they left the stage, the said players formed up in order and to the
sound of trumpets, clarions, minstrels, high and low instruments; they
came to the said church of our lord St. Martin to sing a very devout prayer (salut) to Our Lady that the good weather might come
and they might execute their good and devout intention and purpose
in this said mystery. Which thing God granted them, for the next
day which was Monday the weather was fine again, and it was proclaimed by the trumpeter that by order of the mayor and council
(echevins) of the said Seurre all shops should be closed and no one
should be so bold as to do any work at his trade (oeuvre mecanique)
in the said town for the next three days while they performed the
mystery of my lord St. Martin and that all the actors should go
immediately to the church (moustier) of the said Seurre. Immediately all the people betook themselves to the scaffolds and the actors
to their appointed place, and then they were put in order by the
said Maistre Andrieu who had the book (registre), and they set out
to the sound of trumpets, clarions, buccinas (bussines), organs, harps,
drums, and other high and low instruments playing all round them, as
far as the said playing area where they circled round as is customary; which was such a magnificent and sumptuous array that it is
beyond the wit of man to describe so fine and splendid a matter.
This done, each retired to his marked place (enseigne) and the two
messengers opened the play as is written above in this present book
(registre).

Then Lucifer began to speak, and during his speech the man
who played Satan, when he prepared to enter through his trapdoor
(secret) underground, his costume caught fire round his buttocks so
that he was badly burned. But he was so swiftly succored, stripped,
and reclothed that without giving any sign [of pain] he came and
played his part, then retired to his house.

The players were very frightened by this mishap, for they
thought that such a bad beginning would mean further trouble. Nevertheless, with the help of my lord St. Martin who took the matter
in his hands, things went a hundred times better than expected.
After this the father and mother of St. Martin with their attendants
came onto the said playing area and made such a lively beginning
that everyone--both actors and audience--was very surprised and

indeed, abolishing this former fear, the said actors were filled with such confidence and boldness that no lion in his den nor murderer in a forest was more bold and confident than they were when they performed.

That morning they began between seven and eight o'clock and finished between eleven and twelve. For the beginning of the afternoon session which was at one o'clock the said Satan came back to play his part and made his excuse to Lucifer [*short speech*], and then completed his part in that scene and the other actors after him, each in his place. Then they broke for supper (<u>firent pause pour aller souper</u>) between five and six o'clock, still acting (<u>jouant</u>) and using the time as best they might. And when they left the playing area, the said actors lined up in order as aforesaid and went to the church of my lord St. Martin where they gave thanks to God and sang devoutly the <u>Salve Regina</u>.

The following day which was Tuesday and the Wednesday after, they entered and left the playing area at the aforesaid times. Thus, as is before described, was performed the said mystery of the glorious friend of God, my lord St. Martin, patron saint of Seurre, so triumphantly, authentically, and magnificently, without any fault in the world, that it is not possible for mortal man to describe it in writing as well as it was executed, ending on the 12th day of the month of October, 1496 A.D.

10. PALMA: EASTER CEREMONY (SIXTEENTH CENTURY)

Easter Tuesday ceremony from the Cathedral of Palma, Majorca, preserved in an early sixteenth-century handbook of ceremonial. A much shorter description is contained in an earlier Palma MS. (fourteenth or fifteenth century).

And early, before the offices begin, the person in charge [the sacristan] (lo ragent) is to arrange to have brought to the high altar all the symbols of the Passion of Jesus Christ as noted in Mary's part (consueta). And he is to arrange to have a costume ready in the sacristy for the person taking the part of Mary: a richly worked alb, a dalmatic of green velvet, and a cloak made from a cape of red velvet. And the part of the said Mary is to be taken by a priest chosen by the sacristan, who is to give him one cruat for his work. But the said sacristan is to choose a young boy to take the part of the angel, and is to give him one sou. And when the priest goes to the altar to sing Mass, the subdeacon is to bring the Veronica, and the deacon is to bring him the Gospel. And when Mass has started, the person playing Mary is to put on his costume, and the angel is to do the same, but the angel is to make his way to the Chapel of the Trinity so that when it is his turn to sing he will be high up in the galleries (corradors) on the side of the Chapel of St. Gabriel. And when the Epistle has been concluded, the sacristan with the said Mary, accompanied by two altar boys dressed in surplices and bearing the large silver candelabra with lit white candles, will leave the sacristy to walk to the choir. And they are to leave the cathedral by the Mirador portal. They are to enter the cathedral by the door which overlooks the sea and stop at the gate of the choir in such a way that they cannot be seen from the choir. And the candles are to be lit if they have gone out. And as they are finishing the Alleluia Angelus Domini, the sacristan and Mary, preceded by the altar boys, are to enter the choir. And at the top of the steps leading to the choir, between the seats of the Bishop and the Archdeacon, Mary is to sing Victime paschali laudes, and the choir is to take it up, and the sacristan, Mary, and the others are to walk through the choir on the Bishop's side. And they are to walk towards the high altar past the Chapel of St. Eulalia. And before the high altar there is to be placed a stool on which Mary is to stand, her face turned towards the choir. And the sacristan is to stand on Mary's right to read the script and to hand the symbols of the Passion to her. And at one corner of the altar, on the side on which the sacristan is standing, there shall stand an altar boy to give the symbols to the sacristan. And the said sacristan shall give them to Mary. And at the other side of the altar there shall be another altar boy to receive the symbols from Mary's hand. And just inside the gate of the choir shall stand the twelve priests with cloaks and staffs. They are to question the said Mary. And the

sacristan, reading the script, shall give the symbol to the said Mary
as the script requires.   And when the point is reached where Mary
is to sing of the resurrection of the dead, there are to be ready
beneath the high altar seven or eight altar boys, or as many as is
wished, dressed in albs with their heads covered with amices.   And
when the moment of the resurrection arrives, they are to emerge
from under the altar, roll down to the bottom step, and then walk
to the sacristy.   And the angel is to be ready in the gallery.   When
his cue to sing comes, he is to have his wings full of lit candles
(tindra les ales plenes de candelas encesses).   And when he emerges,
there will be an explosion (feran una bombarde) or some such noise
to mark his appearance.   And when he has sung, he is to withdraw,
and after the ceremony (consueta) is over, Mary, the sacristan, and
the altar boys are to return to the sacristy to change.   And they
are to come down from the altar on the side of the Chapel of St.
Gabriel.   And the office is to continue.

11. BOURGES PARADE: ACTS OF THE APOSTLES (1536)

The description of some of the costumes and floats for the play of the Acts of the Apostles in Bourges in 1536 is taken from Jacques Thiboust's eyewitness account of the parade (monstre) which preceded the performance; his complete text is fifty-five pages long in the 1838 edition. The extracts are given in the order in which they occur in the original; the descriptions of Heaven and Hell will be found in Section B.2 (see pp. 91-92, above). The preliminary address to the reader is in verse and the rest of the account in prose.

Do not imagine, kind readers, that the description hereafter given of the parade (monstre) is a fairytale (fable) or that the directors should have wanted anything written but the truth. It is certain that it has been set down from beginning to end as the eye beheld it, and I would indeed that, as I wish, Almighty God had enabled you to see it yourselves; then you would say: the author of this account has left out more than he has put in.

The order (ordre) of the magnificent and triumphant parade of the mystery of the holy Acts of the Apostles, done at Bourges, Sunday, the last day of April, 1536.

About six o'clock in the morning, the mayor and councillors (eschevins) of the said town, accompanied by the officers thereof to the number of thirty-six, wearing their red and green gowns--that is, the said mayor and councillors on their mules, with saddle cloths, and the said officers on foot, each having a white staff in his hand to keep order and protect the throng of people--made their way to the Abbey and Monastery of Saint-Sulpice of Bourges in which were already the major part of the townsmen who were to portray the characters of the said mystery; all of whom, the said citizens, after having heard Mass, withdrew, each one to the rooms and other places prepared for them, to dress and array themselves, in which place they were all, according to their rank, honorably and with good will, welcomed by the religious of the said monastery who offered them all food and wine in abundance.

Then about nine o'clock there came also to the said abbey the members of the judiciary (messieurs de la justice) to give help and support to the organizers of the said mystery and see how the parade would be ordered. To this end they had the trumpets, drums, and pipes sounded, which was the signal given to everyone to present himself ready to be placed in his order. At which each of them as his duty was came immediately to the place ordained, which was a great open space surrounded by walls in which there were three big gates, by one of which, on the side by the church, all these people entered; and at the second of these gates, giving onto the grounds (partie) and gardens of the said Abbey, surrounded and enclosed by

265

water-filled ditches so that no one could enter them except through
the said gate, was someone, appointed to the task and standing in a
high place, holding in his hands the order of the said parade, the
number, names, and surnames of the characters in it, whom he
called out in turn; the said members of the judiciary, mayor, and
councillors conducted and guided them to the other, third, gate of
the said area, round a lake which was in the said meadow and gardens, so that it was possible to see the whole of the said procession
(ordre) except the horses and triumphal cars, Paradise and Hell which
had remained in the great court in front, which looks onto the district of the said town called Saint-Sulpice, and whose gates were
wide open.   Then, at eleven o'clock, they began to emerge from the
said abbey in the following order.

First, the attorney-general (procureur) of the king and queen
of Navarre on his mule, holding a white staff in his hand and escorted by twelve men-at-arms also with white staves in their hands
who pushed back the people to clear the way, for such a great
number had gathered in this district that only with the greatest difficulty were they forced back into place to clear a way between,
which was indeed but narrow.

First there walked five trumpeters and a bugler (clairon) with
four Swiss drummers and two fifes, followed by two furies from
Hell, who were naked men with here and there on their bodies long
hair, long beards, eyebrows down to their chins, and the rest of them
covered in wounds and gaping mouths from which fire seemed to
issue.

[*The next thirty odd pages describe the devils and the Hell cart
followed by groups of different human beings, good and bad, on foot,
on horseback, and on floats, ending with the float of Herod
Antipas.*]

After them [*the archers of Herod Antipas*] marched a number
of small children, dressed and arrayed like the above, some of whom
carried harps, lutes, rebecs, and bagpipes (cornemuses), which they
played very skillfully; others sang musically.   And on a triumphal car
with blue and gold hangings on which were scattered armorial bear-
ings of the said Antipas was a throne fashioned from flowers (?à
façon de fleurons) on which were seated two small children wearing
blue taffeta tunics, with bare arms and feet, bareheaded and wearing
wreaths of laurel; in front of them on this said cart was a small
table on which stood a spinet (espinette) which they played very
well, each with one hand only, while with the others they held a
triumphal wreath in the middle of which were attached by blue silk
ribbons two white pennons (tollettes = *small cloths*) on which in gold
letters was written, on one:

Dignitas in plures diffusa valescit

and on the other:

Honores non dignitati sed meritis tribuendum est

The said car was guided and pushed by four other archers
(pharétrans) dressed as above.

[*Eight more pages of description of major characters and their attendants then follow.*]

Next came the Eunuch of the said queen of Ethiopia on a-
nother car or chariot, painted to look like red and green porphyry
with great scrolls and gilded foliage in the antique style, representing different birds flying in the air, and his coat of arms. The said
car was pushed by four Ethiopians with naked arms, legs, and heads.
Their bodies were covered in white satin with taffeta sailor-breeches
of the same color and wreaths of laurel on their heads like crowns.
The said car was under the charge of a certain Coridon, who marched in front very orderly in his accoutrements. The said Eunuch was
seated on a chair made in gilded flower-work (?ouvrage de fleurons
dores) covered with a silk cloth. He was dressed in cloth of gold
and silver and over it a gown of crimson velvet, lined in crimson
satin, worked all over in skilled gold work. His doublet was of
fringed cloth of silver; he had a hat of gray-blue (pers) velvet in the
Ethiopian style on which hung many clusters (houppes) of pearls. He
was adorned with chains and rings in great numbers and of great
value and worth. In front of him was placed a reading desk
(pupitre) on two long supports of gilded scroll-work on which stood
an open book, whose cover was of silver gilt worked in large figures
(?ouvré à grands personnages) which weighed perhaps five or six
marks [*1 mark = 8oz.*] which the said Eunuch was reading, turning,
and moving the leaves very often.

[*Ten pages of description follow.*]

Nero came next on a high platform (tribunal) eight feet wide
and ten feet long, covered to the ground with a cloth of gold on
which were embroidered great eagles as lifelike as possible . . . [*one
page description*]. This said platform and he on it were carried by
eight captive kings who were underneath it with only their heads
showing, crowned with gold crowns, and it was followed by another
group of trumpets, bugles, drums, and fifes.

[*The description of Nero's court then follows.*]

Next came Moses carrying a rod in his hand, wearing a long
satin robe with a taffeta mantle over it. His head was bare with
two little horns fixed to it.
Following him walked St. Michael, Gabriel, Uriel, Raphael,
Cherubim, and Seraphim wearing wings moving constantly.

[*Then finally comes the Heaven cart.*]

12. MODENA: CORPUS CHRISTI PLAY (1556)

The company of St. Peter Martyr staged a number of plays at the great festivals in Modena during the sixteenth century. The following description of the Corpus Christi play of 1556 is one of the most detailed preserved in the city records.

At the Corpus Christi procession on 4 June of the year 1556, when Monsignor Gandolfo Sigone was bishop (ordinario), they performed the play (si fece la Rappresentazione) of how Nebuchadnezzar set up the gold statue forcing everybody to adore it; it was a thing (la cosa) no less beautiful and worthy than any other which had ever been performed and it proceeded in the following order. There was a most beautiful cart, surrounded by large canvas screens on which was painted with colors, flowers, and figures the great history of the deeds of the aforesaid king: and these paintings were done by Messer Giovanni Tanasca, one of the Brothers of Charity (fratelli amorevoli). The cart was framed all round by an alabaster frame and at the corners were some heads in relief, all gilded. On the cart there was a tall pillar (pillo), and on the pillar was a statue in relief three ells (braccia) high and all gilded which held a scepter in its hand, and was made by Begarello. Behind the statue was a furnace ingeniously (misteriosamente) constructed and painted in which there were fireworks and people to make them burn at the appointed time. The rest of the play took place as follows. First came the King, richly attired and crowned, riding a most beautiful and finely caparisoned jennet (gianetto); accompanying him there followed twenty noblemen from different nations, dressed in different ways according to the usage of their lands and all armed according to their custom. It was an admirable sight to behold the great variety of dress, all of silk richly adorned with gold and silver, and each wore on his head a helmet, a turban, or a hat following the fashion of his country; for some were Turks, others from Northern Europe, or Tartars, Greeks, Moors, Arabs, and from sundry other nations. These noblemen rode beautiful horses equipped according to their custom and each had his page at the stirrup, dressed in his livery, who carried on his left arm a shield made according to the custom of his land. The King was preceded by four horses more regally adorned than the others on which rode four pages in most beautiful and shining armor, one carrying the King's spear (zagaglia), another his rapier (stocco), another the shield, and another the sallet. On either side of the King there came on foot twenty grooms (palafrenieri) worthily clad in coats and sleeves of mail, and each one of them carried a halberd and the battle-axe with velvet and gold hangings. In this order they left [*the house of*] our Company and with royal magnificence set off to make their appearance in the cathedral. They were preceded, accompanied, and followed by the people of the city in such numbers that it was barely possible and only with great

effort to walk very slowly, so much so that there was much for the
Brothers (fratelli) to do, who in great numbers and armed with
staves (aste) kept the procession in good order. Having arrived at
the cathedral, the King and the King's barons and pages dismounted
and, leaving the horses with the footmen (paggi pedoni), in the same
order accompanied the cart into the cathedral; they arrived before
the Bishop and the other lords, and when the King gave the signal
at the proper time, a proclamation (bando) was made by a trumpeter
that everyone, of whatsoever condition or rank, should obey the
King's command, namely that at the sound of the lute, harp, lyre,
viol (violina), and violin each one should prostrate himself on the
ground and adore the gold statue of the King his master. At the
end of the proclamation the aforesaid instruments, which were accommodated on part of the cart, began to play in a most harmonious manner. As soon as they began to play the King and the
whole Court fell to the ground and adored the golden statue. However, three youths who were present--namely Sidrac, Midrac, and
Edbenego--did not likewise prostrate themselves but remained standing, their eyes fixed on Heaven, inspired to adore the true God and
scorn the statue of the King. When this was noticed they were
immediately accused before the said King of scorning his commands,
and he, having asked that they should be brought before him, told
them that if they did not prostrate themselves with the others at
the sound of the instruments to adore his statue he would have the
furnace made three times hotter (farebbe tre volte più accendered
la fornace) and have them thrown into the burning fire. They very
promptly answered that they would adore no other than the God of
Israel. The King was angry and commanded that they should be
forthwith seized and bound and led to the furnace, which very appropriately sent forth flames in several places in such a way that
they harmed the others but not the three youths, who right in the
middle of the fire began to praise and bless their true God with
beautiful and most learned verses inviting all creatures above and
below the Heavens to share in these holy hymns of praise. On hearing such singing there were but few who did not shed tears of pity
and emotion, moved by the well-sung verses. They finished their
singing while the furnace continued to burn, but the flames were so
carefully arranged that they harmed no one. After this beautiful
and highly praised play (Rappresentazione) a motet was sung and the
litanies were begun with a most harmonious music of voices and
instruments, as beautiful as ever was heard in our city on such a
day. Our Company received signal favor from the Bishop and the
Governor who did not wish the singers of any other Company to stop
and perform except ours. [Our Company] having started the litanies, everyone left the Cathedral, together with the cart, and all
took their places as before and in the same aforesaid order followed
the procession, and the three youths remained in the furnace until
the end of the procession. The matter (la cosa) had a beautiful
beginning and a most beautiful ending, and was praised by the whole
city. Camillo Panizzo devised and directed it. The author of the

verses sung by the three youths was Messer Lodovico Castelvetro.

13. ALCALÀ: MARTYRDOM OF SS. JUSTO AND PASTOR (1568)

In 1568 the remains of the child saints were taken in procession from Huesca (on the western slopes of the Pyrenees) to their original resting place, Alcalà de Henares, close to Madrid. The journey took six weeks. Festivities were organized by the towns along the route to welcome the procession.

This play was an important part of Alcalà's own celebrations, and two accounts of the staging survive. The text of the play includes a description of the pageant wagon and a detailed but puzzling description of a Heaven; these are apparently the accounts of an eye-witness. Ambrosio de Morales, Professor of Rhetoric at the University, recorded his impressions of the festivities, which include comments on the staging.

Both sources give some information about the context of the production. A procession, which included Church, civic, and university dignitaries, and also the pageant wagon (accompanied by two giants, or wild men, on stilts, and by fifteen or sixteen musicians), escorted the party on the last part of its journey into Alcalà; at this point the first part of the play was performed. For the second part, to be performed in the streets, a Heaven was needed in addition to the wagon. Morales describes it thus:

In the middle of the street there was constructed a large round cloud (una gran nuve redonda), which represented the heavens, very well made and equipped, and the whole machine revolved very well.

Owing to the late hour, the second and third parts were postponed, but the whole play was put on in church a week later, using the cart and the Heaven. According to Morales:

The play of the martyrdom of the two saints was acted using the great cloud, which was situated between the two choirs, with the pageant wagon (el castillo) beneath it.

[*Summary of the action of the play.*]

Then the great cloud opened, and the choir began to sing this song (villancico). Two angels came down, received the souls of the saints, and ascended to the cloud with very ingenious artifice.

Descriptions of the wagon and the Heaven were included in the text of the play.

The Pageant Wagon:
A cart (carro) or pageant wagon (castillo movedizo) was made,

entirely of finely worked wood. It was at least ten feet wide and
at least seventeen feet long. [*There follows a very lengthy description of the paintings on the panels of the cart: at the front, the
coat of arms of the church, which depicted the child saints on a
shield; at the back, and on the four side-panels, scenes representing
the martyrdom of the saints.*] These panels were separated by four
pillars (columnas), finely worked and painted. On the cart there
were many railings (berjas) with green boards (?mesas) from which
there sprang some flowers which made a splendid effect. At the
rear of the cart there was a very ornate green seat (silla) with the
same fleurs de lis and other very elegant decorations and carvings.
To get up onto this stage (suelo) there were two doors and ladders,
situated in the cart itself, which could not be seen, as the cart was
enclosed on all sides. These were used by the actors (representan-
tes) to climb up and down to a room (aposento) constructed inside
the cart, built onto the two axles which bore the four wheels on
which the cart moved.

The Heaven:

In this second act the martyrdom of the child saints Justo and
Pastor was represented and also the descent of the angels from
Heaven when they came for their blessed souls, and how Jesus
Christ received them to the accompaniment of loud music and rejoicing from the angelic choirs. For this episode there was constructed a large arch (un arco grande) thirty-six feet high and twenty-eight feet wide in the middle of which there was constructed a
Heaven (un zielo) which was fourteen feet "hollow" (en güeco), ten
feet wide, and seven feet long. It was controlled (se governaba)
from inside and revolved (hazia su arco y daba sus vueltas) like the
real heavens. Inside, there was music, and also people. It had its
doors (puertas) shut, and these could be opened by means of golden
stars with which the whole of one half was studded. That was on
the side where the moon was, for the other half, which belonged to
the sun, was solid blue. The Heaven was made of canvas stretched
over (fundado en) sieve hoops (aros de zedazos). It was made in two
halves, because in any other way it could not have been properly
made. Each half was fixed to (estaba fundado en) two half moons
(dos medias lunas) of wood from which extended many struts
(riostras) to all parts of the curved pieces (arcos), because otherwise
they would not have been secure. Each of these two half moons
fitted into (encajaronse en) a stout, round, long beam which divided
(atrabesaba en medio) the whole arch. In the middle of this beam
there was made a structure (un andamio) on which the people inside
the said Heaven could stand. This Heaven had a little door on one
side, which was kept covered by two angels who were driving the
sky on one side and by two others on the other side, and through
this door they went in and out. For it was necessary, so that nobody would see them come in and out. In the middle of the structure there were two small windlasses (tornillos) on which were two
wire ropes (dos cuerdas de alambre), long and fine, and on the end

of each was an angel carved of wood and about two [*feet*] high,
painted in gold, silver, and other splendid colors.   When the doors
were opposite the angels, they opened at the appropriate moment.

*How was the Heaven constructed?   It is likely that the beam
crossed the arch horizontally, and that the Heaven, probably a hemisphere, revolved on it.   The measurements are also a puzzle.   If the
arch was 28 feet wide, the 14 feet* <u>en güeco</u> *could refer to the
radius of the hemisphere.   Perhaps the other measurements (10 feet
x 7 feet) refer to the dimensions of the internal structure.   Finally,
it is not clear how many doors this complicated Heaven possessed.*

ORIGINALS OF TEXTS NOT READILY ACCESSIBLE

1. The Bordeaux carpenters' contract.

This contract was first mentioned in an article by Madeleine Pourésy in the Revue Historique de Bordeaux *in 1915, but it has never been published. We are most grateful to M. Charles Mazouer of the University of Bordeaux for telling us of the contract and providing us with a copy of his transcription of and notes on the original contract on which he is currently working. This text is published with his permission.*

B.1. The Playing Area (pp. 75-76)
[*f. 239*[v]] Aujourduy quart d'aougst l'an mil cinq cens XXV ont esté presens et perso[nnellement] establys Peyroton de Barety corratier, paroissien de Saint-Michel de Bourdeaux, et Guillem Bergeron, aguilletier, habitant de Bourdeaux, d'une part, et Bernard Gasteau maistre menuisier de Saint-Project et Rousseau, charpentier de grosse fuste de la paroisse Sainct-Maxens dudit Bourdeaux, d'autre part. Entre lesquelles parties ont esté faitz, passez et accordez les marché, pactes et appoinctemens que s'ensuyvent. C'est assavoir que lesdits Gasteau et Rousseau ont promis et seront tenus faire et pouser sur le foussé de Sainct-Eliège[1] au lieu où fut joué le mistère de madame saincte Eula[l]ye les eschaffaulx que s'ensuyvent pour jouer o l'ayde Nostre Seigneur le baptesme et décollation Monseigneur sainct Jehan Baptiste ensemble la conversion de la Magdeleine, mort et resurrection du Lazare en la forme et manière que s'ensuyt. Et premièrement barrer de tables le lieu et place où lesdits mistères se joueront despuis les murailhes de la maison commune de Sainct-Eliège tirant contre le jardin de Lestonar[2], monter sur le pavé de hault de troys pas dans ledit pavé et retourner à l'encontre de ladite murailhe contre ung esguyer qui sort de ladite maison commune de Sainct-Eliège, et ce de dix piedz de haulteur, lesdites tables et barrière de chaffaudage au mesmesme [sic] lieu que lesdits esch[aff]aux se ont acoustumé pouser et mectre.
[*f. 240*[r]] Item plus chaffauder toute la place qui est entre les deux tours qui sont à ladite maison commune ensemble les places qui seront depuis en face jusques à lad. murailhe de la ville et depuis le paradis jusques à icelle murailhe de la maison de la ville. Item plus faire ung eschaffault pour paradis et ung autre pour ung enfer de huict piedz de saillie et de unze piedz de haulteur, et ceux qui seront contre ladite murailhe de six piedz de saillie. Plus sur les deux coings du pavé à chacun coing ung eschaffault de douze piedz de long et la hauteur que s'apartiendra et quatre portes où il leur plaira ordonner. Et lisser la place où se jouera ledit mistère là où il sera besoing. Aussi faire des sièges hault sur ledit pavé

pour seoir le monde qui entrera dans ledit jeu et mistère. Toute
laquelle besongne lesdits Gasteau et Rousseau ont promis et promectent, et seront tenus rendre toute [la besongne] chaffaudage[3] et
pouser sur ledit lieu dans demain en huict jours prochainement
venans et iceulx eschaffaux ainsi faictz laisser en leur estat jusques
au jour de la feste de la décollation monseigneur sainct Jehan
Baptiste inclusivement. Et ce moyennant le pris et somme de cent
francs bourdelois, laquelle somme de cent francs bourdelois lesdits de
Barety et Bergeron et chacun d'eux ont [f. 240[v]] promis, promectent
et seront tenus rendre, bailler, payer et délivrer l'ung pour l'autre
et chacun d'eulx ung seul et pour le tout sans benffice de division
ausdits Gasteau et Rousseau dans ledit jour et feste decollation
monseigneur sainct Jehan Baptiste prochainement venant sans y faire
deffaulte aucune. Item plus a esté accordé entre eulx que s'il y
avoit grosse habundance de pluye les jours des festes que lesdits
mestiers se joueront tellement qu'ilz ne puissent jouer dans ledit
temps obstant ledit empeschement de pluye, lesdits Gasteau et Rousseau seront tenus laisser lesdits eschaffaulx audit lieu jusques à la
complément de cinq jours de festes dans lesqueulx ilz prétendent
jouer lesdits mistères après prouchains. Item plus a esté dit et
accordé entre lesdites parties que si lesdits eschaffaulx se rompent
par faulte et coulpe desdits Gasteau et Rousseau, en icelluy cas
seront tenus ester ausdits de Barety et Bergeron, aussi si aucunes
tables, membrures ou autre boys estoyt brisé, gasté, rompu ou
derrobé despuis que lesdits eschaffaulx auront esté faitz jusques à
la fin dudit jeu, en icelluy cas ont promis et seront tenus lesdits
de Barety et Bergeron satisfaire, esmender et payer lesdits Gasteau
et Rousseau desdits dommaige et interestz[4]. (...)

Notes:
1) Il s'agit des fossés de Saint-Eloi, comblés à cette
   époque, qui couraient le long de la deuxième enceinte de
   Bordeaux. A proximité se trouvaient les bâtiments com-
   munaux (*la maison commune*).
2) Le jardin des Lestonnac, dont la localisation précise est difficile
   à établir.
3) Le mot *besongne* a bien été rayé, pour être remplacé par
   chaffaudage; mais l'adjectif *tout* est resté au féminin et l'article n'a pas été rétabli.
4) Nous avons réduit à l'extrême la modernisation de la graphie
   et de la ponctuation du contrat.

2. **The Paris Resurrection:**
Bibl. Nat. fonds français 972 (1491).

*The originals of the quotations from this unpublished MS. are given
in the order in which they appear in the text. They have been
edited according to standard French practice.*

B.2. *Individual Locations.*
Hell's tower and Limbo (pp. 90-91)
[*f. 41*^{v}] Icy l'ame de Jhesus doit bouter Sathan de dessus la marche
du puytz dedans et doit cryer Sathan horriblement. Lequel puitz
doit estre fait entre le portal d'Enfer et la tour du Limbe par
devers le champ du jeu pour mieulx estre veu. Et doit estre fait
ledit puitz en telle maniere qu'il semble par dehors estre maçonné
de pierre de taille noire et doit estre fait de telle maniere que on
fourme et partout dedans separacion de bousilles sans qu'on l'apper-
çoive. En l'une des parties l'ame de Jhesus gectera les diables et
par l'autre se gectera souffre flambé, canons, tonnerre et aultres
tempestes terribles tant que Sathan et les aultres y soient tous gec-
tés. Apres laquelle chose soit fait silence et lors l'ame de Jhesus
doit rompre avec la croix l'uys de la tour du Limbe, de laquelle tour
la façon est cy apres divisee et en ce faisant l'ame de Jhesus dit ce
qui s'ensuit:

> 'Sus Adam, et ta compaignie
> De votre prison serez hors
[*f. 42*^{r}] > Car ceans nous sommes les plus fors
> Et si viendrés avecques moy.'

Icy l'ame d'Adam commencera a chanter cestuy respont: <u>Libera me</u>
. . . [*several lines of Latin*]. Et les ames bien chantans luy aide-
ront a chanter ledit respont et nota que le Limbe doit estre au
cousté du parlouer d'Enfer qui est sur le portal, en une habitacion
qui doit estre en facon d'une haulte tour quarree environnee de rethz
afin que parmy lesdiz rethz on puisse veoir du parc les ames qui y
seront quant l'ame Jhesucrist y sera entree a force. Mais par avant
sa venue ladite tour doit estre garnye tout entour de rideaulx noirs
de toille qui couvrirons lesdis rethz et empescheront qu'on ne les
voit jusques a l'entree d'ame de Jhesus. Et lors seront lesdis rideaulx subtillement tirez par annelez a cousté tellement que les
gens du parc pourront veoir dedans ladite tour par les dis rethz. Et
oultre a la venue de l'ame de Jhesus doit avoir en icelle tour
plusiers torches et falotz ou gros flambeaux ardens et derriere ladite
tour en aucun lieu doivent estre gens cryans a haulte voix come
desesperés, que ceulx dudit parc ne verront point et ne doit [*f.
42*^{v}] gueres durer ce cry et puis l'ame du mauvais larron dira tout
hault pour soy et pour les aultres dampnés ce qui s'ensuit:

Earthly Paradise (pp. 92-93)
[*f. 84*^{v}] Duquel Paradis par dehors les murs doivent estre blans. Et
par dedans y doivent estre arbres, les ungs fleuriz, les aultres plains
de fruitz de diverses especes come cerises, prunes, pommes, poires,
allemandes, orenges, figures, grenades et rasins et aultres arbres vers
come rosiers, fleurs, romarins, mariolaines. Et doivent estre si
haultes qu'on les voit par dessus le mur de par tout le parc. Et y
doit estre une fontaine qui se divisera en quatre ruisseaux.

B.3. *Machinery*.
Entry into Paradise (pp. 95-96)
[*f. 292^r*] Et le doit on tirer peu a peu et luy doit on veoir les
jambes par dessoubz l'engin et par dessus le chef et les mains
joinctes. Et par dessus l'engin en la toille partout doivent estre
painctes les ames des saincts peres qui entreront en Paradis
secretement par eschielles soubz Paradis et les cordes qui
tireront l'instrument ou Jhesus sera doivent estre mussees de
toille en maniere de nue et doit sortier du lieu ou sera Jhesus
par dessus et par dessoubz manne blanche et jaulne comme
grans blans en forme d'or et d'argent et la Vierge Marie et sa
noble compaignie estans a genoulx et les mains joinctes doivent
regarder ainsi monter Nostre Seigneur tant qu'ilz l'auront perdu
de veue.

Movement Underground (p. 97)
[*f. 98^v*] Ce fait, Jhesus acompaigné de ces trois anges doit
cheminer par le parc et en allant par engin s'en doit aller par soubz
terre pour visiter Notre Dame sa mere estant seule ou cenacle et
soy monstrer resuscité quand temps sera.
[*f. 97^v*] Et Jhesus vestu de blanc ou tout nud acompaigné des
anges Michel, Raphael et Uriel doit resusciter subtillement et soub-
dainement du tombeau par dessus par une trappe de boys colleysse
qui incontinens se fermera apres qu'il sera resuscité et s'asserra
Nostre Seigneur dessus le tombeau sans le froisser ne entamer
aucunement et aussi en celluy instant resusciteront Carinus et Leoncius en Jherusalem, chacun de son tombeau.

Joseph's tower (p. 100)
[*f. 141^r*] Icy Jhesus s'apparoist a Joseph d'Arimathie en la tour ou il
est en prison, portes closes . . . [*f. 142^r*] Icy se levera la tour par
engin de fil d'archal en l'air subtillement fait et Jhesus prant Joseph
par la main et le meynt en sa cité d'Arimathie, les anges chantans
melodieusement . . .

B.4. *Special Effects*.
Tongues of fire (p. 107)
[*f. 314^v*] Icy doit descendre ung brandon de feu de Paradis qui sera
ront comme ung cercle et doit estre tout baigné d'eau vive brulant
et ou millieu de ce cercle ardant doit estre ung pigeon de fer blanc
environné de feu qui ne le consume point et tout autour du cercle
doivent estre langues ardentes qui doivent tomber sur Notre Dame,
sur les femmes, sur les apostres et disciples . . .

Red faced angels (p. 109)
[*f. 84^r*] Icy Seraph, garde de Paradis terrestre, aians vestement et
visaige rouge, tenant une espee blanche toute nue en sa main, par-
lera . . .
[*f. 98^v*] Ce pendant dit Dieu le Pere a Gabriel vestu de blanc aiant
la face vermeille ce qui s'ensuit . . .

Peter walking on the water (pp. 114-15)
[*f. 250^r*] Icy va Sainct Pierre par sus la mer a Jhesus sans moiller
la cheville par une grant haies mise subtillement et chevillee en
l'eau et les apostres mectent leur poisson en ung aultre reth venant
tousiours a la rive de la mer puis s'agenoillent tous devant Nostre
Seigneur sans parlement et dit Jhesus . . .

B.7. Costumes.
Christ's wounds (pp. 143-44)
[*f. 291^v*] Icy chantent les sainctes ames doulcement ceste hymne:
Jhesus Noster Redemptor, amor et desideratio. Et doit estre Jhesus
vestu de la robe [*f. 292^r*] en laquelle il apparoissoit a Notre Dame
apres sa resurrecion et doit avoir ses cinq plaies ouvertes et rouges
et doit estre avec luy Gabriel, Raphael, Carinus et Leoncius.

B.10. Movement.
Harrowing of Hell (p. 162)
[*f. 34^v*] Icy tous les diables excepté Sathan portent colevrynes et
aultres ferremens en Enfer et ferment leurs portes a gros correilz.
Et l'ame de Jhesus avec les quatre [*anges*] aus-dessusdits et l'ame
du bon larron vont en Enfer tenans Sathan lyé et dit l'ame de
Jhesus en frappant la porte d'Enfer avec la croix . . .
[*f. 35^r*] Icy l'ame de Jhesus rompt les portes d'Enfer avec la croix
et entre avec les quatre anges et l'ame du bon larron dedans.   Et
lors les ames du Limbe chantent melodieusement ceste hymne: Conditor alma sidera.   Puis l'ame de Jhesus se doit arrester empres la
chambre du Limbe tant que les diables s'en vueillent fouyr.

Mary Magdalene in the garden (p. 170)
[*f. 125^v*] Icy Magdalene cerchant ainsi par le jardin ou estoit le
tombeau, apparceut les deux anges qui s'enclinerent devant Jhesus
qui venoit par derriere la Magdalene en guise de jardinier.   A l'occasion duquel enclinement elle regarda derriere por scavoir devant
qui ilz s'enclinoient.   Jhesus comme jardinier parle a la Magdalene.

3. *Le mystère de S. Crespin et S. Crespinien*,   ed. O. Ostrowski,
Greifswald dissertation, 1909.

*Text of parts of prologue from MS. C (Chantilly, Cabinet des Manu-
scrits, Vol. II, 619).*

B.1. The Playing Area (p. 78)
Bonnes gens, afin que soiez   74
Chartains de ce que verrés chy,
Je nommeray les personnages
Et l'estat de chascum aussy.
Les ungs sont en ce lieu bas cy
Par le champ qui est lonc et larges.

Autres plusieurs sont autresy
Cy entour en ces hauls estages.
Et pour commenchier en hault lieu
Le premier ve(e)z là paradis!
Angelz y sont avecques dieu,
Nostre dame enprès luy assis; . . .
Les deulz bons freres que l'en nomme   90
Crespin ausy Crespïnien,
Veez là où il sont à Roume . . .
En ceste costé cy est la ville   98
De Soissons où paiens plusieurs
Sont et ausy (y) a plus de mille
Sarrasins tant grans que mineurs; . . .
Veez là le roy Maximïen,   106
Avecques luy ses conseill(e)ez; . . .
Le prevost dont j'ay devant dit   114
V(e)ez le là en moult grant aroy! . . .
Des tirans qu'oy dit vela quatre! . . .   162
Le geollier voy là endroit   170
Qui est garde de la prison! . . .
Deulx proudes gens a en cest lieu,   178
De bon vouloir et bonne vie, . . .
V(e)ez là le pape en son manoir . . .   196
V(e)ez là ung archevesque ausy,   202
Qui sert dieu comme bon preudon! . . .
Sixte que bien noumer me plaist,   214
V(e)ez le là! En son lieu le voy. . . .
Puis vez là enfer le puant!   234
Foyson y a diables dedens; . . .

4. Autun, 1516; Play of St. Lazarus.

This description of the theater at Autun is taken from the Catalogus
Gloriae Mundi. *It is given in a French translation in Petit de Julleville (I, 405). Part 12, section 66, from which this description is
taken, is mainly concerned with classical theaters, but there are one
or two other references relevant to the medieval stage.*

A.3. The Audience. (p. 63)
Nos autem Hedui, anno Domini millesimo quingentesimo decimosexto,
excellens et magnificum amphiteatrum in campo sancti Lazari, qui
est in medio civitatis nostrae, construximus, et erat e ligno quadrato
artificio solenni fabrefactum impensis ecclesiae, et civium, nec in
Gallia fuit simile. Ducentenarias enim cellulas cum quadraginta in
superiori parte habuit, parietibus e ligno intermedijs divisas, et tabu-
latis coopertas, quae loca erant viris Ecclesiasticis, Nobilibus, Sena-
toribus, Equitibus, et Gentibus civium patricijs. In cavea vero seu
inferiori parte, erant gradus et sedilia ita disposita, ut altiora in
ambitu semper excrescerent, ubi plebs promiscue sedebat. Quae

habuit et velaria lintea, quibus substantes seu subsidentes adumbrantur, et ne a pluvia offenderentur. Etiam ludentes in medio Cavee, seu Theatralis Scenae ijsdem tantum tegebantur quos fossa aquis vallata, et alijs obstaculis a plebijs discriminabat. In eo amphiteatro octoginta millia hominum non gravate collocari poterant, et quia indicta fuerant spectacula finitimis, spectatores prope infiniti affuerunt, quae spectacula fuerunt excellentissima causa divi Lazari patroni Heduorum facta, ubi vita eiusdem dignis versibus non ad Pompam, sed ad divinae maiestatis laudem, et beati Lazari, vehementissime, et gratis, quatuor diebus recitata fuit. Unde a Deo datum est, ut nulla exibilatio, nulla plebis consternatio, aut derisiorie quid gestum fuit, et licet nocte pluebat, tota die tamen nulla aeris serenitatis major ijsdem diebus visa fuerit, de quo aliquid iam supra tetigi in 60 consideratus est et in precedenti parte in 52 consideratus est.

Bartolomeus Cassanaeus, Catalogus Gloriae Mundi *(Frankfurt 1597), Duodecima pars; no. 66, p. 362 (copy in Edinburgh University Library, shelf mark: JY 100; transcribed by Graham Runnalls).*

5. The Mercadé Vengeance: Chatsworth MS. 48B.

Chatsworth MS. 48B (2 vols.) was copied for the Duke of Burgundy in 1464. It contains the Mystère de la Vengeance Jésu Christ *attributed (in the slightly shorter version of Arras, Bibliothèque municipale, MS. 697) to Eustache Mercadé (d.1440). The relationship between the two texts is fully discussed in E. B. Ham's "The Basic Manuscript of the Marcadé 'Vengeance'," Modern Language Review, 29 (1934), 405-20. The Vengeance deals with the events in Josephus' The Destruction of Jerusalem, interwoven with the apocryphal trials and death of Pilate. The play is remarkable for its many battle scenes, and the Chatsworth version of it for the quantity and unusualness of its stage directions. The following passages have been transcribed from the MS. in the library at Chatsworth by Jane Oakshott.*

B.4. Special Effects.
Dummy bodies (pp. 112-13)
[Vol. II, f. 49ᵛ] Trompetes sonnent dedens et dehors et ilz assaillent la seconde foys tant que bon leur semble par ordonnance comme l'aultre assault et drescent eschieles et doit durer tant que bon semble et getent faulx corps vestuz comme aulcuns de ceulx de dedens. Jus des murs aussi en doivent tirer ceulx dedens avecques eulx ung ou deux de ceulx de dehors et faire semblant de les tuer et puis geter jus faulx corps ainsi vestus que les tires a mort.

[Vol. II, f. 13v] Adoncques Pylate se fiert d'ung cousteau et doit avoir quelque chose sur lui dont il isse sang et se doit mettre en lieu quant il se frappa qu'on le puist veoir comme s'il fust tué.

B.12. Mime and Gesture (p. 178).
[*Vol. II, f. 91*] Cy assemblent les ungs aux aultres et adonc se
combatent ensemble et en abatent d'ung les et d'aultre de ceulx qui
pas ne doivent parler. Trompetes sonnent dehors et dedens yoieuse-
ment tant que la bataille dure a la voulente des meneus et sans
blecier l'ung l'aultre se doit faire. Et faintement se laisier cheoir.

APPENDIX II

Cysat's Stage Plans for the 1583 Performance
of the Lucerne Passion Play

By the middle of the sixteenth century the tradition was established that the Town Clerk of Lucerne should be the director of the performances of the Passion Play. By 1583 Cysat was only 38, and even though the intervals between performances had lengthened from the five years which had been usual earlier in the century, he could reasonably expect to be required to organize further performances in his lifetime. As an aid in planning Cysat drew a plan of the *Weinmarkt* square for each of the two days of the performance. That he set great store by them is evident from several extant notes he made about keeping them safe; he succeeded in doing so and used the plans again when organizing the performance which took place in 1597 after postponement.

That the plans were made before the 1583 performance is clear from some of the changes which can be seen on them. On the plan for Day 1, for example, the group of names beginning "Moses" was first included near the top of the right-hand side of the plan (above Caiaphas' group), but has been transferred to a new location exactly opposite. On the plan for Day 2 in contrast the stalls of the Herald's group and of Caiaphas' group are adjacent to one another. Definite proof that this change was made for the 1583 performance comes from the relevant section of Hardmeyer's "Layout of the Places" (see above pp. 81-82). However, other alterations on the plans must date from 1597 since they refer to scenes included for the first (and only) time as part of Cysat's major revision of the text for this performance--e.g., the reference to the execution of Haman added beside the tree used for Zacheus and Judas Iscariot.

In making this translation of the plans, everything except the writing was traced from a xerox copy of the originals kindly provided by the Zentralbibliothek Luzern. Examination of the originals in Lucerne enabled us to decipher all the writing on the plans. What is deleted on the originals we enclose in square brackets, e.g., the names of the group beginning with Moses in their original position; what is demonstrably an alteration or later addition we enclose in parentheses (round brackets), e.g., "also execution of Haman" already mentioned. Biblical characters whose names have accepted English forms are translated accordingly, e.g., "Johannes Baptista" as "John the Baptist," "Pylatus" as "Pilate," and "Herodes" as "Herod." However, where names from the Old Testament are used as the names of members of the crowd of Jews, these have been left in the form used by Cysat, e.g., "Ozias" and "Salmon" as names of Jews in the Temple remain thus and are not changed to "Hosea" and "Solomon." The usage of u/v has been modernized, and Latin names

(e.g., "Pater aeternus," "Salvator," "Proclamator," "Legis peritus")
have been translated.

Particular care is needed in dealing with the alterations and
additions to the plans. As already suggested, it is vital to read the
plans in conjunction with Hardmeyer's "Lay-out . . . " (above, pp.
81-87). Only in this way do we discover, for example, that the
position of the stall reserved for the City Councillors at the foot of
the steps leading up onto the stand on the fountain dates from 1583,
since on the plans it appears only on Day 2 and in the ink of the
later alterations.

The fact that Cysat drew the plans essentially for himself
provides the apparent explanation for the absence from the plans of
some details we might expect to appear on the complete diagram of
the square. The plans give no clue regarding the relationship between the actors' stalls, the spectator accommodation, and the
buildings around the square. On this point Cysat was in no doubt
and saw no reason to record it.

Further difficulties of interpretation arise because the two-
dimensional plans represent a three-dimensional reality. Therefore,
for example, they do not show clearly the relationship between the
moveable Mount Sinai/Mount of Olives which is depicted flat against
the *Haus zur Sonne* and the stalls in front of it. Furthermore the
fourth dimension, time, is not taken into account on the plans, as
they do not show unambiguously which structures remained in position throughout the twelve hours of a day's performance and which
were put in position by the stage staff only for specific scenes. In
the middle of the square on Day 1, for example, not far apart are
the locations of the sacrifice performed by Cain and Abel and that
performed by Abraham. The structures shown look remarkably similar, and stage directions and notes (p. 148, above) elsewhere make
clear that it was indeed the same altar which was used in different
positions at different points in the action. The cost-conscious organizing committee would never have permitted otherwise. The plan
for Day 2 shows the three crosses in their dominating position at the
top of the square. But since we know from elsewhere that a light-
weight cross was used for the journey to Calvary and was then to be
spirited away quickly, and that the Savior is attached to the cross
before it is erected, it seems that the crosses were not in position
throughout the whole day's performance.

A final example of the kind of care required in examining the
plans is provided by the left-hand (northern) side of the square. At
first sight the plan for Day 2 seems to show part of this side empty. But closer examination reveals that, for example, "the house of
the late Sebastian Knab" and "the tree of Judas" are significantly
higher up than on the plan for Day 1. Cysat has simply filled in
the information he wished to record concerning this side of the
square starting from the top and taking up as much space as this
required.

These stage plans, therefore, are far from being simple "dia-
grams" of the stage; but carefully interpreted they do contain a

quite remarkable amount of information about the staging of the 1583 and 1597 performances in Lucerne.

296

INDEX OF CHARACTERS AND STAGE STAFF NAMED ON LUCERNE PLANS

Day and position on plan are indicated thus:

1 = day 1, 2 = day 2.
L = left-hand side of sheet; R = right hand side; T = top; and F = foot of sheet.
Erased names are indicated by references in square brackets.

300